CHURCHILL'S GRANDMAMA

Frances, 7th Duchess of Marlborough

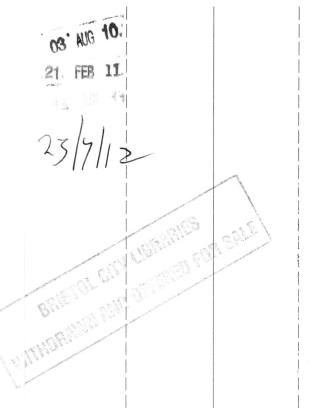

CHURCHILL'S GRANDMAMA

Frances, 7th Duchess of Marlborough

MARGARET ELIZABETH FORSTER

Foreword by His Grace The Duke of Marlborough

To dearest John, Simon, Benedict, Nicholas
my support and inspiration

First published in 2010

The History Press
The Mill, Brimscombe Port
Stroud, Gloucestershire, GL5 2QG
www.thehistorypress.co.uk

© Margaret Elizabeth Forster 2010

British Library Cataloguing in Publication Data.
A catalogue record for this book is available from the British Library.

ISBN 978-0-7524-5552-5

Typesetting and origination by Phillimore & Co. Ltd.
Printed and bound in Great Britain.

Contents

LIST OF ILLUSTRATIONS

Plate section between pages 72-3

1. Frances, 7th Duchess of Marlborough, aged about twelve
2. Wynyard Hall and Park, a watercolour by J.W. Carmichael
3. Charles, 3rd Marquess of Londonderry, 1819, by Sir Thomas Lawrence
4. Frances Anne, 3rd Marchioness of Londonderry, 1819, by Sir Thomas Lawrence
5. John Winston, 7th Duke of Marlborough, 1843, marble, Lawrence MacDonald
6. Frances, 7th Duchess of Marlborough, 1843, marble, Lawrence MacDonald
7. Londonderry House, Park Lane, London
8. Frances, 7th Duchess of Marlborough, by Buckner, 1840s
9. Silver centrepiece, Blenheim Palace, by Robert Garrard
10. 3rd Marquess of Londonderry, 10th Hussars, a bronze
11. Frances, 7th Duchess of Marlborough in her boudoir, Blenheim Palace, by Sir George Scharf
12. Frances, 7th Duchess of Marlborough, photographed in the 1860s
13. John Winston, 7th Duke of Marlborough, photographed in the 1860s
14. Frances, John Winston and members of the family, *c.*1860
15. Lord and Lady Randolph Churchill, 1874
16, 17. Pages from the Visitors' Book at Blenheim Palace
18. Royal Yacht Squadron yacht *Wyvern*, 1876

Illustration Acknowledgements

Many of the photographs in this book have been taken by Richard Cragg, my friend and colleague at Blenheim Palace to whom I express my deepest gratitude. Without his skill, talent and unfailing enthusiasm a great many of the illustrations simply would not have been possible. I am grateful, too, to my son, Simon Forster, for his discovery and photography of the Famine Memorial sculptures in Toronto.

The author and publisher are grateful for permission to reproduce images:

Illustration number 28 is reproduced by gracious permission of Her Majesty Queen Elizabeth II.

Alamy, 33; Churchill Archives Centre, 15; Richard Cragg, 10; Rowan Gillespie, 22 (and inset); the Reverend Canon R. Humphreys, 32; Library of Congress, 28; His Grace The Duke of Marlborough, 1, 5, 6, 8 (photographed by Porter-Design), 9, 12-14, 16-17, 20-1, 23, 24-7, 29-30; National Portrait Gallery, 3; National Portrait Gallery and Yale University Press, 11; Private Collection, 2, 4, 7; R. Shepherd, 18; TopFoto, 19, 31.

ACKNOWLEDGEMENTS

My grateful thanks to the following:

His Grace The Duke of Marlborough, for generous access to the Archives and Library at Blenheim, for permission to reproduce a great deal of material from these sources, and for writing the Foreword;

Lady Soames, Lady Henrietta Spencer-Churchill, Lady Mairi Bury, Celia Sandys, Anthea Morton-Saner, Hugo Vickers, Professor Anthony Fletcher, and those who prefer not to be named, for their invaluable help, encouragement and advice;

Frances Harris (Head of Modern Historical Manuscripts at the British Library), Richard Olney (Historical Manuscripts Commission), Allen Packwood (Director of the Churchill Archives Centre) and Caroline Herbert, Carole Kenwright (Property Manager at Chartwell), Francesca Odell and Gudrun Muller (National Portrait Gallery), Dawn van Ee (Library of Congress), Richard Edgcumbe (Victoria and Albert Museum), Lucy MacMillan, Henry Porter and Els Rowlands (Porter-Design), Rowan Gilhespie and Louise Holbrow, Roger Shepherd, Maldwin Drummond, Shaheeda Sabir (Churchill Permissions), Rev. Roger Humphreys, Richard and Marie Cragg, John Forster (Archivist to the Duke of Marlborough), whose specialist knowledge has been given so generously;

the staffs of Oxfordshire Records Office, Durham Records Office, Oxfordshire Centre for Local Studies and Woodstock Public Library (especially Gill Morris and Anne Elsmore), and Dr Melanie White of the Sorbonne, my researcher in Dublin, and the many individual members of the public who wrote to me of their own accord or responded to the TV documentaries about Blenheim;

my many colleagues at Blenheim Palace, in particular John Hoy, Dominic Hare, Heather Carter, Victoria Bellamy, Sandra French, Antonia Keaney, Caroline McCormack, Tim Mayhew, Hannah Payne, Odette Christie de Rivas, Cathy Tuckey, Karen Wiseman;

the Palace Guides, in particular Marae Griffin, Sue Thorne, Veronica Thorneloe, Ros Campbell, Lesley Deane, Jenny Grubb, Liz Chapman, Christine Gadsby, Julia Lennon, Wendy Neale, Sumie Smith, and the welcoming Guides at Floors Castle;

Sue Hawker, headmistress now retired, Tracey Smith her successor, Maureen Clifford, Wendy Heppell, Caroline Hudspeth and all the staff at Bladon C.E. Primary School, Oxfordshire;

my family and friends, my sister Wendy Heslop, my brother Jack Heslop, Mary and Nicholas Grey, Eileen and Bob Mason, Carol and Allen Mason, Robert and Ann Parkin, Jeri Bapasola, Gill Brounger, Monica and Gerard Coleman, Tineke and Peter Gill, Alan Jamieson, Sarah and Michael Lyon, Irene and Tom Maddison, Harold and Pamela Redwood, Mary and Chris White, Ann and George Wilson, my sons Simon, Ben and Nicholas for their unfailing encouragement and support, often of a very practical kind, and my husband John, who devoted so much time and patience to researching illustrations.

Finally, to Shelley Grimwood of The History Press, whose experienced advice and insight over many months has been invaluable to me, and to all her colleagues, I offer my most grateful thanks.

Margaret Elizabeth Forster
2009

Blenheim Palace.

FOREWORD BY HIS GRACE THE DUKE OF MARLBOROUGH

I am very pleased to introduce this book about my great great-grandmother, Frances, 7th Duchess of Marlborough and grandmother of Sir Winston Churchill. Almost an exact contemporary of Queen Victoria, she has never had the recognition she deserves. The picture of her in the public eye is of a Victorian martinet, unbending and rather cold. This book throws a clear and rewarding light on a lady who, it is now revealed, had the warmest of hearts and a most generous nature. By examining her commitment as a caring grandmother, notably of Winston Churchill, by demonstrating her commitment to the local community, especially in the field of education, and by sharing the sadness in her life, when she buried her five sons as well as her husband, this book brings alive the personality of a truly admirable woman.

However, it was the breaking out of famine yet again in Ireland during her husband's term as Viceroy which moved her on to the world stage and drew from her talents and qualities hitherto unrecognised. In her speedy and effective creation and administration of her Famine Relief Fund on an international scale, she revealed not only her warmth and compassion but also qualities of leadership, judgement and organisation of the highest order. The letters of thanks and farewell she received throughout the Irish press, from all shades of political opinion, are particularly illuminating and make moving reading.

I welcome this publication with its vivid and stimulating insights into a hitherto overlooked member of my family.

Marlborough

Spencer-Churchill/Londonderry Family Tree
Dukedom of Marlborough (Selective)

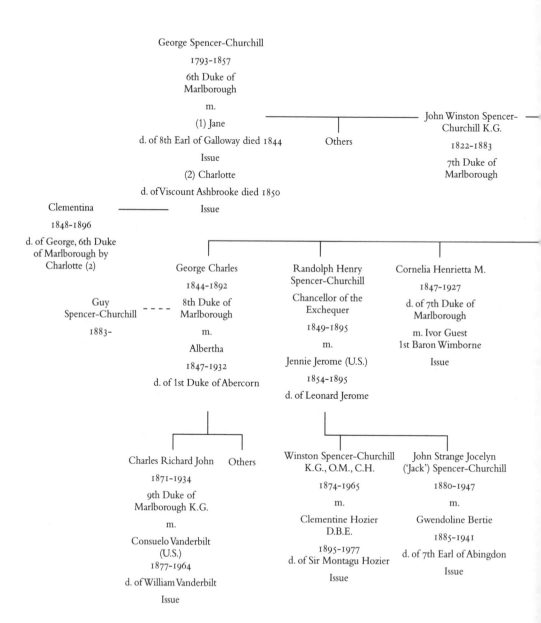

George Spencer-Churchill
1793–1857
6th Duke of
Marlborough

m.

(1) Jane
d. of 8th Earl of Galloway died 1844

Issue

(2) Charlotte
d. of Viscount Ashbrooke died 1850

Issue

Others

John Winston Spencer-
Churchill K.G.
1822–1883
7th Duke of
Marlborough

Clementina
1848–1896
d. of George, 6th Duke
of Marlborough by
Charlotte (2)

Guy
Spencer-Churchill
1883–

George Charles
1844–1892
8th Duke of
Marlborough
m.
Albertha
1847–1932
d. of 1st Duke of Abercorn

Randolph Henry
Spencer-Churchill
Chancellor of the
Exchequer
1849–1895
m.
Jennie Jerome (U.S.)
1854–1895
d. of Leonard Jerome

Cornelia Henrietta M.
1847–1927
d. of 7th Duke of
Marlborough
m. Ivor Guest
1st Baron Wimborne
Issue

Charles Richard John   Others
1871–1934
9th Duke of
Marlborough K.G.
m.
Consuelo Vanderbilt
(U.S.)
1877–1964
d. of William Vanderbilt
Issue

Winston Spencer-Churchill
K.G., O.M., C.H.
1874–1965
m.
Clementine Hozier
D.B.E.
1895–1977
d. of Sir Montagu Hozier
Issue

John Strange Jocelyn
('Jack') Spencer-Churchill
1880–1947
m.
Gwendoline Bertie
1885–1941
d. of 7th Earl of Abingdon
Issue

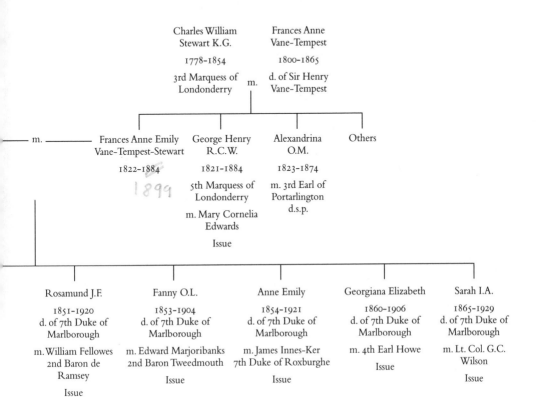

Charles William
Stewart K.G.

1778-1854

3rd Marquess of
Londonderry

m.

Frances Anne
Vane-Tempest

1800-1865

d. of Sir Henry
Vane-Tempest

— m. —

Frances Anne Emily
Vane-Tempest-Stewart

1822-1884

1899

George Henry
R.C.W.

1821-1884

5th Marquess of
Londonderry

m. Mary Cornelia
Edwards

Issue

Alexandrina
O.M.

1823-1874

m. 3rd Earl of
Portarlington
d.s.p.

Others

Rosamund J.F.

1851-1920
d. of 7th Duke of
Marlborough

m. William Fellowes
2nd Baron de
Ramsey

Issue

Fanny O.L.

1853-1904
d. of 7th Duke of
Marlborough

m. Edward Marjoribanks
2nd Baron Tweedmouth

Issue

Anne Emily

1854-1921
d. of 7th Duke of
Marlborough

m. James Innes-Ker
7th Duke of Roxburghe

Issue

Georgiana Elizabeth

1860-1906
d. of 7th Duke of
Marlborough

m. 4th Earl Howe

Issue

Sarah I.A.

1865-1929
d. of 7th Duke of
Marlborough

m. Lt. Col. G.C.
Wilson

Issue

CHRONOLOGY

1815   Battle of Waterloo; Defeat of Napoleon; Peace in Europe; Congress of Vienna.

Lord Charles Stewart, Adjutant-General to the Duke of Wellington in the Napoleonic wars, is appointed British Ambassador to Austria with special reference to the Congress of Vienna.

1819   Frances Anne Vane-Tempest (born 1800) meets and marries Lord Charles Stewart. They arrive in Vienna, having first restored the estates and collieries at Wynyard Hall, the Vane-Tempest home near Durham.

1820   Death of George III; accession of George IV.

Charles sent to Italy to facilitate King George's divorce from his wife Caroline.

1821   Birth of Harry Vane-Tempest-Stewart, eldest son and heir to Charles and Frances Anne. Family returns to England.

1822   Birth of Frances Anne Emily, eldest daughter to Charles and Frances Anne, in London. Birth at Blenheim Palace of John Winston Spencer-Churchill, eldest son and heir to the 6th Duke of Marlborough.

Purchase by Charles Stewart of Seaham estate from Sir Ralph Milbanke. Purchase of houses in Mayfair.

Death of Lord Castlereagh, Charles' stepbrother, British Foreign Secretary. Charles resigns from embassy at Vienna but is ordered to Congress of Verona. He becomes 3rd Marquess of Londonderry in place of Castlereagh.

Family travel across the Alps to Verona. Frances Anne meets Tsar Alexander I for the second time. Family returns to England.

1823   Birth of Alexandrina, second daughter, with Tsar as godfather.

1825   Stockton and Darlington railway opens.

Birth of Adolphus, second son, with two royal Dukes as godparents, York and Cambridge.

1826   Housewarming of Wynyard Hall, rebuilt in classical style.

1827   Duke of Wellington visits Wynyard.

1830   Death of George IV. Accession of William IV. Whigs in power under Earl Grey.

Birth of Adelaide, daughter, with Queen Adelaide as sponsor.

1831   Liverpool and Manchester railway opens. Seaham Harbour constructed and opened. Cholera epidemic in Sunderland.

1832   Great Reform Bill enlarges political franchise and restructures representation in Parliament. Charles stoned in Whitehall by angry London mob.

1833   Beginning of Oxford Movement in Church of England.

1834   Slavery abolished throughout British Empire.

1836   Wellington, Prime Minister, offers Charles the Ambassador's post in St Petersburg; he courteously declines. Private family visit to Russia in Tsar Nicholas' (brother of Tsar Alexander) yacht.

1837   Death of William IV. Accession of Queen Victoria.

1840   Penny post introduced.

1841   Conservatives in government; Robert Peel Prime Minister.

Wynyard Hall burns down; rebuilt by John Dobson and Ignatius Bonomi.

1842　Harry Vane-Tempest-Stewart's coming-of-age celebrated at Wynyard. Beginnings of first Irish potato famine.

1843　Frances marries John Winston Spencer-Churchill, Marquess of Blandford and heir to the 6th Duke of Marlborough, attended by royal and aristocratic guests. The couple take up residence in Hensington House.

1844-80　Development of British coal industry and the railways. London docks built.

Birth of George Charles, first son of Frances and John Winston, and heir to the dukedom and Earl of Sunderland.

1846　Whigs in government.

Birth of Frederick John, second son of Frances and John Winston; dies 1850.

1847　Birth of Cornelia Henrietta Maria, first daughter of Frances and John Winston.

1848　Revolutions in Europe.

1849　Birth of Randolph Henry, third son of Frances and John Winston.

1850　Frances Anne builds Garron Tower, near Belfast, to help relieve Irish unemployment.

1851　Great Exhibition, organised by Albert, Prince Consort.

Birth of Rosamund Jane Frances, second daughter of Frances and John Winston.

1852　Earl of Derby Prime Minister. Death of Duke of Wellington. Charles is honoured to receive Wellington's Order of the Garter. He cuts the turf to begin the Seaham to Sunderland railway.

1853　Birth of Fanny Octavia Louisa, third daughter of Frances and John Winston.

1854   Death of Charles Stewart, 3rd Marquess of Londonderry. Frederick, Charles' son by his first marriage, becomes 4th Marquess of Londonderry. Harry, Frances' brother, becomes Earl Vane. Frances Anne, her lands and collieries restored to her, establishes herself at Seaham Hall.

          Birth of Anne Emily, fourth daughter to John Winston and Frances.

1854-6   Crimean War.

1855   Viscount Palmerston becomes Prime Minister.

1856   Frances Anne entertains 4,000 miners to dinner at Chilton Moor.

          Birth of Charles Ashley, fourth son to John Winston and Frances; dies 1858.

1857   Death of 6th Duke. John Winston and Frances become Duke and Duchess of Marlborough.

1857-83   Restoration and development of Blenheim and its neighbourhood.

1858   Indian Mutiny.

          Augustus Robert born, fifth son of John Winston and Frances; dies 1859.

1859   Publication of Darwin's *On the Origin of Species*.

          Opening of Bladon School.

1860   Duchess's school established in Woodstock to train girls for posts in domestic service.

          Birth of Georgiana Elizabeth, fifth daughter of John Winston and Frances.

1861   Death of Albert, Prince Consort.

1863   Randolph attends Eton.

1865   Death of Palmerston.

          Death of Frances Anne.

Birth of Sarah Isabella Augusta, sixth daughter of Frances and John Winston.

1866-8   Derby minority Conservative government.

John Winston now Lord Steward of the Royal Household.

1867   John Winston becomes Lord President of the Council, with responsibility for education. Randolph attends Merton College, Oxford.

1868   Disraeli becomes Prime Minister (Conservative) but resigns in same year. Gladstone's first Liberal government.

John Winston becomes a Knight of the Garter.

Movement of Blenheim household staff to lodges and independent homes outside the Palace.

1869   Suez Canal opened.

1873   Randolph Spencer-Churchill meets American Jennie Jerome and proposes marriage.

1874   John Winston refuses post of Viceroy of Ireland because of expense. Randolph becomes Member of Parliament for Woodstock. Randolph and Jennie marry at the British Embassy in Paris.

Winston Churchill born at Blenheim Palace.

Great Western Railway disaster at Hampton Gay, near Blenheim.

1875   Disraeli buys shares for Britain in Suez Canal, to gain a controlling interest. John Winston sells Marlborough Gems and also sells land to Lord Rothschild to build Waddesdon Manor.

1876   Queen Victoria is proclaimed Empress of India.

Lord George Blandford and Lord Randolph attract the anger of Edward, Prince of Wales.

1877   Despite the efforts of Queen Victoria, the Prince of Wales refuses to be reconciled and makes the Spencer-Churchills social outcasts in London.

1877-80   Disraeli appoints John Winston and Frances Viceroy and Vicereine of Ireland to protect their reputation. They work hard and receive a warm response from the Irish.

1879   Irish potato crop fails, raising fears of recurrence of 1840s famine. Frances establishes her Famine Relief Fund, appealing for international support. With her voluntary helpers she raises £130,000.

1880   With a change in government the Marlboroughs have to leave Ireland. Queen Victoria awards Frances the Order of Victoria and Albert.

Disraeli becomes Lord Beaconsfield and moves to the Lords.

John Winston and Frances return to Blenheim to recover from the heavy expense of the Ireland posting.

1880-   The Liberals sweep into power with a majority of 146; Gladstone becomes Prime Minister. Sir Stafford Northcote replaces Disraeli. Randolph forms the Fourth Party and gains support for the Conservative opposition. Randolph and Jennie enjoy a hectic public and social life.

Frances brings Winston and his younger brother Jack to Blenheim. Winston suffers poor health at school and returns to Blenheim.

1881-2   John Winston sells the Sunderland Library.

1883   John Winston dies. Randolph begins to rise in Parliament.

1886-92   Conservatives return to power with Lord Salisbury as Prime Minister. Randolph is appointed Chancellor of the Exchequer and Leader of the House of Commons.

George, now 8th Duke of Marlborough, sells off pictures and porcelain from Blenheim. Frances goes to live in the London house.

Randolph threatens to resign over budget proposals and Salisbury accepts.

1888   Winston attends Harrow School.

1892   Gladstone becomes Prime Minister (Liberal).

George, 8th Duke, dies. Randolph's health begins to decline.

Frances writes regularly to Winston, now at Sandhurst.

1893   Independent Labour Party founded.

Randolph and family move into Grosvenor Square with Frances for financial reasons.

1894   Earl of Rosebery becomes Prime Minister.

Jennie takes Randolph on a yachting holiday.

1895   Salisbury becomes Prime Minister.

Randolph returns home and dies. His funeral is held in Westminster Abbey and he is buried in Bladon churchyard.

Winston commissioned into 4th Hussars; he progresses with distinction in his Army career but then decides to settle to writing and politics.

1896   Winston serves in Bangalore, India.

Charles (son of George), now the 9th Duke, brings Consuelo, his wealthy American bride, home to Blenheim.

1898   Winston in Sudan, attached to 21st Lancers, takes part in last regimental cavalry charge at Omdurman.

1899   Death of Frances in London. Her body is brought back to Blenheim to be buried in the crypt beside John Winston.

Winston resigns from Army. Fails at first attempt to be elected to Parliament. Goes to South Africa as war correspondent for *Morning Post* to cover Boer War; is captured and escapes. Commissioned into South African Light Horse.

1900   Winston returns to England in July; elected to Parliament in October as a Conservative.

1901   Death of Queen Victoria. Accession of Edward VII.

INTRODUCTION

This is the biography, and I have found no other, of Sir Winston Churchill's grandmother, Frances, 7th Duchess of Marlborough. As the eldest daughter of the 3rd Marquess of Londonderry, popular soldier and diplomat, she grew up in one of the major social and political families of the nineteenth century; in addition, her mother the Marchioness was one of the wealthiest women in England. Her childhood was therefore steeped in great historical occasions and names: the Congresses of Vienna and Verona, Tsar Alexander of Russia (with whom her mother was rumoured to have had an affair), the Duke of Wellington (her godfather), Lord Castlereagh (her uncle), Queen Victoria (a personal friend from childhood), Disraeli (her mother's grateful protégé) and later Gladstone.

History has not been kind to Frances. Largely owing to the misinterpretation of early accounts the modern record relegates her to obscurity. This book aims to restore her to the position she deserves. It is based on previously unpublished material at Blenheim Palace, graciously given by the present Duke of Marlborough.

Frances' arrival at Blenheim as the Marchioness of Blandford in 1843, at a particularly depressed point in the Palace's history, resulted in its regeneration as a family home; subsequently, as 7th Duchess of Marlborough, she revived it as the social and political focus of both a neighbourhood and nation. Winston's mother Jennie reveals that 'She ruled Blenheim and nearly all those in it with a firm hand. At the rustle of her silk dress the whole house trembled,' but then she adds that she was 'a very remarkable and intelligent woman with a warm heart, particularly for members of her family'.

It is this latter aspect of her which forms the basis of my book. She is revealed not only as a force to be reckoned with but also as a woman of great sensitivity and compassion, responding quickly to the distress of the deprived. As a caring and progressive Duchess, she attended to the needs of her staff and estate workers as well as of those in the neighbourhood. As a loving mother, she was extended at times to the limits of her resilience and knew both pathos and tragedy; she was a caring surrogate mother not only to Winston but also to other orphaned or abandoned members of the family. 'I keep Winston in order because I know you like it,' she wrote to Randolph one Christmas, a time which Winston often spent with her. 'He is a clever boy but he needs a firm hand.' At times she was simply the rock upon which others found strength.

Towering over all this is her achievement as Vicereine in Ireland, where her husband was serving as Viceroy. Her interest in and care for the weak and deprived are well documented. Her crowning achievement, fully and dramatically retold in this book, is the humanity and leadership together with administrative and organisational skills she showed in effectively averting a potato famine in 1879 which threatened to repeat the wholesale loss of life in the famine of the 1840s. It was this most public international performance which brought her the award of the Order of Victoria and Albert from Queen Victoria herself, normally reserved for members of the Royal Family.

From her glamorous background, through the dramatic incidents and turmoil of her family and public life, to the years committed to her grandchildren, particularly Winston, this hitherto undisclosed story gives us an indication of the strength of character of this talented woman consigned by history to the shadows. Hers is a story that deserves to be celebrated.

A note on names: throughout *Churchill's Grandmama* I have consistently referred to the 7th Duchess as Frances in order to distinguish her from her mother, Frances Anne, and her daughter Fanny.

A note on monetary values: figures are quoted as the values of their times; the modern-day equivalent of Frances' Famine Fund would be approximately £9-10 million and John Winston's income of £40,000 in the nineteenth century would be equal to around £2 million today.

Chapter One

A GLAMOROUS BEGINNING

O n a bitterly cold evening in the winter of 1822 a tiny horse-drawn carriage was making its way along a narrow valley in the Austrian Alps, slowly but steadily approaching the small town which still lay a considerable distance ahead. The overhead sky was gradually darkening to leave a clear but heavily frosty night. The distant mountains, so enchanting during the day, seemed to be closing in and threatening those less imposing aspects of nature.

The most noticeable occupant of this small vehicle, sitting in the corner of the carriage and anxiously watching the approach of night, was a man of average height and weight, dark in colouring but with a rare animation which was overlaid by an expression of grief and sadness only discernible at close quarters. This was Lord Charles Stewart, brave and brilliant soldier of the Napoleonic wars, Adjutant-General to the British Expeditionary Force under the Duke of Wellington, 3rd Marquess of Londonderry and, until recently, His Majesty's Ambassador in Vienna. This was the man who had fought so courageously alongside Wellington at Waterloo. The heartbreak in his face was for his step-brother Castlereagh, British Foreign Secretary, whose sudden death had left him totally bereft, not only in personal terms but also in terms of his career. As a result he was moving his family to the town of Verona in Italy, where he had been directed by Castlereagh's successor at the Foreign Office to attend the Congress there before he relinquished his duties.

Not everyone in the carriage bore such responsibilities. The small cradle opposite him contained a very lively occupant, carefully swathed in blankets to protect her from the weather but nevertheless managing to surface sufficiently to take a keen interest in her surroundings. Two huge blue-grey eyes, resting at the moment on her father's aquiline profile, took in every aspect of the world around her. Lady Frances Anne Emily was very much awake and alive; this was the future 7th Duchess of Marlborough. At present history scarcely acknowledges it, but she grew to be a remarkable and fascinating woman of considerable achievement, not the least of which was the vital influence she was to have on her grandson, Winston Churchill.

Her elder brother Harry, her father's son and heir, was sound asleep in the opposite corner, his blonde hair falling across his forehead in an unconsciously innocent way. Last, but certainly not least, the baby's mother, the new Marchioness of Londonderry, Frances Anne, was fully awake but had her eyes fixed anxiously on her husband's face, deeply concerned for the man, 20 years older than herself, whom she loved so passionately and had fought to marry against the advice of her guardian aunt; she had slept no more than he had and was increasingly anxious to reach their destination.

When one enters the chapel at Blenheim Palace, two statues immediately draw the eye: they are of John Winston Spencer-Churchill, 7th Duke of Marlborough (1822–83), and his second son Lord Randolph Henry Spencer-Churchill (1849–95), father of Sir Winston Churchill. Of the wife and mother who placed them there, very little trace can be found, and yet the infant with the blue-grey eyes in this frail-looking carriage became one of the most influential duchesses ever to rule 'this wild and unmerciful house', as Sarah, the 1st Duchess called it.

Duchess Frances, as she came to be known in later life, was born Frances Anne Emily Vane-Tempest-Stewart on 15 April 1822 at 21 St James's Square, London, into a family which had always been significant both socially and politically. The house was rented for her birth by her parents, who wished to be near Charles' step-brother and his wife, Viscount and Lady Castlereagh, and it cost what her mother described as the 'immense' rent of £500 per month. Frances, the second child and eldest girl in a family of six children, was the daughter of two very interesting parents, both of whom emerge from nineteenth-century history as highly colourful characters who certainly left Frances with significant genes to enjoy and pass on to her descendants. Her background provides considerable insight into how she became the remarkable force she did. The qualities and personality she grew up to demonstrate are founded in her own family and the life and experience she gained with them: her strength of character, her strong sense of family, her confidence, her poise, her fortitude, her compassion for the deprived, all were the product of the inheritance and environment which surrounded her childhood.

Her father, Lord Charles William Stewart, was a member of the Scottish-Irish family of Stewart of Mount Stewart in Ireland, whose members made substantial contributions to British national life in both military and political matters. His reputation was that of a glamorous British soldier, fighting companion of the Duke of Wellington in the Napoleonic wars against France. Born in 1778 and younger by nine years than Castlereagh, his step-brother, he was deeply devoted to him. Although not as intellectual as Castlereagh, he acquired a reputation at Eton for courage and physical prowess, narrowly escaping death when he rescued a schoolfellow from drowning.

His military career reads like a roll of honour. He joined the 18th Dragoons and in 1803 was made a colonel and ADC to George III. He preferred action to office and in 1809 joined Sir John Moore in Portugal, distinguishing himself in battle and, after Sir John's death at Corunna, becoming Adjutant-General (i.e. second in command) of the British Forces in the Peninsula to Sir Arthur Wellesley, later Duke of Wellington. At the age of 32 he was promoted to Major-General and only ended his military career when, three times wounded, he was invalided home in 1812. At almost the same moment his wife died suddenly and unexpectedly, leaving him with one son, Frederick. Castlereagh, at that time Foreign Secretary, made Charles a Knight of the Bath and sent him to Berlin to liaise diplomatically with the Prussian and Swedish armies. In 1814, as the war with Napoleon was brought to an end, he entered Paris with the conquering forces. He was given the position of Privy Counsellor GCB, the title of Baron Stewart of Stewart's Court and Ballylawn in County Donegal, and appointed British Ambassador to Austria, with special reference to the Congress of Vienna.

Such a man, of sound character and well respected, could expect to be welcomed by the family of his future wife, but her aunt and guardian, Mrs Angelo Taylor, showed considerable resistance. Lady Frances Anne Vane-Tempest was descended from more than one distinguished line and was one of the wealthiest heiresses in the country. The Vanes were Earls of Darlington; in the seventeenth century Sir Henry Vane of Raby Castle in Durham was Secretary of State to Charles I. The Tempests dated from medieval times in both Durham and Yorkshire; Sir Piers Tempest had fought with Henry V at Agincourt and had been knighted on the battlefield. The vast estates of her grandfather, John Tempest of Wynyard Hall and Brancepeth Castle, came to Frances Anne's father, Sir Henry, on condition that he added the name of Tempest to his own name of Vane. He also 'inherited' John Tempest's parliamentary seat for Durham City and later, in 1799, married the 18-year-old heiress Catherine, Countess of Antrim. Frances Anne, born in 1800 in St James's Square, was the only child of this wealthy pair; she did not see much of her mother, who led a frantic social life, but became very attached to her aunt, her father's sister Frances, Mrs Angelo Taylor, who nursed her through smallpox and later became her guardian. This was the lady who questioned the marriage: Frances Anne was fatherless, she was extremely wealthy, there were almost 20 years between Frances Anne and Charles Stewart, and he already had a son by his first marriage who was only a little younger than Frances Anne.

Frances Anne did not inherit the exceptional beauty of her aunt or the arresting good looks of her father, but her portrait by Sir Thomas Lawrence at the time of her engagement to Charles Stewart shows an attractive young woman with considerable humour and character in her face, a gift which was to serve her much more effectively than beauty, and would be inherited by her daughter Frances. This was the woman and role-model Duchess Frances had before her eyes for the first half of her life; it must have had a profound effect on her.

What is now known of Lady Frances Anne Vane-Tempest is to some extent drawn from her Journal, which she wrote in 1841 at Wynyard Hall, the family home near Durham, towards the end of her life, because it would be a 'souvenir of a long, brilliant existence', intended only for her children.

Lord Charles Stewart and Lady Frances Anne Vane-Tempest, aged 17, met in 1818 at her mother's house in Bruton Street, Mayfair. At the age of 41 he was a dashing, handsome man with a brilliant career as soldier and diplomat already established; he was British Ambassador to Austria, based in Vienna, a post from which he supported Castlereagh at the Congress of Vienna in 1815. Their further acquaintance led to attachment, but Frances Anne's aunt and guardian was not impressed. Frances Anne was heiress to an immense fortune in land and productive collieries, providing her with an annual income of £60,000 compared with Charles's £18,000 and, under the law as it then stood, on marriage her property would belong to her husband; furthermore, she was a ward in Chancery, which enabled her aunt to delay the marriage by legal proceedings.

Finally, however, Frances Anne, whose resolve had only been strengthened by this opposition, married her Charles quietly in London in April 1819, when she was given away by the Duke of Wellington, her aunt having been satisfied with a stringent marriage settlement which would protect her fortune from misuse. This meant, in effect, that Charles became tenant for life of his wife's estate, but the trustees were empowered to suspend his authority if they considered he had acted imprudently in his management of the estates, especially the collieries; nor was he allowed to sell any portion of the landed property unless he made good the sale by the purchase of land or government stock of equivalent value. Charles in due course carefully honoured this agreement.

Castlereagh, who provided his country house for the honeymoon, wrote at the time about Frances Anne:

She is not a beauty but she is extremely well-looking, mild and intelligent and innocent ... and for her time of life, she seems to have a great deal of decision and character. The situation in which she is placed will require a large share of both.[1]

By the time Charles and Frances Anne had spent a week of their honeymoon at Cray in Kent, the Castlereaghs' delightful country house, and for a second week at Wildernesse, Lord Camden's property, where the estate workers strewed the ground with flowers to welcome the new bride, they were expected at the Pavilion in Brighton to stay for a few days with the Prince Regent. Returning to town, they prepared for their visit north. The journey took four days, but they were given the traditional splendid reception: the tenantry took the horses from the carriage and drew it themselves to the tremendous accompaniment of bells. Frances Anne sadly recorded in her diary that she had not seen Wynyard for five years, when she had left it at 14, after her father's death; she was appalled to see that her mother had stripped it, selling all the plate and many other valuable things.

This did not, however, prevent them giving a magnificent ball to the county and visiting Durham and Sunderland, where again they were received with great enthusiasm. It took a considerable time to restore the estates and collieries, which had been neglected and plundered during her minority; they had to write off whatever money was owed to them by her mother and appoint new agents. Finally back in London, having been presented at court by Lady Castlereagh and having attended a fancy dress ball at Carlton House, they were ready to leave England in July 1819.

Frances Anne soon had plenty of adventures to reflect upon, beginning with the long, slow journey to the British Embassy in Vienna, where her husband was to return to his ambassadorial duties. They reached Paris in the middle of August, where they spent three weeks dining with the 'corps diplomatique', which Frances Anne found 'boring', and being presented to the Bourbon monarch, Louis XVIII and 'Madame', his queen, and the other members of the Orleans family, who were 'very kind' to her. In early September 1819 they crossed the inhospitable Jura mountains to Geneva, where Frances Anne discovered she was pregnant. Resting here for a few days, she was delighted at the scenery, the high mountains and the blue waters of the Rhone.

On through Schaffhausen, Augsburg, Munich and Salzburg, where Frances Anne became ill and where they decided to push on to Vienna, arriving on 10 October. A miscarriage soon followed, and the newly decorated, newly furnished British Embassy, a large house in the Minoriten Platz, was no consolation to the unhappy young bride.

Time passed, however, and Charles and Frances Anne gradually settled down to embassy life. There was entertaining to do and balls to attend. Vienna, the musical capital of Europe, resounded with melody. Frances Anne, used to a high standard of living, and Charles, who loved fine clothes, were soon the centre of local discussion. The observations of Martha Bradford, wife of the Reverend William Bradford, embassy chaplain, have been recorded:

'Tis plain she is not free from caprice, and 'tis equally plain that she is a completely spoilt child with fine natural qualities and excellent abilities, and with a quickness of perception and sense of the ridiculous, which makes her at once entertaining to a degree and perhaps a little dangerous.[2]

Certainly, the fact that Frances Anne was only 19 years of age and in possession of a huge fortune attracted attention and some degree of envy wherever the couple went. Charles's diplomatic position gave plenty of opportunities for the display of finery and jewellery and Frances Anne was later to record her regret that she had not spent her leisure time more profitably in furthering her education. There was also the strange story of Tsar Alexander I of Russia ...

In 1820 the Russian Tsar Alexander I called on them on his way to the Congress of Laibach in Slovenia and thus gave rise to the rumour of an affair between himself and Frances Anne that was to persist and become an important part of both their lives. He was to be a familiar figure to our Frances in her early years. It so happened that two years previously the Tsar had sat for his portrait by Sir Thomas Lawrence and had been greatly taken by an unfinished portrait of a lady which stood on an easel in the studio. Since Sir Thomas refused to identify the lady or to sell the picture, Alexander insisted on having the portrait placed in front of him as he sat and later confessed that he felt a great disquiet about it. Now, two years later, in the British Embassy in Vienna, he came face to face with Frances Anne, Lady Stewart, and recognised her as his mysterious lady in the portrait of two years earlier. This was to lead later to a much closer association.

Chapter Two

FROM CRISIS TO CRISIS

The period just before Duchess Frances' birth was to prove both busy and eventful for the Stewarts. In Britain in 1820 George IV acceded to the throne and began proceedings for divorce against his wife Caroline. Since this involved gathering information from northern Italy, where she had been living, it fell to Charles to travel there, collect the necessary witnesses and ship them off to London. At the same time he was instructed to attend the Congress of Troppau as an observer. Frances Anne, now pregnant again, missed him dreadfully, with the result that at the end of each week he made considerable overnight journeys to be with her.

More adventures followed when a fire broke out in the Embassy, starting in Frances Anne's bedroom, next door to where she was sitting with her companion Ellen Cade, daughter of her old governess, who had come out from England to keep her company. As the flames burst into the boudoir where they were both sitting, they rushed out, but at the head of the stairs Frances Anne fainted. The two rooms where the fire began were entirely consumed; the adjoining ones were badly damaged. Her clothes and laces were burnt but her jewels were saved. As for the pregnant Frances Anne, she was carried to a nearby house, where a Dr Forbes tried in vain to bleed her in both arms but managed to give her 50 drops of laudanum. She could not rest until she returned home, to a bed on the ground floor. Violent spasms and shivers brought back Dr Forbes, this time with one hundred drops of laudanum, which 'composed and under God's blessing, saved me'.

It says a great deal for the future son and heir that he survived all this; perhaps he gained the strength from it to face further ordeals ahead. He was finally born in April 1821 to his ecstatic parents. His father gave his mother a set of pearls which cost £10,000. The layette cost £2,000. He was named George (after the King) Henry Robert (after his two grandfathers) Charles William (after his father). Martha Bradford again shares her rather sour observations at the christening, recording, rather acidly, that everyone assembled at nine o'clock in the evening arrayed in gold, silver and diamonds, and was received by Lady Stewart, dressed in Brussels lace over white satin, and £10,000 worth of pearls. Charles was in full Hussar uniform, yellow boots included.

This splendid event was followed by the journey back to London to attend the Coronation. George Henry, however, was vaccinated, a daring act for those times, and reacted by catching cold. The wet nurse 'failed' and he became quite ill. On his recovery they finally departed in June 1821, accompanied by the Embassy Secretary, a doctor and several nurses, too late for the Coronation but happy to arrive at Cray after a rough and boisterous crossing lasting five hours. Frederick, Charles' son by his first marriage and now at Eton, was waiting at Cray to welcome them.

By this time Frances Anne was again pregnant and this pregnancy was also to have its adventures. Charles's regiment, the 10th Hussars, were stationed at Brighton and he took the opportunity to review them. She wrote to her mother that the occasion was absolutely splendid. All the officers came to breakfast and then everyone proceeded to the review. Charles, in his full General's uniform, was mounted on a beautiful Arabian horse covered with trappings and Frances Anne followed in an open carriage, in a habit made up in the uniform of the 10th Hussars. She was delighted when the officers seized her carriage and paraded with it up and down the ranks. After Charles had reviewed them and addressed them, to thunderous applause, everyone proceeded at five to the Riding School, where Charles gave them dinner. Frances Anne wrote to her mother to say how delighted she was, but added:

> The quantity of people, the lights, the band, the row, finished what the fatigue of the day had begun; and as soon as dinner was over I was taken ill and this was increased by the difficulty of getting me into my carriage. This increased my illness by fright so much that by the time Lord Stewart could be called to me I was almost senseless. Some other Hussars seized him, stuffed him into the carriage, shut the doors, and harnessing themselves

to the carriage, flew with us all the way to Brighton through the streets to the door of the inn, screaming and hurrah-ing … Dr Turney, who very fortunately was at hand, said nothing could save me but losing fourteen ounces of blood immediately. This was done, and I have taken quantities of laudanum and as yet nothing fatal has occurred.

She adds loyally:

Notwithstanding all my sufferings, I have been very much delighted. Indeed, since I have been out of England, nothing I have witnessed has given me half the pleasure of seeing this magnificent Regiment receive Lord Stewart with such enthusiasm as their commander … 'L'homme propose et Dieu dispose' is an old proverb. Still I cannot help settling that, if I am so fortunate as to go on well and have another boy, his destiny shall be to become a Hussar.[1]

It wasn't another boy, of course; it was the future Duchess Frances. If her brother Harry had gone through fire before his birth, then Frances had experienced the celebrations of the wild Hussars. It speaks volumes for the fortitude and tenacity of both mother and daughter that they survived unharmed.

That same year of 1822 saw the purchase of the Seaham estate from Sir Ralph Milbanke for £63,000; it was to prove a most profitable investment. The Vane-Tempest collieries, which were developed there, producing more than a quarter of a million tons a year, made Frances Anne the second largest exporter of coal from the Wear. They were situated in the Rainton and Pittington areas of Durham and it cost £10,000 per year to bring the coal in wagons to the staithes at Penshaw on the Wear; there it was loaded on fleets of keels and brought downstream to Sunderland, where it was reloaded into larger vessels for the onward sea voyage. Milbanke had originally planned to build a harbour at Seaham and to this Lord Stewart wanted to add a railway to avoid the heavy charges on these overheads. Castlereagh supported him in this because he saw the advantage to Frances Anne's interests and there was no opposition from her guardian. Indeed, it turned out to be one of Charles's best investments for the neighbourhood. This is only one example of how Charles Stewart was faithful to his marriage settlement and how early fears of him were unfounded. Not only did he prove a skilful manager but he also demonstrated his integrity and commitment to his adored wife's estate.

Meanwhile the small family had moved back to London and rented a house in St James's Square, near the Castlereaghs. Princess Lieven, wife of the Russian ambassador, always anxious to keep everyone informed, wrote to her lover Prince Metternich in Vienna, saying that Frances Anne 'was wearing enough jewellery to buy a small German principality'.[2]

The unborn Frances had another narrow escape when her mother stumbled and fell on the steps of her sister-in-law's house. She was taken up insensible, much cut and hurt, but the baby, Lady Frances Anne Emily, finally arrived safe and sound on 15 April 1822, 'the most diminutive object ever seen!' Her mother recovered very well, and they had a lavish christening on 18 May, Charles's birthday. Frances Anne's Journal continues:

> Considering our fine linens and plate were at Vienna, it did very well. We had 34 people, Esterhazy, Becketts, Lievens, Munster, Duke of Wellington, Camdens, Belgraves, Howdens, etc. The Bishop of Lincoln performed the ceremony, and the baby was called Frances Anne Emily, the last name being our gesture to Castlereagh's widow, whom we love very much.[3]

Charles immediately entered upon the purchase of a London residence, Holdernesse House, on the corner of Park Lane and Hertford Street. Frances Anne complained to her mother that it was dirty, but that the luxury of having a home of one's own, with five large windows overlooking the Park, and a garden, covered many defects. The garden was on the other side of Park Lane, and Charles also purchased the house next door in Hertford Street, bringing the total purchase cost to £43,000. Later the two houses were combined into a harmonious, more convenient whole and in 1872 this was renamed Londonderry House by Harry, the 5th Marquess.

Misfortune was to follow swiftly. It began with the King's mistress, Lady Conyngham, who hated Emily Castlereagh and wanted her and her husband to be excluded from a diplomatic dinner being held for Prince Christian of Denmark. Although her demand was completely out of the question and the matter was swiftly dealt with, it had a profound effect on Castlereagh, who as Foreign Secretary and Leader of the House of Commons, naturally expected to be present and was deeply shocked that his omission should even be contemplated. Rumours of blackmail and homosexuality followed;

subsequently his nerves seemed shattered and he began to show signs of a mental breakdown. After Charles and Frances Anne had set off back to Vienna, complete with two children and a rather large retinue, word reached them of his death. The fact that he had committed suicide had to be communicated gradually to Charles, who was devastated. The rumours of blackmail and homosexuality, spread eagerly by the Whigs, were firmly dismissed by the Duke of Wellington and other close friends, but the emotional blow was a heavy one. Frances Anne, comforting and supporting her husband, not surprisingly suffered a miscarriage. The Duke of Wellington replaced Castlereagh at the Congress and subsequently George Canning, Castlereagh's hated political rival, took his place as Foreign Secretary. Charles felt he had no alternative but to resign.

All this happened within a fortnight. When Charles had said goodbye to his step-brother in London it was with the expectation of seeing him again, his normal and confident self, in Vienna on the way to the Congress in Verona. It had taken only a short time for the gossip to take effect and for Castlereagh's mind to give way completely, causing him to put an end to his own life and also, since Canning expected to appoint his own man, to Charles's diplomatic career. Needless to say, the political scene was rife with factions and rivalries. Castlereagh's rapid rise to office had been facilitated by his brother-in-law Earl Camden's appointment as Lord Lieutenant of Ireland. Nevertheless, his intelligence and background had enabled him to serve in the British Cabinet, where he held office from 1802 till his death 20 years later. It was largely due to Castlereagh's firmness and energy that the war with France terminated and Europe was saved from the domination of Napoleon. As an experienced diplomat at the Congress of Vienna in 1815, he also laid the foundations of all future schemes of international government. He was buried in Westminster Abbey, where Charles, his devoted step-brother, later raised a statue to him.

Since Castlereagh was childless, his Irish titles now passed to Charles, who became 3rd Marquess of Londonderry while Frederick, Charles's only son by his first wife, became the new Viscount Castlereagh. Later, after Castlereagh's widow Emily died, the magnificent jewels presented to Castlereagh by the allied European monarchs at the time of the overthrow of Napoleon would pass to Charles to be worn by successive marchionesses of Londonderry. The fact that his brother was succeeded at the Foreign Office by George Canning, an old rival, did not help mitigate his grief. Charles was requested to attend the Congress of Verona as Ambassador as originally intended and the Duke of Wellington was also appointed to attend in Castlereagh's place. Later the Duke's youngest brother, Sir Henry Wellesley, would follow Charles as British Ambassador in Vienna. Sharing her husband's grief, Frances Anne sadly packed the furniture and linen and sent it back to England. Later she set out for Verona in the company of her husband, children and all their retinue.

Chapter Three

AN EMOTIONAL FAREWELL

———————————

S uch were the circumstances that led to this small family party crossing the Alps on that cold winter's night in 1822, and so it was that Duchess Frances had such strange and romantic memories of the earliest months of her life. On 25 October the Stewarts, now the Londonderrys, arrived in Verona after a fatiguing journey of ten days, during which they travelled from six and seven in the morning until eight and nine at night. The weather was very cold, the roads 'detestable', the inns 'execrable'; notwithstanding, the country was 'magnificent' and 'so different' that Frances Anne could only be glad that she had seen the Tyrol. She wrote, however, that this pilgrimage, as she called it, in the mountains was 'formidable' at that time of year, and that crossing the Alps when covered with snow was not easy.

To her mother the Countess Frances Anne wrote:

This town is a beastly, hateful place. Everybody is equally badly lodged, not a good house in the town, cold stone floors with dirty mats which swarm with insects. Conceive the horror of being indifferent to such pests as fleas, bugs, mosquitoes, etc. but expecting at every step to find scorpions and lizards! The former get into beds, drawers, etc. and the latter come in at the windows as they crawl up the walls. Not a door or window ever shuts, the wind comes in at every cranny, not a comfort to be had for love or money and the smells are insupportable.[1]

The next letter was equally depressing, written a week later on 3 November. Frances Anne had been ill and had been bled by her doctor.

She complained of the lack of comfort around her, of the fact that neither doors nor windows shut properly but provided a draught wherever she tried to settle. The house itself comprised several small rooms of various shapes: Frances Anne had two rooms, each 'the size of a Wynyard pantry'; the mattress lay on the floor in the bedroom, with a wash-stand, two chairs and an imperial (wardrobe) providing the rest of the furniture. It was impossible to have a (wood) fire because of the smoke from it. The second room served as everything else – drawing-room, dining-room, kitchen – and was furnished with green baize carpet, white dimity curtains, 12 little high chairs and a hard sofa. Frances, Harry and their nurse had three rooms elsewhere in the house. Charles had a den situated over the kitchen with its accompanying smells. As for the food, sour bread and bad butter made it impossible to eat breakfast but they did compensate for this by having French chocolate and green tea.

Such was Frances' and Harry's introduction to European winters and the questionable delights of diplomatic life. The end of this letter, however, sees the natural resilience reasserting itself: their mother looks forward to being settled again in England and itemises the furniture which Charles had collected in Italy – the fine bed, armoires and commodes of buhl, vases without end, marble tables, alabasters, statues, candelabras and loads of plate, linen, wine and china.

There were other incidents occurring around Frances and Harry at this time, one of which was to cause international scandal. Their mother had first met Tsar Alexander I in 1820 when she was considerably pregnant with Harry. Now, two years later, she had two small children, Harry and Frances, and the Tsar was to make much of both. He arrived in Vienna in mid-September on his way to the Congress of Verona and immediately sent word that he would call on the Londonderrys that same afternoon. Why this visit was so precipitate can only be the subject of conjecture. He arrived alone and spent two hours with Charles, Frances Anne and the children. Such attention was unusual and of course noticeable. A week later he came to dinner, attended by several of his staff, when Frances Anne was the only woman present, a daring thing for her to do. A few days later he wrote to her, in French, which was the language they conversed in, thanking her for the gift of a briefcase which he had admired at their home. His last visit in Vienna took place while Charles was away attending an official dinner. She writes in her Journal:

He sat with me above two hours. He certainly is a very fine-looking man if not positively handsome, his countenance remarkably pleasing, his manners at all times affable and agreeable, when he addresses a woman captivating, his conversation perfectly beautiful … During this interview we had a long explanation, and he gave me to understand the extent of his feelings of attachment for me and the strong impression I had made upon him.'[2]

There is considerable emotion here and it is tempting to believe what the rest of Vienna believed. He looked forward to meeting her again in Verona, and when he did, his visits were of great comfort among the miseries of the house she was occupying. He told her the strange story of her portrait which had so impressed him and how he had never felt drawn to any other woman. In the meantime, she writes that Charles was deep in gloom, which for some reason made her 'very uncomfortable'. Did he sense his wife's infatuation and was troubled? Had the gossip reached him?

Frances Anne's days were otherwise filled with social activity, involving the Emperor and Empress of Austria, the Duke of Wellington and other diplomatic personnel. Rumour was rife that she was now the Tsar's mistress, and certainly if they had followed the custom of the day she would have been. It is certainly true that the situation was watched by the Austrian secret police, but it is not known precisely why. Anita Leslie, in her book *Edwardians in Love*, records that Frances Anne received gifts of jewellery (now in the Victoria and Albert Museum) from the Tsar, which were added to the Londonderry collection. In Frances Anne's Journal, however, she gives her own very intimate and revealing description of the deep feelings that lay between them when she describes their final separation. So frankly does she reveal their emotion that, not surprisingly, the Journal remained private for years after her death, and was only published by Edith, 7th Marchioness of Londonderry, approximately three generations later.

Frances Anne's account of their parting is so raw in passion and so complete in her grief that it still moves the reader deeply today almost two hundred years after the event. Very poignantly and convincingly she conveys the deep emotion and uncontrollable grief that consumed them both. She describes how, when Alexander came to bid her farewell, he found her in a deep depression and spoke to her with a tenderness that became melancholy. He assured her of his love, maintaining that 'while life shall last' her image should rest in his heart. Neither could bear the parting: 'my agitation quite unmanned him', reducing him to tears. Neither could control feelings and, after trying twice to leave, the Tsar 'once more strained me to his breast' before rushing out of the room. Frances Anne describes herself as 'stupefied by grief', her remembrance of the scene being 'like a faded dream'.

Her description of a consuming love that cannot rest but must be released by some action or demonstration is psychologically very true to life. She needs to find some kind of release for her feelings and she finds it by pouring them out in writing her Journal. 'In truth I loved him,' she writes quite bluntly, without restraint, and confesses herself completely taken over by an overpowering feeling. She cannot believe that she is loved by such a man in whom she finds perfection in every way that would 'captivate the heart'. Neither could he contain his love for her. She recalls intensely his being 'at my feet, kneeling before me' and 'covering my hands with kisses'. Frances Anne describes how for long after this parting she remained depressed, felt as if her emotions were frozen and was consumed by a terrible lassitude.

After reading this unrestrained and compelling account of this scene, it comes as a surprise to read her final words: that she could only rejoice and wonder that they came out of the ordeal innocent of grief. So it seems their relationship was purely platonic! But can this final remark be accepted with certainty? On the face of it, an affair seems to have been unlikely. Both Frances Anne and Alexander were married and he in particular was renowned for his austere and ascetic character. Both were high-ranking and public figures; to keep such an affair private would have been very difficult and Frances Anne categorically makes the nature of the relationship clear at the end of her account. Yet, from the depth of passion and the physical demonstration of it that Frances Anne describes, it is not too difficult to entertain at least the possibility of a sexual fulfilment.

It is impossible to know the truth. Clearly, however, the Austrian secret police were aware of the relationship; they kept the couple under surveillance and, according to the custom and mores of the day, few eyebrows would have been raised anyway, always with the proviso, of course, that nothing became public. Yet Frances Anne makes it clear very forcibly at the end of her account that there was no sexual relationship. Supporting this is the fact that she has just given such a vivid account of her feelings in a document which, although private, she did not destroy but left for posterity. Would she have done this if her behaviour had been seriously questionable? Or is this a final subtlety, an escape clause to disguise the truth?

There is one last detail. In her account of their parting, Frances Anne describes how she became so uncontrollably agitated that Alexander implored her to be calm and 'consider the wickedness of endangering the infant within my bosom for I was above two months with child'. The baby girl, born some seven months later, was baptised Alexandrina and the Tsar became her godfather.

And so the infant Frances and her elder brother Harry not only crossed the Alps in winter, a hazard at any time but in their early childhood doubly so, but were then some kind of party or witness to these dramatic scenes and the inevitable tensions that followed. At the end of her account of this episode in her Journal, Frances Anne's husband Charles emerges as a man commanding respect. Whatever suspicions he had, despite the depression, gloom and feverishness that followed, he remained unfailingly caring, never voicing any criticism: on the contrary, she insists, his kindness was unwearied and his attentions unremitting.

Chapter Four

A Privileged Childhood

Even from her early days the young Frances and future Duchess mixed at a level in society which produced the poise and confidence that characterised her as an adult. There is a significant account of her and her brother being taken to see the Empress of Austria in Verona. Harry was dressed in a short cambric frock with blue ribbons let in down the robings, trimmed with lace and hanging buttons; his trousers had three rows of lace, his stockings a jour and little black shoes, a broad light blue sash and shoulder knots and his hair nicely settled. Frances had a cambric worked frock, blue satin sash and shoulder knots, a pretty cap trimmed and lined with blue, with a matching necklace and bracelets.

On the whole Frances' manners were better: while Harry cried and hid his face in his mother's gown, she submitted to being picked up and petted and coaxed by the Empress, an early indication of her natural diplomacy. Nevertheless, returning from another freezing excursion, this time to Venice, Frances Anne wrote to her mother that she found both children quite well, '… the former delighted to see me, the latter I can hardly flatter myself either prettier or cleverer than I left her. She is so different from Henry that, while I reproach myself for it, I cannot love her as well as Henry.'[1]

Such an admission for a mother to make! Is this the reason why there is only one surviving portrait of the young Frances while Harry's good looks are displayed frequently?

In some respects this is an echo of Frances Anne's comments about herself at the age of 12:

I was a woman in size, thoughts and feelings. I was singularly ugly –
broad, fat, awkwardly made, with immense feet, huge purple hands, greasy
stubborn hair and a fixed redness in my face.[2]

Neglected by both her parents, Frances Anne had been taken under the
wing of her aunt, Mrs Angelo Taylor, a singularly beautiful woman who later
became her guardian, but *her* daughter Frances may not have been so fortunate.
There is some evidence, however, that she was her father's favourite.

They set off on the long journey home from Verona. In Florence in 1823
Harry caught a cold and by the time they reached Milan this had developed
into a bad cough which it was feared would settle on his chest. Charles,
anxious to cross the Alps before Frances Anne's most recent pregnancy
developed too far, was forced to wait three weeks before Harry, having had
leeches applied to his chest, was pronounced fit to travel. After a further delay
of two weeks in Paris, Frances Anne finally reached Dover with a bed in the
carriage and six nurses. Charles, full of relief at arriving in England, wrote to
Emily, Castlereagh's widow, living at Cray, that he could not bear to pass her
by without communication, but that to go to her so soon after his brother's
death would be more than he could bear. He adds his news: his wife has
crossed the Channel in safety and, although very ill, was not in danger of
miscarriage; Harry was still recovering from his bout of illness, but Frances
also was poorly:

and I am afraid she is not nor will she be a beauty. But she will be, I hope,
quick and clever and amiable and will find favour in your eyes.[3]

Charles Stewart's judgement of his eldest daughter was to prove very true.
Obviously he loved her unconditionally.

From this point of infancy until the year of her marriage, in 1843, only
mere glimpses of Frances' existence are known. These very formative years
were largely spent in either Wynyard Hall near Durham, Mount Stewart
near Belfast, or Londonderry House in Mayfair. All three homes exuded
a rare degree of wealth, comfort, privilege and social contact. While
Frances in her youthfulness would not have the experience to evaluate
these advantages consciously, nevertheless they would have an impact and
influence upon her and would form attitudes and qualities which would
always stay with her.

Frances Anne, returning to Wynyard after five years absence, found it almost unfurnished. The result of this was that she and her husband commissioned Benjamin and Philip Wyatt to demolish the old house and rebuild more grandly: the Tempest mansion, built in the Flemish rural style, was to be replaced by a classical Greek shape. This was not finished until 1825, when Frances was three years old and Harry was four. There is no surviving description of this house of Frances' childhood; it was destroyed by fire in 1841. A very attractive watercolour of Wynyard Park itself does exist, however, dated 1840, by the local artist, John Wilson Carmichael. The Durham Directory of 1894 records that it stood on the site of the present Hall, 'delightfully situated in the centre of the home park, near a large artificial lake, which is crossed by an elegant suspension bridge'. The area of the site was 2,500 acres, and an obelisk standing 127 feet high on the highest point in the Park commemorates a visit in 1827 by Londonderry's old friend, the Duke of Wellington.

Wynyard was the ancestral seat and home of the family. Here were hung the portraits of Frances Anne and Charles, painted on the occasion of their engagement in 1818 by Sir Thomas Lawrence; it was Tsar Alexander's first sight of this portrait of Frances Anne that inspired his deep attachment to her. They are seen exactly as described by contemporaries: Charles is the handsome, dashing cavalry officer, and Frances Anne, although not pretty in the conventional sense, has a face full of confidence, character and humour. Also here were the twin portraits of the couple painted by Ender in 1820 in their rooms in the British Embassy in Vienna, when Charles was British Ambassador there. The original painting of Tsar Alexander I by Sir Thomas Lawrence also hung at Wynyard. To these was added later a portrait of eldest son and heir Harry, the future Viscount Seaham, an attractive, delicate-featured boy.

Perhaps it was the staircase which fascinated the young Frances. Tiny as she was, she would surely love to climb each stair, holding tightly to the banister and looking to left and right, enjoying the improved view of each portrait and particularly that of Mama by Sir Thomas Lawrence, smiling affectionately out into the world, her eyes dancing with kindliness and humour. Frances was surrounded by love and goodwill, particularly from her father, whose portrait hung close by, his army uniform splendidly decorated with honours and his commanding profile staring confidently into the middle distance. These were some of the qualities that the girl inherited from her parents. The third portrait of fascination to the children would be that of Tsar Alexander I, Alexandrina's godfather, a tall, imposing figure of dignity and strength.

There seems to have been no portrait of Frances at Wynyard. She was said by several people, including the Tsar, to resemble her mother, Frances Anne, but this does not appear to have drawn affection from that quarter. It probably meant that she had brains and character rather than beauty, and this was certainly borne out in later life.

In July 1823 Frances Anne's baby was born in Londonderry House, a girl, Alexandrina Octavia Maria, and the Tsar was reminded of his promise to be godfather. In the meantime, in the House of Lords, the Londonderry wealth was considered too great for Charles to be given the usual diplomatic pension: on the other hand, the Prime Minister, Lord Liverpool, agreed to the unusual step of creating Charles an earl with special remainder to Harry, the eldest son of his second marriage. This delighted Frances Anne, who rejoiced in her son's recognition. It was perhaps more an expression of regard for Charles than the pension, which he did not need. It meant that both sons would now have a peerage, his elder to succeed him as Marquess, the younger as Earl.

The nursery now had three occupants: Harry, Frances and Alexandrina. They were not isolated; in common with the great houses of the nineteenth century, Wynyard teemed with life and was a community in its own right. There were many rooms and innumerable staff, all of whom lived in and received bed and board as well as their annual wage, which was strictly scaled according to their status on the staff. In a good house a servant was comfortable, preferring this life to one outside on the farms.

Frances' upbringing was consistent with that of girls of her class. With the other children, she was looked after in the nursery wing by nursery maids and Nanny. Just as she was to find years later as Duchess, with her own huge household at Blenheim, girls and women had many fewer opportunities than boys and men. In later childhood she remained at home with a governess responsible for her education, often restricted to such ladylike subjects as music, embroidery, art and some knowledge of European languages.

Harry, however, was sent to Eton, his father's public school. Here the emphasis was on developing the self-confidence and self-reliance of the public leaders it was assumed the boys would become. A domestic role in their own households was the assumption, and usually the reality, for girls.

An important preparation for this was what they absorbed, subconsciously, in their childhood environment in all its aspects, from day to day routine to the grander occasions.

The next major event in the Londonderry household was a typically grand ceremonial occasion. In the summer of 1825 the new London home, Londonderry House, was opened with a great banquet and ball. This was originally Holdernesse House in Park Lane, bought by Charles at about the time of Frances' birth, and combined with the house next door to provide an impressive and fashionable London base for the family. Benjamin and Philip Wyatt were the architects, both here and at Wynyard, and certainly no expense seems to have been spared. Besides the initial purchase price of at least £43,000, no less than £200,000 is said to have been spent: a new entrance was created from Park Lane and given a splendid staircase; a ballroom, gallery and banqueting hall provided the means to entertain on a grand scale. The paintings and sculptures collected by Charles during his ambassadorship in Vienna were displayed here, together with portraits of George IV, the Duke of Wellington and Tsar Alexander I, the latter having been shipped from St Petersburg in 1824 to hang at Wynyard.

A contemporary newspaper account describes this housewarming as being of 'a style of extraordinary magnificence and taste', attended, among others, by HRH The Duke of Gloucester, the Duke and Duchess of Wellington, Prince and Princess Lieven and Emily, Lady Castlereagh; these were the friends and relatives of Frances' parents and it was on a similar base that she built her social life at Blenheim. The account continues:

> Every apartment was illuminated with girandoles or sidelights, except the first which contained an ormulu chandelier of great dimensions. All the interior was illuminated with wax candles. At eleven o'clock the company began to arrive; the dancing commenced half-an-hour after with quadrilles and ended with waltzes. A regular supper was set out in the banqueting hall at two o'clock. Covers were laid for fifty and the tables were replenished six times; on the whole three hundred supped, which was the extent of the party. The dancing was afterwards resumed and kept up till five o'clock.

This was the basis of the social confidence which characterised Frances throughout her life. All these sights and sounds would register over time in Frances' mind, some to be recreated at Blenheim a generation later.

That same summer, in July, Frances Anne produced her second son and fourth child, Adolphus Frederick Charles William; his godparents were the two royal dukes, York and Cambridge.

In 1826 the new building at Wynyard was completed and there was another housewarming celebration which, this time and typically of Charles and Frances Anne, included their tenants and work force (demonstrating a concern for ordinary people that was to become characteristic of Frances). Again, a newspaper account described the event:

On Monday last the third inst., being the seventh anniversary of Lord and Lady Londonderry, they gave a splendid and friendly treat to their tenantry and tradesmen in the neighbourhood. As the foundation stone of the new mansion had never been laid, it was determined to commemorate the building by depositing the current coins of the realm, and an appropriate inscription, under one of the immense blocks which form the portico. At half-past five o'clock this ceremony took place; Lady Londonderry placed the stone assisted by Mr P. Wyatt, the architect, in the presence of a large concourse of gentry, workmen, tenants, etc. At the conclusion of the ceremony, and after an address from the gentlemen present, the company gave three times three cheers, his Lordship's band playing 'God save the King'.

At seven o'clock, a large party sat down to dinner in the new dining-room, where it is unnecessary to say that they were treated with every delicacy and every friendly attention by the noble host and hostess. At nine o'clock the tenantry began to assemble – the company left the dining-room, which was immediately fitted up for a ball. Dancing commenced about ten, and continued without intermission, except during the time of supper and occasional refreshment, until six o'clock next morning.

The house, or rather palace – for it is the most splendid mansion in the north of England – reflects infinite credit on the taste and abilities of the architect: it combines, with singular felicity, the comforts and convenience of a country gentleman, with the splendour and magnificence of a palace.

That she grew up in a family environment in which grand events such as these were taken for granted explains the easy and natural control for which Frances was renowned as Duchess at Blenheim some 30 years later. She was part of a way of life which bred ease and confidence, a confidence which in Frances was to transcend mere control of a household and family, albeit a ducal one. Years later, when her husband became Viceroy of Ireland, she found within herself the confidence to be effective in averting a national disaster.

Frances Anne followed up these celebrations four months later with the birth of Sophia Henrietta Charlotte, third daughter and fifth child, who sadly did not survive an illness, probably pneumonia, at the age of eight months. The family was now at the peak of its wealth and social status. Apart from the expense of Wynyard and the London house, Mount Stewart, seat of the Londonderrys near Belfast, had been enlarged, Seaham Hall bought and refurbished and, finally, the Seaham harbour constructed at a cost of over £118,000.

Chapter Five

AN EVENTFUL ADOLESCENCE

F rances grew up in an environment in which the comforts of wealth and familiarity with the most powerful, rich and high ranking people in the land were normal. The household clearly lacked for nothing. Even so, there were considerable drains upon the combined income of Frances' parents of over £80,000 per annum, the basic costs being considerable. It cost £200 per month to run Wynyard; in addition, the housekeeper was paid ten shillings a week and the housemaids seven shillings. An inventory in 1841 shows the house equipped with 68 mattresses, 136 pairs of blankets, 602 towels, 80 damask tablecloths, 463 napkins, 910 pieces of china and 600 pieces of silverware.

The long line of distinguished visitors to Wynyard included Prince Louis Napoleon, George III's daughter the Duchess of Gloucester, his brother the Duke of Cambridge, the portrait painter Sir Thomas Lawrence, the poet and novelist Sir Walter Scott, and the statesman and reformer Sir Robert Peel. Nor was this wealth used solely for the comfort of the Londonderrys and their friends: the conditions in the Vane-Tempest collieries were better than most. Free education was provided for the children of workers and free medical treatment for the miners was provided at the local infirmary. The new pits sunk at Seaham were paying off: from 1845 onwards profits rose annually and were reflected in improved conditions.

Family life followed the recognised pattern of most nineteenth-century aristocratic households and Frances' opinion of it is reflected in what she chose to establish at Blenheim. The triumvirate of the three eldest children was a natural consequence of their closeness by birth: Harry, the eldest son and heir, pale blonde and handsome, the darling of his mother and an acceptable leader to the two girls; Frances, a true and loyal supporter in every adventure, confidante and loving sister, the apple of her father's eye, with Alex, or Alexandrina, a more delicate and less confident child, but nevertheless providing a different perspective equal in value to that of the others. Frances benefited from her siblings: on the one hand an older brother to add vitality and drive to the world, and on the other a younger, quieter sister, providing for Frances a balanced childhood, reflected in the stable, sensible adult she became.

Wynyard Hall, their idyllic childhood home, occupied a Park of two and a half thousand acres, the large lake providing a most pleasurable view from the main windows, an elegant, arching bridge crossing to the greater part of the Park. The children's daily walk or ride took them across the bridge and beyond, where they could play happily and enjoy their freedom and safety without being disturbed. All too soon the grooms called them to retrace their steps and they climbed back up the hill, the serene panorama of their home a constant image before them. Back in the stable yard, they dismounted and helped lead the horses back into the stables, where they would rub them down under supervision and look after them, an important part of their upbringing. The afternoons in the early days would be taken up with Nanny and basic nursery lessons, but soon their mother would introduce them to the world outside and to the people for whom they would one day take responsibility. Typically their mother, Frances Anne, took them in the carriage to visit neighbouring villages, carrying gifts of food and clothing; farmers' and miners' families alike benefited from this service. As Harry left for Eton and more masculine company, Frances and Alex accompanied their mother to the wider world of newly built schools. It was a stable, sociable and busy life which taught an unforgettable lesson of service and compassion to those less fortunate than themselves.

From her earliest years Frances was surrounded by people of influence and wealth. In 1827 the Duke of Wellington arrived at Wynyard to lay a foundation stone, which was actually an obelisk 127 feet high, standing on the high ground of the Park. He was given a tremendous welcome locally with several civic receptions and a huge roasted ox. A ball in his honour drew guests from the whole of the county, while his visits to the collieries were greeted with great warmth. Although Charles did not benefit from Wellington's appointment as Prime Minister, a few months later his eldest son, Frederick Castlereagh, was given the junior office of a Lord of the Admiralty.

In May 1830 Frances Anne's new baby was baptised Adelaide for the Queen, who came to Londonderry House with her husband William IV and stood sponsor to the child. In contrast to all this royal favour and aristocratic splendour was the London public's perception of Charles's opposition to Parliamentary reform and the Reform Bill of 1832 in particular. Riding down Whitehall to the House of Lords in 1832, he was stoned by a London mob during the riots which followed the Lords' rejection of the Reform Bill; on another occasion the windows of Londonderry House were smashed. Charles did not suffer fools gladly and could be very tactless; he certainly made enemies among those with whom he was not personally acquainted. On the other hand, he was a man of high principles, rooted in honesty and fair dealing; in this respect his daughter Frances identified with him. Always a scrupulous land and colliery owner, as far as he was concerned there was no need for so-called reform.

On the North Sea coast, meanwhile, Charles was taking great financial risks. The previous owner of the Seaham estate, Sir Ralph Milbanke, had had plans drawn up for the building of a harbour at Seaham and Charles had long nursed the ambition to carry out this project, perceiving that it would connect Frances Anne's collieries with the sea independently of Sunderland and its heavy port dues. His financial advisers were against it on the grounds of risk but leading engineers such as Rennie, Telford and Logan, whom he consulted, supported the project. It was an undertaking that also had strong public support and in 1828, when Charles laid the foundation stone of the north-east pier, he was supported by an immense crowd which included the Mayor and Corporation of Durham and all the principal county families, as well as Frances Anne and her three older children. Frances and her brother and sister watched their father perform his public duties, just as the young Winston Churchill, Frances' grandson, was to do half a century later in Ireland when his grandfather, the 7th Duke, carried out his responsibilities as Viceroy. Both occasions had a profound effect on the young spectators.

The chief agent and colliery manager, Mr Buddle, was the spokesman, handing the Marquess the traditional silver trowel, voicing appreciation for the risks and the expense involved, and reminding his audience that a few years previously no fewer than 11 ships had been wrecked with loss of life less than a mile away from where they were standing: 'It will become a harbour of refuge, into which vessels may flee for safety in times of difficulty and danger.'

Charles rose magnificently to the occasion with a remarkable speech, and was given an equally remarkable reception, both of which were recorded by the *Durham Advertiser*. He begins by expressing the emotions and commitment that he feels at the fulfilling moment:

> Gentlemen and friends, it would indeed be an effort of the greatest difficulty for me to convey to you, in any adequate language, the gratitude I experience for the kind and flattering manner in which you have been pleased to receive me; and in expressing my heartfelt and cordial thanks to this immense concourse of wealthy and respectable persons who I see around me, for the warm interest which has been shown in the important proceedings of the day, I am fully sensible of the inability of language to do justice to the feelings of my heart. (Cheers) It has fallen to my lot, during the period of an eventful life, to be frequently placed in critical situations; but I never felt under the influence of more overpowering, I may say of more aweful feeling, than at the present moment, when I contemplate the warmth of your kindness and support, coupled with the magnitude of this undertaking in the hands of an individual. Believe me, my friends, the impression is indelible and it will descend with me to the grave. (Immense cheering)

He continued:

> My great object – and it is an object of which any man may be proud, and which will be a consolation to me, as a resident of this county, to the last moment of my existence – that I have attempted, and mean to persevere in a bold effort, to add greater facilities to the export of the staple commodity of this part of England; and if we ourselves should not reap all the benefit which we have a right to hope and lay a fair claim to, still our children, and our children's children, may look back to this day as an important epoch in the annals of the county and in the records of their prospects; and while they may receive the full benefit of our honest endeavours, we may repose under the best of all reflections – we have done our duty by them.

He concluded by commending his son Harry to them:

To this boy (pointing to Lord Seaham) who will, I hope, hereafter be as dear to your hearts as his grandfather was before him, and on whom the present moment must make a long and lasting impression ... I shall ever instil into his mind the debt of gratitude which you have imposed upon me, and which he must repay to your children.[1]

Loud applause and a 34-gun salute marked the end of his speech, and there is no doubt about Charles's commitment and sense of public service. He strongly identified with County Durham and the interests of its people, something which emerges clearly from this occasion as well as the warm reception which he enjoyed. He could well have been addressing his soldiers, as he did so long ago. This, allied with his eloquence, acumen and drive, must explain his popularity. Certainly his children witnessed this public display of commitment by their father. It would be demonstrated to them that public responsibility was a natural consequence of wealth and they would be left in no doubt as to their father's sentiments on the subject. Later in her life, when she was Duchess of Marlborough, this moment would certainly be one of Frances' proudest memories of her father. Where else could she have found the courage, the acumen and the drive 50 years later to come to the aid of the Irish in the way she did?

Almost immediately the harbour was an asset: in the first three months of its opening 209 vessels with a registered tonnage of 31,000 had made use of the port's facilities. A new town, Seaham Harbour, grew up. In 1842 Frances Anne wrote that 14 years previously there was not a 'house or a path on these rugged cliffs', and that the project to create a port was treated as visionary and absurd. Lord Londonderry's risk, however, had been justified and as the years passed and the town and harbour had grown it had been crowned with success.

In 1831 an epidemic of cholera was at its worst in Sunderland, eventually carrying off a national total of 50,000 victims. This served to whet Charles's appetite for a fight. He wrote from Wynyard with his usual spirit:

The cholera at Sunderland has added much to my private anxieties, as well as the state of public events, which has made my thoughts most gloomy on general politics. Although I am persuaded the accounts have been largely exaggerated, still that an unusual epidemic reigns there cannot be denied, and with wife, children and servants, who are all of the weaker and timid nature, it is not easy to eschew all rumours, apprehensions and daily histories that arise. Still, I felt that, had I abdicated and given way to the alarm, the mischief that it would have occasioned in this county would have been incalculable. It would have been the tocsin for a general emigration. Neither Lord Cleveland, Durham, Ravensworth, nor any person of note, is now resident here, but my family and myself, and, with the large number of persons in my employ, my fears would have given general dismay. Whatever I may, therefore, individually feel, and however I may be ill at ease in my own mind for those I love and cherish far more than myself, and whose early years may make their lives valuable while mine has run more than half its course, I have determined to put the best face I could upon the general position, and place my faith in Providence more than in any of the doctors and their reports ... By going over to Seaham and Sunderland two or three times a week I show no outward apprehension, while I trust my children are as safe here as they well can be.[2]

This is another display of Londonderry's values, his clear-minded attitude about where his duty lay, and his determination to fulfil it.

Emotions also ran high in a different direction. In 1836 the Duke of Wellington had come under considerable fire in the House of Commons when he offered Charles the Ambassador's post in St Petersburg; despite the considerable respect for Charles's reputation as a soldier and diplomat, his wealth nevertheless continued to attract considerable hostility. He courteously declined, but after the birth of their third son, Ernest McDonnell, in 1836 he and Frances Anne arranged a private visit to Russia. From Stockholm, Tsar Nicholas' own private yacht, the *Ischora*, took them directly to St Petersburg, and Frances Anne happily recorded in her letters that she did not know she could be so happy at sea.

The visit to Russia was of particular significance to Frances Anne and a chance to see the places about which her friend Tsar Alexander I had spoken more than ten years earlier, when she saw so much of him in Vienna and Verona. Edith, 7th Lady Londonderry, wrote that the gossip had not evaporated. In 1825, when the Tsar was reported as having died of a fever at Tagenrog, there sprang up a rumour that the body brought back to St Petersburg for burial was that of another man, leaving Alexander to disappear secretly to Siberia and live out his life in a monastery there. Travellers who visited the monastery at Tomsk brought back tales of a monk there who bore a remarkable resemblance to him. Furthermore, in 1921, when the Bolsheviks opened up all the imperial tombs in the old Russian capital, that of Alexander was found to be empty. It has been suggested that Alexander left Tagenrog for a secret destination in an English yacht registered at Lloyds in the name of Charles Stewart, and that the Londonderrys facilitated his disappearance.

Edith insisted that the Londonderrys had no part in this mystery, but of course the rumours persisted and there is no doubt that the visit to Russia was an emotional one. If this gossip were true, then this would have been Frances Anne's last meeting with Alexander. As for Frances and Harry, whatever they knew about this romantic story has never been mentioned, and so the denials of both Frances Anne and her biographer Edith Londonderry stand as the final word on the subject.

Chapter Six

A MARRIAGE HAS BEEN ARRANGED

B y 1837 Frances was 15 years old and sufficiently mature to be taking an interest in what was going on around her. Her life was divided between Wynyard, the family home and estate, and Londonderry House in Park Lane, the social and political focus of her parents' lives, a place which her mother had made the glittering centre of London society. It was a significant year nationally as Victoria came to the throne; her coronation was celebrated in splendour at Londonderry House. After a military review in Hyde Park, in which Charles's regiment, the 10th Hussars, played a prominent part, the Londonderrys hosted a dinner for 150 guests.

One of the guests was the young Benjamin Disraeli, a friend of Charles's eldest son Frederick Castlereagh, and later to become such a devoted correspondent to Frances' mother. Frances Anne promoted his political career when it was just beginning, and from this time the relationship between Disraeli and the family, particularly with Frances Anne, grew and deepened into a lifelong friendship. Disraeli wrote to his sister, vividly bringing out the spectacle and excitement of the occasion, describing it as 'the most magnificent, most recherché conceivable', and saying he felt privileged to sit down at the table with the other guests, surrounded by exquisite sculpture. The setting, in the newly built and refurbished Londonderry House, was magnificent: Londonderry's regimental band was playing, this time on the huge double staircase, the background enhanced by orange trees and cape jessamines; their dashing cavalry uniforms evoked a spectacular scene.

Among this magnificent company would have been Frances, the eldest daughter of a substantial family. This was the world to which Frances was becoming accustomed, one in which she acquired the social confidence and poise that characterised her as an adult, not only in the fashionable situations over which she was to preside so successfully but with regard to her responsibilities and interests. These were precious and important years for Frances as she entered into womanhood. She was remarkably well equipped for life. At Wynyard were all the pleasures and pastimes of the Park, such as walking, riding, hunting; then the classically styled house furnished in excellent taste with portraits, several by Sir Thomas Lawrence, furniture which the Marquess had collected on his various travels, and gracious windows with their uninterrupted views of the surrounding countryside. Wynyard was also the social centre for the neighbourhood, the country house towards which the county families would gravitate, giving the Londonderrys an experience different from that of London.

There was also Seaham Hall, the centrepiece of the estate bought from the Milbankes with the sale of land for the development of the railway. It was situated on the headland above the harbour, looking out over the North Sea, or German Ocean as it was sometimes called, and was Frances Anne's favourite home, comfortable in its size and simplicity. Here were the beginnings of a seaport, complete with piers and a lighthouse, around which the sea birds circled with their loud, piercing cries. The place had its own, quite different appeal.

Disaster struck suddenly and unexpectedly. In 1841, when the Londonderrys were travelling extensively in Europe, word was brought that Wynyard Hall had burnt down. A flue connected with the conservatory had overheated and two thirds of the mansion was consumed by the subsequent fire. Staff and neighbours loyally fought the flames but their cause proved hopeless. The total damage was estimated at £150,000. The portrait of the lost heir, John Wharton Tempest, perished, together with other precious portraits and much of the fine furniture. Abroad in Italy, the Londonderrys were shattered but eventually summoned their resilience, supported by their neighbours and friends. It was characteristic of Charles that during these dark days he should dedicate his written account of his travels to his beloved Frances Anne, to whom he owed 'more than I can repay', the partner of his joys and sorrows.

The house was rebuilt with speed, fortunately with the talents of, among others, John Dobson, the gifted architect from Newcastle, and Ignatius Bonomi, from Durham City with an equivalent reputation; as a result, the final structure was even more splendid than the first. It was typical, too, of the Londonderrys that they should enter at this moment upon one of the most significant periods of their lives.

It was in 1842 at Wynyard, still only half restored, that the coming-of-age of the son and heir Harry was celebrated. In spite of the shortage of accommodation for guests, the event was honoured by royalty in the person of the Duke of Cambridge. Nor did the Londonderry estate workers and tenantry fail to acknowledge this landmark: the survival of the heir into adulthood meant continuity of employment, security of tenure for all, and the occasion was celebrated with the traditional roasted ox.

On this important occasion, Frances, aged 20, the eldest daughter of the 3rd Marquess of Londonderry, had her own special guest. There is no official record of where and how Frances Anne Emily Vane-Tempest-Stewart met John Winston Spencer-Churchill, Marquess of Blandford, heir to the 6th Duke of Marlborough. No doubt they frequented the same social circle and had mutual friends. There is evidence in the Londonderry Papers in Durham Records Office that Harry, Viscount Seaham, Frances' brother, was a friend of John Winston's, probably from their Oxford undergraduate days. Also, in the private apartments at Blenheim Palace hangs a picture of two gentlemen painted by John Wootton and dated 1735. One is Charles Spencer, Earl of Sunderland and later 3rd Duke of Marlborough, and the other is Lord Henry Vane, Frances' ancestor. This would indicate an acquaintance between the two families over at least one hundred years, one point of common interest being the hunter and hounds which make up the rest of the picture.

John Winston Spencer-Churchill, the 7th Marquess of Blandford, was descended from a long line of proud ancestors, ambitious high-achieving men in some cases, yet he was a fiercely individual politician with a reputation for stability and, unlike most of his ancestors, conscientious industry. Contrary to family tradition, he did not go to Christ Church, Oxford, that stronghold of broad-mindedness, but to Oriel, the centre of Tractarianism at the height of the Oxford Movement during the days of John Henry Newman. There he would absorb an awareness of the need for reform in the Church of England, something which preoccupied him in Parliament. His new father-in-law, the 3rd Marquess of Londonderry, with his Scottish and Northern Irish background, was also known for his high principles and honourable dealing, qualities which reappeared in his daughter and became one of the factors which made theirs such a strong marriage.

This marriage had none of the insensitivity of that in 1895 of the 9th Duke and the American Consuelo Vanderbilt, in that neither party was coerced, either by a socially ambitious mother or the desperate need for money. *Jackson's Oxford Journal*, precursor of the *Oxford Times*, gives a comprehensive report of the wedding, which was held at St George's, the fashionable 'society' church in Hanover Square, at 11 a.m. on 12 July 1843. As might be expected, for a marriage between two of the most notable families in the country, it was a grand affair. The ceremony was conducted by the Bishop of London; the bridesmaids were Lady Alexandrina Vane (Frances' sister), Lady Louisa Churchill (John's sister), Lady Adelaide Vane (Frances' younger sister), and the Hon. Miss Liddell (eldest daughter of the Dean of Christ Church, Oxford and sister to Lewis Carroll's 'Alice'); the groom was supported by his brother, Lord Alan Spencer-Churchill. As well as receiving presents from Queen Victoria, Frances and John enjoyed the support of guests including His Majesty the King of Hanover and, in addition to the Londonderry and Marlborough families were the Duke of Wellington, the Marquess of Salisbury and Lady Blanche Cecil, the Marquess and Marchioness of Ely with Lady Anna Loftus, and many other aristocrats. There was a splendid wedding breakfast at Londonderry House, attended by Her Royal Highness the Duchess of Kent, Her Royal Highness the Duchess of Gloucester, Their Royal Highnesses the Duke and Duchess of Cambridge and the Duke and Duchess of Northumberland. The list was long and impressive.

The characters of the two main participants meant that the main purpose of the ceremony would not be forgotten. John Winston, because of his education at Oxford at a time when the Church of England was in the process of reform, and Frances, because of the attitudes and practices with which she had grown up, were both aware of the importance and solemnity of the vows they were taking. There is no doubt that each of them made a serious and wholehearted commitment to their marriage which was to strengthen and support them through the troubled times which lay ahead.

In an age when it was acknowledged that not all children would survive infancy, John Winston and Frances, the new Marchioness of Blandford, had a large family: five boys and six girls, but three male children died in infancy. George, the eldest surviving male, was set to inherit the dukedom, and Randolph, the younger survivor, was born five years later. They grew up with their six sisters in Hensington House, which their father was given as Marquess of Blandford until he became Duke of Marlborough. It was a gracious, sensible, unpretentious family house just outside Blenheim Park, which allowed daily access to the Park, a spacious and attractive playground. Designed by Sir William Chambers and built by John Hooper, a local mason, the house occupied land acquired by exchange from Merton College. It can be clearly seen on the 1920 map of Woodstock, occupying the site of the present Cadogan Park.

Discovered between the pages of a book in the library at Blenheim Palace were a few sheets of paper with dates of birth, probably destined for the family Bible. They are headed BLANDFORD and prefaced by a quotation from the Old Testament book of Job (Chapter 1, verse 21): 'The Lord gave, and the Lord hath taken away; blessed be the name of the Lord.' After this there follows:

George Charles	Born in London May 13th 1844
Frederick John	Born in London Feb. 2nd 1846
	Died at Alverstoke, Hants. Aug. 12th 1850
Cornelia Henrietta Maria	Born in London Sept. 17th 1847
Randolph Henry	Born in London Feb. 13th 1849
Rosamund Jane Frances	Born in London Nov. 9th 1851
Fanny Octavia Louisa	Born in London Jan. 29th 1853
Anne Emily	Born in London Nov. 14th 1854
Charles Ashley	Born in London Nov. 25th 1856
	Died at Blenheim March 11th 1858
Augustus Robert	Born in London July 4th 1858
	Died in London May 12th 1859
Georgiana Elizabeth	Born in London May 14th 1860

To these was added later the last child: Sarah Isabella Augusta, born in 1865. It is sad to note the early deaths of three of the boys, but this was common in Victorian times, and it endorses the wisdom of the parents' policy of having a larger family than we would have today.

Three years younger than Queen Victoria, Frances was very much in the same mould. They were already linked socially, as indicated by the wedding guest list, and were following similar life patterns: the large family, the social conscience, the strong sense of duty. It was in 1853 that Queen Victoria led the way with the use of chloroform in childbirth; Frances would not be slow to follow this example.

Upon his graduation John Winston had become MP for Woodstock and immediately identified his priorities as being those of church reform. Everything he did as an MP was supported by Frances; they frequently discussed politics and possible reforms together. The Bill which actually bears his name, of Blandford, was passed in order to strengthen the Established Church through the fairer distribution of parish finance by the creation of smaller parishes out of larger ones, particularly in large cities. Later, in 1850, he vehemently opposed the introduction of a Radical bill which would have removed Christian teaching from schools. Both he and Frances were shocked by the revelation of the over-generous income of senior churchmen: the Archbishop of Canterbury's average salary was £22,907 per annum and the Bishop of Durham's £26,786. John Winston's proposal that the management of church lands should be placed in the hands of the laity was defeated in the Lords, but as a result of his efforts the properties of the Church are now administered by its Commissioners and the church hierarchy lives on fixed stipends.

John Winston was strong in his convictions and energetic in his approach, and supported by a wife who was as intelligent and informed as himself. He observed in 1856 that over the past 30 years, £191,000 had been paid to the Dean and Chapter of Durham alone, simply for fines on the renewal of leases, none of which had been for the benefit of the Church. This was the world of novelist Anthony Trollope's *Barchester Towers*, of the Mrs Proudies and underpaid starveling curates, that he was seeking to reform. He was opposed to any form of Sunday trading, and Lord Palmerston came in for his fierce criticism when he tried to celebrate the end of the Crimean War without a national day of thanksgiving.

Here was a member of a premier dukedom who would become a national political figure of some importance. Peregrine Churchill and Julian Mitchell, writing for a TV series in the 1970s, called him 'serious and puritanical'. He was encouraged in his political career by his mother-in-law, Frances Anne. Frances' mother, the 3rd Marchioness of Londonderry, was the leading political hostess of the period and a close friend of Disraeli, whose political career she had promoted from his early years. John Winston's own political career foreshadowed those of his son Randolph and his grandson Winston.

It would seem from the number of Spencer-Churchill babies born in the years following the marriage that Frances might have been fully occupied; however, other events are recorded for this period. The Londonderry family events in Durham continued, of course, and this played a substantial part in the lives of the Marlboroughs in Oxfordshire.

From 1843 onwards, the collieries which Frances' mother had inherited showed considerable prosperity, grossing in 1844 an annual profit of £33,400 and in 1854, the year Charles, Marquess of Londonderry, died, a working profit of over £60,500. By this time women and girls were forbidden to work underground and the employment of boys was restricted to those over 12 years of age. Victorian working-class women, however, were expected to work, family or no.

In Durham, various amenities were provided for the miners by the humanitarian Londonderrys: free medical treatment at the local infirmary and practically free education for children in the schools built and maintained by Frances Anne, who also defrayed the cost of books and masters' salaries. A miners' hall was built locally for meetings and recreation, and a needlework guild introduced for the free distribution of warm clothing for miners, their wives, children and elderly people, which was still in operation when the mines were nationalised after the Second World War in 1945. In return, she expected loyalty and usually obedience. Edith Londonderry relates an amusing story about a page-boy who was kept on duty outside the door of Frances Anne's room and summoned from time to time by a handbell to carry out messages. One day, irritated by his repeated absences, she sent him to her husband with a note saying 'Flog this fellow for me; he has been quite unendurable.' The page read the note and asked a rather large footman to deliver it for him, with the result that it came back from the Marquess after he had added 'I'm afraid!' Frances' father and mother continued to hold huge parties at both Wynyard and Londonderry House, to which many people aspired to be invited, and from her position Frances Anne promoted the interests of the young, promising politicians who gathered around her, including Benjamin Disraeli.

In 1846 two more Londonderry weddings occupied the family: Harry, Viscount Seaham, married a Welsh heiress, Miss Mary Cornelia Edwards, only daughter of Sir John Edwards, Bt, of Garth and Machynlleth. A year later he entered the House of Commons as MP for North Durham, which he continued to represent until his father's death. In 1846, also, Frances' sister Alexandrina, the late Russian Tsar Alexander's goddaughter, married an Irish peer, Lord Portarlington. The wedding took place at Wynyard, to which a huge party, including the influential Sir Robert Peel, was invited. It was also a house-warming, for this was the first time the reconstructed mansion was thrown open. Disraeli, jealous at what he saw as conspicuous favouritism of his rival Peel, wrote to Frances Anne, expressing admiration at the heroic resurrection of Wynyard and pleading that he should always be allowed to remain her special friend.

Nor was Frances' maternal grandmother, the Countess of Antrim, forgotten. In 1850, at the height of the potato famine in Ireland, Garron Tower was built in her memory in an attempt to diminish the unemployment crisis. Standing in a spectacular and dominating position on land inherited from the Countess, at Garron Point just outside Belfast, it overlooked a great overhanging cliff with a 300-feet drop to the sea below. Built in the style of a fifteenth-century castle, it forms two sides of a quadrangle, with a high octagonal tower. The grand hall and staircase are decorated with the old arms and flags, including the colours of the 18th and 25th Light Dragoons and the 10th Hussars, all regiments which Charles Stewart, 3rd Marquess of Londonderry, had commanded. On the first landing of the main staircase was a huge stained-glass window showing Frances Anne's illustrious ancestor Sir Piers Tempest receiving the accolade of knighthood from Henry V on the battlefield of Agincourt in 1415. There was a great house-warming in the summer of 1850, when the Lord Lieutenant of Ireland, the Earl of Clarendon, was the guest of honour.

This grand occasion, a vivid memory in any young woman's impressionable mind, contributed to Frances' and John's commitment to the Irish people in the 1870s, when they took their turn as Viceroy and Vicereine of Ireland and Frances became so unexpectedly active on behalf of the Irish. Garron Tower also became a significant factor in the life of their grandson, Winston Churchill, over 70 years later.

Chapter Seven

FRANCES AND BLENHEIM

F rances and John Winston (as Marquess of Blandford) began married life at Hensington House, which, although relatively tiny, was an important Blenheim property. It was conveniently located on the land now occupied by Cadogan Park, a short distance from the Palace, the seat of the Marlborough family and home of Frances' father-in-law, the 6th Duke. It was a substantial house of three storeys, with a central clock and wings to each side, and occupied attractive spacious grounds. It had been built in 1768 by the 4th Duke and only used for the most senior staff. In location, size and status it was ideal for the young couple as their first home.

In these early years of the marriage an important role for Frances was to support her 22-year-old husband in his political career. He was elected MP for Woodstock, the local town, almost immediately in 1844, and held the seat with only a short break until 1857 when, on succeeding to the Marlborough title, he continued his career in the House of Lords. To give her husband a full measure of support would not have been easy for Frances since she was busy producing and bringing up a large family.

In the 14 years, from 1843 to 1857, they lived at Hensington, Frances gave birth to eight of their 11 children. All accounts agree she provided a loving, happy, well-adjusted and well-guided childhood for them here, as she later did at the Palace itself. One of her great personal qualities was her maternal instinct, the ability to reach out and care for all children, not just her own. From the moment of her arrival, Frances' home became Blenheim. Although she revisited Wynyard, and no doubt remembered it with affection, her love and attention were focused on this lovely palace and its environs. Much has been said elsewhere about Blenheim, more graciously and at greater length, but the purpose here is to emphasise the significance of her arrival, her substantial contribution to its life and community, and her well-deserved place in its history.

Blenheim Palace, the family seat of the Dukes of Marlborough, is situated a few miles north-west of the city of Oxford; the park on which it stands has a clear perspective of 12 centuries of history. It had been a royal hunting forest from Saxon times. In the Middle Ages Henry II built the royal manor of Woodstock where Elizabeth I was later imprisoned by her half-sister Mary. When John Churchill, the 1st Duke of Marlborough, as leader of the allied forces against Louis XIV, was victorious in the critical battle of Blenheim in 1704, he was rewarded by a grateful Queen Anne and nation with the gift of two and a half thousand acres of land and the means to build the palace, which was to be huge and imposingly baroque. It would be built on a scale to symbolise for posterity the glory of the Duke's achievement and, perhaps more importantly, serve as a reminder of Queen Anne, the last of the Stuarts. Sir John Vanbrugh, the chosen architect, built for them this dramatic palace, overwhelming to many. For Frances, however, brought up in a world of power, status and magnificent houses, her new married world was one she not only adjusted to but also warmly welcomed. She was aware and appreciative of the palace's fascinating history. The park at Wynyard had been comparable to that at Blenheim, and in later years Benjamin Disraeli, Prime Minister, was to describe Wynyard as 'a palace in a vast park', with a feudal air of forest rides and antlered deer.

It was thanks to the 1st Duchess Sarah's close friendship with Queen Anne that the Churchills' Blenheim inheritance survived in the early days. When John and Sarah's remaining son died, and the dukedom was threatened with extinction, Queen Anne made it possible for the title to pass through the female line, so that at her father's death his eldest daughter, Henrietta, became Duchess in her own right. Her son in turn predeceased her, and so on her death Charles, the oldest surviving son of Anne, the second daughter, came from Althorp to become the 3rd Duke of Marlborough. Since he was a Spencer, the family name ultimately became Spencer-Churchill. Anne's second son, John, remained at Althorp to continue the family line which is now that of the present Earl Spencer and his famous sister, the late Diana Princess of Wales.

It was the 4th Duke of Marlborough, George, succeeding to the title in 1758 and living until 1817, who made a most substantial contribution to Blenheim. In his 59 years at the palace he improved the park, firstly bringing in 'Capability' Brown, the famous landscape gardener, to create the lake in particular and provide the lovely views on all sides. His celebrated style of tree planting in belt and clump; his skill with water, that we see in the lake and the glorious cascade; his topographical talent with rise and fall of land created the remarkable and impressive sight we enjoy today, a vista which is man-made but convinces us it is totally natural. Secondly, the three Greek temples in the gardens and the elegant Bladon bridge were built by the Duke's architects, Sir William Chambers and John Yenn. The cost of it all exceeded £100,000. He was thorough in his stewardship of the palace also, investing in furniture, antique gems and pictures. The portrait of this Duke and his family by Sir Joshua Reynolds is one of the present treasures at Blenheim.

His son, the 5th Duke, was an outstanding horticulturist, bibliophile, talented musician and spendthrift; he caused severe financial problems for the family for generations to come. Lady Mary Soames has outlined his lamentable career in her book *The Profligate Duke*; suffice it to say here that his extravagance was a cruel legacy for his descendants, and his shortcomings forced the subsequent sale of important Blenheim art treasures in years to come.

Of Frances' five sons three had died very young: Frederick at four, Charles before he was two and Augustus at only ten months. Fortitude was one of Frances' strengths throughout her life and it was a quality she needed in the face of the bereavements she had to endure. There were great moments of pathos in her life.

For now, though, she was free to concentrate mainly on her family although time would be given to duties assigned her by the 6th Duke and her husband John Winston. She would come to know the people in the surrounding villages of Bladon, Combe, Long Hanborough, Church Hanborough and Hensington, which is now part of Woodstock. Often she would walk by the lovely lake created by Capability Brown in 1764, when Blenheim underwent a transition from formality to naturalism. She would take pleasure in the wildfowl, probably feeding them, in particular the wild geese that reminded her of the sea birds that flocked around Seaham Hall: cormorant, seagull, guillemot and tern. Rosamund's Well would be a favourite place, sheltered and peaceful, where one might imagine the thoughts and feelings of lonely Rosamund as she marked the passing of the years. Frances would study the developing shape of Brown's beeches, growing in clumps in the distance and turning in autumn to those familiar and glorious shades of bronze and gold. It is very easy to come to love Blenheim Park in every season, but perhaps the most splendid is the late summer and autumn when the leaves linger in glowing colours and the eye is drawn to the warmth and beauty of the trees in the dying moments of the year.

The location of Hensington House was fortunate because it brought John Winston and Frances into easy contact with John's father, the 6th Duke, at the palace a short distance away. There seems to have been a good relationship between them, although in some ways the Duke was not an easy man. The proximity had another consequence for Frances in that it placed her at the heart of the Blenheim community in which, as Duchess, she was later to have responsibilities. Over the 14 years at Hensington House she came to know the ordinary people and the reality of their lives in Woodstock and the surrounding villages. Concern for the needy and deprived was to characterise all her years in the Marlborough family as it had characterised her ancestors' lives.

On one occasion her husband was addressing a gathering of prosperous farmers. He thanked his wife for her presence and support but said they should know that her real care and concern was not for them but for their workers and families, the more vulnerable, where she found there was often more need and more hardship.

As the family grew older and her sons went to preparatory school and Eton, it was the mother's responsibility to educate her daughters; in this respect Frances was fortunate, being both intelligent and well educated. Education was one of her passions and, of course, she started with her own family. She was fortunate also to have at Blenheim what was described as one of the finest private libraries in Europe, and this storehouse of Victorian thought and literature echoed and reinforced Frances' own ideals and sympathies.

From the 1850s onwards the prosperity and power of the Victorians showed an astonishing increase; they looked back on a poverty-stricken agricultural past and flocked to the new industrial regions to enjoy new prosperity and security. They became confident, dynamic, ambitious, wealthy and internationally respected. The military glory of the eighteenth century was followed by the growth of the British Empire, which came to rule almost half the world. Founded on natural resources – mainly coal, iron and wool – British exports increased ten-fold. The year 1825 had seen the first public railway, from Stockton to Darlington, and now science and technology made great strides. Brunel and the Stephensons erected magnificent bridges over rivers and valleys; Faraday in 1837 introduced electricity. Britain hummed with activity and pride. As an educated, aristocratic woman, wife and mother, Frances took great interest in this exciting social and cultural change.

In the arts the output was prolific. At the centre of intellectual life were Thomas and Jane Carlyle, Scottish by birth but established from 1834 in Cheyne Walk, Chelsea. Here Thomas wrote his defence of the industrial poor, *Past and Present*, published in 1843 and destined to become a beacon for the new social consciousness; he became a passionate reformer, both spiritual and prophetic. In 1849 John Ruskin published *Seven Lamps of Architecture*; he became the first Slade Professor of Fine Art at Oxford in 1870 and his struggle for Christian social ideals against competition and self-interest was his greatest characteristic. Also in Oxford were the Tractarians, a movement generating profound reform in the Church of England. Led by John Keble, John Henry Newman and Edward Pusey, it used sermons and published pamphlets to provoke concern and discussion throughout the Christian Church. The impact of the Oxford Movement, as it came to be called, was immense upon both religious and cultural life and it directed thought and research back to the times before the Reformation. Alongside it, the Pre-Raphaelite movement was a brotherhood of artists dedicated to the reflection of nature and moral seriousness, represented most often in medieval subjects and imagery. Associated with it are the names of Dante Gabriel Rossetti, J.E. Millais, W. Holman Hunt, Edward Burne-Jones and, of course, William Morris, the multi-talented craftsman who married the lovely Jane Burden in St Michael's Church in Oxford in 1859 and in 1871 brought her and their two daughters to live at Kelmscott Manor on the banks of the Thames. It was the Pre-Raphaelite Brotherhood who painted the murals in the Oxford Union in 1857. Throughout society a fresh wind of enterprise and initiative, of creativity and precision, of energy and enthusiasm was blowing, which was to have a profound effect on those generations following.

The family at Blenheim grew up surrounded by books and newspapers. The work of writers and poets in this literary golden age rank among the familiar classics of today: Emily Bronte's *Wuthering Heights* (1847), Charlotte Bronte's *Jane Eyre* (1847), the products of that dramatic but tragic vicarage in Haworth; William Makepeace Thackeray's *Vanity Fair* (1848) and later *Henry Esmond* (1852); Lord Alfred Tennyson's poems of lyrical beauty, *Ulysses*, *The*

Lotus-Eaters and his grief-stricken *In Memoriam*, published in 1850; Robert Browning's highly original poems, mostly written after he had eloped with Elizabeth Barrett in 1846, a romantic marriage which ended with her death in 1861; Elizabeth's own *Sonnets from the Portuguese* (1860); the fiercely intellectual Mary Ann Evans, forced into the nom-de-plume of George Eliot, for *Adam Bede* (1859), *The Mill on the Floss* (1860) and *Silas Marner* (1861); Matthew Arnold, reformer in education and poet, and his *Forsaken Merman* (1849), *Sohrab and Rustum* and *The Scholar-Gipsy* (both 1853); Elizabeth Gaskell, pre-occupied with social problems in *Mary Barton* (1848) and *North and South* (1855); and, most prolific of all, Charles Dickens with his monthly magazine instalments, beginning in 1836 with *Sketches by Boz* and continuing through to 1865 and *Our Mutual Friend*.

All these volumes would have been read by Frances and her daughters, who lacked a formal education and remained at home; the richness of the literature would have made an important contribution to their thinking and conversation, and books would be eagerly read and discussed at the dinner table. Serial publication in magazines was common, and the whole family would look forward to the arrival of the weekly or monthly instalment, delivered by that great Victorian invention the Royal Mail. Reputed to have had brains rather than beauty, Frances would have relished the opportunity to follow the progress of contemporary arts in particular. She passed on her love of the theatre, whose heartland was London, and adored Gilbert and Sullivan, which says something about her sense of humour. It seems likely the London houses in Mayfair were used by Frances and John Winston from the beginning of their marriage; after all, the children were born in London and she had spent a great deal of her own childhood there. It was doubtless a family treat to attend the theatre regularly; she enjoyed taking her grandson Winston and his cousins years later.

Sadness was not far away from the Londonderrys. In 1849, when Queen Victoria visited Ireland, Frances' father Charles rode with her in the royal carriage through Belfast. Relations with the Queen, a contemporary of Frances, had always been cordial and at this point Charles enjoyed affection and respect from that quarter. But, in November 1852, the Duke of Wellington died and Charles, in his seventies, served as pallbearer to his old friend and ally in the magnificent public funeral which followed.

The Whig government had fallen and Lord Derby became Prime Minister, with Disraeli as Leader of the House of Commons and Chancellor of the Exchequer. The question of who should succeed Wellington as a Knight of the Order of the Garter arose, and, remembering Londonderry's courteous withdrawal from the post of Ambassador to Russia in 1836, Queen Victoria agreed immediately that he should be appointed. Derby wrote to him that he could not more appropriately dispose of Wellington's Garter than to one of the 'most distinguished of his old companions-at-arms'. Life had come full circle, and Londonderry was reminded of his beloved brother Castlereagh and the glories of military and diplomatic Europe. He replied with great pleasure to Derby that although he had been fortunate to receive the highest decorations from the sovereigns of all the countries of Europe he would value Wellington's ribbon as worth them all put together. The idealism and integrity which Frances inherited from her father are evident in this reply.

The shadows were closing in on Charles Stewart, however. In February 1853, his last public appearance, he stood in a biting north-east wind to cut the first turf of the railway which was to link Seaham with the port of Sunderland. In his speech, delivered with his usual charismatic commitment, he was cheered and carried along by his audience almost sentence by sentence. He concluded:

> I beg pardon for having troubled you at such length; but the moment is one of great importance to myself. It may be the last time I shall have the opportunity of addressing you. I have told you without reserve every feeling that has directed me, and also the history of my latest undertaking. If I live to see this last project successfully accomplished, I shall cheerfully lay my head on my pillow and resign life, conscious that, so far as concerns those whose interests Providence has committed to my care, I have to the fullest extent of my means discharged the duty which has devolved upon me.[1]

He had spoken for over half an hour, bare-headed in a cruel wind from the North Sea, and then he came down from the platform, cut a piece of turf with his spade and threw it, with appropriate style, into a handsome mahogany wheelbarrow. The loud cheering followed him as he wheeled it across the field to his carriage, on top of which he flung it with a heroic flourish, together with the spade. For him it was the triumphant moment for which he had waited so long.

Christmas and New Year were spent as usual at Wynyard and, although Charles was unwell, he struggled up to Londonderry House in February 1854 to attend Parliament. A bad attack of influenza unfortunately turned to pneumonia and he died on 6 March 1854 in the presence of his wife and children, deeply mourned. The Crimean War was beginning, and the Indian Mutiny a year away. The same black horses that had drawn the coffin of the Duke of Wellington through the streets of London now conveyed the Marquess of Londonderry to his final resting-place.

Chapter Eight

DUCHESS OF MARLBOROUGH

Three years later, in 1857, the 6th Duke was also dead; John Winston and Frances became the 7th Duke and Duchess of Marlborough. They were fortunate in that they had had time to become familiar with the estate and neighbourhood and were in a position to effect a smooth transition into the next generation.

The will of the 6th Duke provides an interesting insight into John Winston. His relationship with his father reveals a degree of trust and understanding which speaks well of John Winston. In some ways the Duke was a troubled and difficult man, especially towards the end of his life when he was an invalid, largely confined to a bathchair, but there is absolutely no indication of anything other than harmony between father and son; Frances, with her strong sense of family loyalty, became part of this harmony. The Duke's will placed some interesting responsibilities on Frances and John Winston, one of them very moving.

The Duke had married three times and at his death at 63 was leaving a daughter Clementina, only nine years old. She was now an orphan as her mother, the Duke's second Duchess, had died when she was only two. In his will the Duke requested that Clementina should be cared for by John Winston. John and Frances, typically, brought the little girl into their own family and she remained happily with them as their ward until her marriage some years later. Her affection for her guardians was lifelong; the visitors' book at Blenheim is peppered with references to her staying there as Lady, later Countess, Camden, now in a marriage arranged for her by Frances. No doubt the magnificent diamond tiara she inherited from her mother at the age of 21 was a reminder of Blenheim and the happiness she enjoyed there with Frances and John Winston.

It seems that any human need met with response from John Winston, something in which he enjoyed Frances' support; she was sensitive to any form of personal deprivation. The dying Duke was also anxious for the future of his housekeeper, Sarah Licence, who had been with him for many years, and directed in his will that she be given an estate cottage and a pension for life; on the other hand he stipulated that his own funeral expenses should not exceed £100. His son duly fulfilled both requests.

Frances had chosen her husband well, despite a comment written 70 years after his death which has unfairly and inaccurately coloured the image of John Winston. Dismissing him as 'a complete full-blown Victorian prig',[1] the writer makes the mistake of judging some of the Duke's views on aspects of Victorian belief and behaviour by today's more accommodating standards. In his time, his views were common, and there is no evidence of their causing any particular antipathy; a current view sees him as one who 'to a large extent sympathises with the progressive tendencies of the time'. Nothing could be clearer than that!

He was a devout member of the Church of England. Educated at Oriel College, Oxford, focal point of the powerful Tractarian Movement, he was familiar with the free and vehement religious debate of his time and considered and established his own position, which he then lived up to with integrity. A lifelong Conservative in Parliament, he nevertheless reserved for himself 'a general liberty of action, particularly on foreign and church policy'. His daughter-in-law Jennie, Lady Randolph Churchill, described him as having a 'grand seigneur appearance and manner', and he certainly had a rather formidable manner, but she acknowledged him as 'extremely kind and most courteous'.[2] Even the writer who dismissed him recognised 'a faint hint of kindliness' about the eyes in one of his photographs. He was, in fact, an admirable man, a loving, understanding and caring father to whom his family were devoted, and a very popular Lord Lieutenant throughout Oxfordshire. He had a serious attitude towards his public duties, and his strong character could produce a single-mindedness in pursuit of principle, leading occasionally to obstinacy, which he passed on to his ultra-decisive grandson Winston.

In Frances he found the ideal wife; she shared his intense love and loyalty for the family and for Blenheim. Robert Rhodes James, biographer of Randolph Churchill, describes Frances as highly intelligent and resourceful, ruling the households of first Hensington House and then Blenheim with a firm hand, adored by her children. One is reminded of Lord Castlereagh's comment about the Duchess's mother, Frances Anne Vane-Tempest: when she married his step-brother Charles, he said that she had a great deal of decision and character about her, and she would require both.

Her daughter-in-law Jennie, Randolph's wife, wrote in her *Reminiscences* that 'at the rustle of her silk dress the whole house trembled', but added that a warmth of heart 'overcame any overmasterfulness of which she might have been accused'. She was deeply respected by her husband's family and an amusing instance provides evidence for this. Her father-in-law's third wife, Jane, was an amiable woman who did not share Frances' intelligence. When the Duchess asked Frances why she was not invited to Court balls, but only to drawing-rooms, Frances patiently advised her to write to the Lord Chamberlain. A few days later Frances received a letter from the Duchess, thanking her for the advice, which had been effective. 'I am told it was a clerical error,' she wrote, adding that she couldn't see what the clergy had to do with it. Frances' reply is not recorded!

Under the circumstances of her marriage, Frances had brought a degree of relief to the Marlboroughs. The 4th Duke had made over Cornbury, a Blenheim estate of 5,000 acres, to a younger son who established the cadet branch of the Churchills with a separate peerage; the extravagance of the 5th Duke was legendary. With the marriage of John Winston, things took on a more prosperous appearance. Mortgages were called in and debts repaid; items such as the magnificent silver centrepiece in the Saloon at Blenheim, wonderfully crafted by Garrards, the Crown Jewellers, appeared in 1845. The register of the Royal Yacht Club at Cowes shows the yacht *Wyvern* registered in the name of the 6th Duke of Marlborough from 1845 to 1854, and John Winston continued this tradition: from 1843, the year of his marriage, to 1882, the year before he died, he had several yachts registered. The *Wyvern* was one of the 15 starters in the original 1851 yacht race which is now known as the 'Americas Cup'.

John Winston had chosen his life partner with characteristic care. She had contributed in real terms to the financial security of Blenheim; moreover, her nature and family background ensured she was instinctively committed to the future of her new home and the members of it for whom she was directly responsible. Under her perceptive gaze and influence the fortunes of all began to revive both politically and socially.

Frances found, on assuming the title of Duchess of Marlborough in 1857, that she had a more public profile than her predecessors, certainly since the death of the 4th Duchess, Caroline, in 1811. Like Frances, Caroline had arrived at Blenheim from a major aristocratic family and home, being the daughter of the 4th Duke of Bedford, of Woburn Abbey. She had married her husband when he was already Duke and had the advantage of youth, becoming Duchess and arriving at Blenheim when she was only 20. Her successor, Susan, 5th Duchess, had little time to make any impact at Blenheim. Tiring of her husband's profligacy and infidelity, she left him and Blenheim for good in 1819. Jane, the 6th Duke's first wife, was in her fifties before she became Duchess and died four years later. His second wife, Clementina's mother, died after fewer than four years as Duchess, and the Duke's third wife left him after only two years, when he was 60.

Coming, as she did, after this rather barren period, Frances was looked to with anticipation and readiness by a neighbourhood deprived of a strong female figurehead for so long, and she was of the calibre to respond. Over the next 26 years she established a loved and respected place for herself in the community. She had enormous advantages from the start. Living just over the road from the Palace for the last 14 years, she and her children had already settled in the local community. She had come among them as a young bride of 22 and now, as Duchess, was still only 35 years old. The local community would be aware of her background as daughter of one of the richest and most successful men in the country and of the legendary nature of her family home at Wynyard. Her father's fame as a soldier and partner in Wellington's triumph over Napoleon lived on in the national memory; Wellington had died fewer than five years earlier, his military successes crowned by his later political achievements. The neighbourhood welcomed this new Duchess with anticipation and Frances lived up to their expectations.

The town of Woodstock had always had close associations with Blenheim, being developed by Henry I to provide lodgings for his retinue when he was in residence at what was originally Woodstock Manor. Since the building of the Palace (1705-22), Blenheim had been central to the fortunes of the local town and the surrounding area. It had introduced a large labour force to the neighbourhood, which brought prosperity. The town sustained a favourable population level, and Blenheim and its gardens, park and estate was always the biggest employer.

In 1713, as the Palace was being built, architect Sir John Vanbrugh had wished to improve the town. The main streets of Woodstock were paved at the Marlboroughs' expense, retaining a central channel with a gradual rise to the buildings on each side; this had cost £1,000 but it served until the middle of the nineteenth century. The Marlboroughs also transformed the town's public buildings. The old Guildhall, demolished in 1757, had eventually been replaced in about 1766 by the present Town Hall, built by the 4th Duke on the site of the High Cross and the Penniless Bench. Park Street, opened up by the removal of the main park gate from its west end in 1723 and then by the demolition of houses to open up the north side of the church, had been further enriched in the 1780s by the rebuilding of the church tower in the classical style, the work of John Yenn and Sir William Chambers. Two rows of almshouses had been built by Caroline, the 4th Duchess, in the 1790s, one of which still survives as Caroline Court.

Woodstock had often reflected the rise and fall of Marlborough fortunes; the death of the 4th Duke in 1817, for instance, threw between 80 and 100 people on to poor relief. The absurd extravagance of the 5th Duke, which brought him virtually to bankruptcy, meant that almost all Blenheim staff were laid off and the neighbourhood suffered in consequence; it was not until the middle of the nineteenth century that there was any revival of prosperity under the 6th Duke. From John Winston and Frances' time until well into the twentieth century, however, there were over 40 gardeners alone.

A field in which Frances was particularly interested and active was education, and her concern was inevitable. She was much influenced by her parents, particularly her mother, having observed Frances Anne's concern for the miners and farm labourers around their estate in Durham, and she was aware of her efforts to provide health care and education for the workers and their families. This example, and Frances' own sensitivity towards those in need, particularly children, moved her to provide for and support schools in Woodstock and the local village of Bladon. In this she was closely allied to her husband.

Evidence is provided by the records of Woodstock National Schools, which were built in 1854 by subscription on a site presented by the 6th Duke of Marlborough, a fact commemorated by a plaque on the school wall overlooking the Oxford to Stratford road. The minute book of the committee that met in Woodstock Town Hall on 29 January 1853 to raise subscriptions was chaired by John Winston, then Marquess of Blandford. He was almost certainly the driving force, as his father was by then in poor health; there is clear evidence that both he and Frances later helped, visited and showed considerable interest in the new school. The architect was Samuel Sanders Teulon, who had started to re-model Blenheim Palace chapel in 1850. The school was an ambitious project, intended to accommodate 380 pupils. The infants were to occupy the smallest room on the west side, the furthest from the road. The girls and boys had the two long rooms with a smaller room off for the headmaster. There were separate entrances, toilets and playgrounds. The heating was by open fires and lighting was provided by oil lamps.

On 1 May 1858 Frances laid the foundation stone for a school at Bladon, just a few yards away from the site where her famous grandson was to be buried 107 years later. Although the Duke gave the address, he was careful to reflect her interest and commitment by including Frances in his speech: 'It would afford himself and the Duchess great pleasure to erect this school', and 'this school ... he and the Duchess would feel true gratification in promoting'. As the Duke, it was inevitable that he would be at the forefront, but he was no mere figurehead: his zeal for education was well known and he had been much involved, as Marquess of Blandford, in the school ostensibly built by his father in Woodstock. He had the status and influence to promote it and only he could donate the land on which it was built. However, the support for the running of the school and the practical contact with its pupils came from Frances.

Probably because of this, the school was known, and still is, as 'The Duchess of Marlborough's School'. It is recorded as such in the inscription on the exterior of the building which is still a substantial part of the present school: 'The Duchess of Marlborough's School, erected 1858, enlarged 1889 and 1894.' The previous school had been destroyed in a fire in 1853 and some 80 children under the age of 11 had been attending school in a temporary cottage room. As the inscription implies, the school flourished. Although it was designed for 64 pupils it opened with 84. By 1871 there were 96 children; by 1890 it could take 130, and by 1895 there were 172. The Marlboroughs had made a far-sighted provision.

The rules of the school reflect the Duke rather than the Duchess: 'The school should not be altogether free, because people always value most that for which they had to pay something.' Such a view reflects John Winston's High Victorian attitudes more than those of Frances, whose instinct was to react to need. The Duke's address at the opening of the Bladon school had included the hope that it 'would be the means of training the young in those ways which should prepare them for a course of Christian usefulness on earth and a life of eternal happiness in heaven'. He was aware of the reality of those hard times, however, and acknowledged the need for education to provide temporal as well as spiritual improvement.

A particular value for the school, reflecting what Frances had seen in Durham, was its use as a centre for the wider community. One contemporary commented that local families 'have their children trained there ... but they also enjoyed the use of it for missionary and other pleasant evenings'. There are reports of the school being used for the Feast, 'in the presence of the Duke and Duchess of Marlborough, the kind donors of the feast'. And on another occasion, after the Harvest Thanksgiving in the school, 'a public tea was held by kind permission of Her Grace The Duchess of Marlborough'.[3] Frances and John Winston had done much to improve the quality of life in a small, not very affluent, village for which they clearly felt a responsibility.

It is evident that Frances had strong views about the importance of education and that in Bladon she found a wonderful outlet for her enthusiasm. Stories are still told in the village of the traditions she established, of regular visiting, for instance, and a keen interest in the welfare of the pupils, followed up by practical help, which were continued by subsequent duchesses for many years to come.

Although the Bladon school log book is missing for this early period it is obvious that Bladon and Woodstock schools received identical treatment and the log books of Woodstock school in this period have survived. From 1863, when log books became compulsory, we have a clear portrait of Frances and a wonderfully entertaining picture of life in this little school until 1880, when the next log book disappeared. The 1863 log records numerous visits by the 7th Duke and Duchess, both separately and together, over a period of almost 20 years. In 1864 Frances, Duchess of Marlborough, a frequent visitor to Woodstock School, brought with her 'five dozen yards of calico, two dozen yards of flannel, wool and stockings. Calico and flannel to be made into useful articles of clothing for charitable purposes; wool and stockings to be used to teach the girls to darn.'

An entry in 1865, an extremely severe winter, tells us: 'Several children go at quarter to 12 a.m. to fetch soup from Blenheim.' Local historian Norman Roast refers to the Duchess as 'her charitable self', and in a later entry the 'ever faithful Duchess visited the school this morning, gave a reading lesson, corrected the first class dictation, looked over the copy books and needlework and heard the infants sing.'[4]

Nor was this courtesy one-sided. There are frequent occasions when pupils were taken to Blenheim for tea parties and, sometimes, special occasions. In 1870, when the Prince and Princess of Wales visited Blenheim, the pupils marched there in twos and sang the no doubt well-rehearsed 'God Bless the Prince of Wales'. Nor would these duties have been a burden on Frances. Throughout her life she was drawn to children; her affectionate nature established an immediate rapport with them and made every visit a pleasure on both sides.

The deep feeling of responsibility Frances and her husband displayed for children in their community as well as in their family, of compassion and care for them, emerges time and again throughout their lives. Even the most conservative interpretation of their private annual accounts reveals their commitment. In 1861 they built another new school, at Ardley, a small village on an outlying part of the estate ten miles from Blenheim. Frances had a special interest in this village, later repairing the church there after a serious fire. The support for schools continued regularly over the years. In 1865, 26 local schools received direct financial support to a total of £220 14s. Indirect support with such things as coal and clothing funds, teachers' salaries, furniture, etc. increased this by a further £1,000.

A regular, exciting and much enjoyed aspect of their commitment to schools was the regular provision of events in the Park, variously described as 'School Teas' or 'School Feasts'. A charming series of sketches drawn at Blenheim in 1973 by Sir George Scharf, Director of the National Gallery, still survive in the Gallery archives. They record vividly the children's pleasure in a typical 'School Feast'. Several of the sketches show large numbers of children enjoying their activities in the Park. One sketch shows a band which had been brought in to add to the occasion; another shows tea in the Riding School.

Frances' involvement with schools in the years still to come, as Vicereine of Ireland, was based on long experience.

Chapter Nine

THE TRIUMPHANT REVIVAL

T he more domestic face of Blenheim Palace was to take on a new appearance at this point in its history. The 6th Duke had already begun on the restoration after his father's sad reign, but only by obtaining an Act of Parliament could he finance repairs by mortgages and timber sales. The fact that this Duke had all his papers destroyed at his death has made it difficult to assess the extent of his contribution, but we do know that in his relatively short time as Duke (1840-57) the Palace was renovated 'at immense expense', reputedly £80,000. It is not possible to define exactly what he did, but there is one known detail which was to benefit Frances when she arrived at Blenheim after her marriage. The 4th Duke had developed the former Orangery into a theatre, but this was now redundant and so the 6th Duke converted it into offices and moved the Palace administration there from Hensington House. This resulted in the large and attractive house, so conveniently located, becoming available to Frances and John Winston when they were married.

The period 1857-83, when John Winston and Frances inhabited Blenheim as 7th Duke and Duchess, brought significant changes and improvements. The 7th Duke continued his father's work of developing and restoring the Palace and Park after years of neglect by the 5th Duke. This was a world foreign to Frances. There was no question of any need for remedial or restoration work on the houses and farms where she had grown up. Nothing was allowed to deteriorate there: everything was in good order. The financial basis of the Londonderry estate and houses was different, the family not depending on their land and agricultural income. The income from industry was huge, particularly the collieries of her mother's family, the Vanes, which her father, the Marquess, had developed so successfully. When her father-in-law and then her husband were struggling to find necessary finance, the Londonderry collieries were employing over 4,000 miners at the height of the nineteenth-century boom. As usual, there was only support from Frances for the measures her husband had to take.

In their years at Blenheim there were great changes for the staff who had always lived in the Palace. In the early nineteenth century there were said to be 187 furnished rooms in the Palace and a staff, not all resident, of about 80; the 1871 census return records at least 30 servants living in the Palace itself. Now the Duke was building lodges and estate cottages on the Park and in nearby villages. Springlock Lodge, or Cottage, was built near High Lodge in the 1840s; Middle and Eagle Lodges before 1863; Hensington Lodge from 1876-7. Ditchley Lodge, at the northern boundary to the park, was rebuilt closer to the gate before 1863; Woodstock Lodge, at the Town Gate, so called by 1863, was rebuilt in the 1880s; Bladon Lodge was much restored in 1888; the Bothy, north-west of the kitchen garden, was built in the late nineteenth century. Staff, household and otherwise, could now move out of the Palace and enjoy a new degree of freedom, no longer under the same roof as the Duke; in many cases there was easier access to local amenities such as schools and shops. Among the houses were the Duke's 'Model Cottages', of which he built 20 or more, not only in Woodstock but in villages on the outlying estate. These were built for families, and provided a much greater opportunity for staff to marry and have children.

This period also saw a great deal of restoration and alteration within the Palace. Frances and John used it as the home for a family (a family with eight children), and also made comfortable provision for guests, both family and formal, of whom there were many. They enjoyed a reputation for their welcoming hospitality at the Palace as well as for the grand society occasions they hosted. To this end, the circuit for visitors of public rooms was curtailed and the whole east front reserved as private apartments. The large drawing-room west of the Grand Cabinet Room, and the present Green Drawing Room, became a billiard room. The Saloon, known as the State Dining Room, was refurnished as a drawing-room. The former billiard room became a library, designed in Gothic style by S.S. Teulon, who also made substantial alterations in the Chapel. The principal staircases were altered around this time, the one in the north-west of the main block being entirely reconstructed. It is also possible the Duke installed a system of underfloor heating of the main corridors. By the 1880s the present China Ante-room linked the hall to the rooms beyond. Before 1860 an Italian garden was laid out on the east front and a circular rose garden with radiating paths and a central fountain constructed.[1]

The local town of Woodstock seemed to emulate the Duke's energy and began to improve considerably. Several Nonconformist churches were built, a police station appeared, and in 1853 there was a gas works on Brook Hill. Houses in the main streets were demolished and rebuilt, and there was gradual residential development along Hensington Road. A large union workhouse appeared on what is now the site of the fire station. Later, in 1890, a single track railway was opened from the Great Western Railway at Woodstock Road (renamed Kidlington) station to Blenheim and Woodstock station, built on the Duke's land on the east side of Oxford Street.

In 2001 a letter arrived at Blenheim from a correspondent in Warwickshire, containing photocopies of a prayer book presented to the sender's great grandmother in 1880, 'With best wishes from the Duchess of Marlborough at her leaving the Duchess's School of Industry'. Previous generations of her family said the great grandmother had been provided for by the 7th Duchess of Marlborough, at a boarding school she had established in the 1860s at 22 Park Street in Woodstock, just outside the Park gates. The school trained girls, aged 13 and usually local, at Frances' expense for posts in domestic service which required high levels of skill or responsibility. In 1873, on one of his frequent visits to Blenheim, Benjamin Disraeli visited the school, which continued for at least 20 years. Clearly Frances was providing sought after and valued opportunities. One of her frequently demonstrated qualities was common sense; her altruism was often based on practicality. This was to stand her in good stead in her greatest challenge, soon to come.

The period between 1850 and 1886 was the high point of Victorian energy and achievement. It was characterised by exciting and powerful initiatives and achievements nationally and overseas: the Great Exhibition (1851), the opening of the Suez Canal (1875), Queen Victoria's reign as Empress of India, and the growth of Britain's exports throughout the world. Between 1844 and 1880 Britain's coal production was half as great again as that of France, Germany, Belgium and Russia combined. Huge London docks were built to facilitate export: Royal Victoria (1855), Millwall (1868),

Royal Albert (1880). All this activity was typical of the Victorians: they built with confidence and foresight; they invested in the future and, in Blenheim's case, they put right the neglect of the past. Both John Winston and Frances took their responsibilities seriously, their attitudes and decisions reflecting the ambition and achievement of the times. So the Palace and Park were an urgent priority; a considerable number of staff were housed comfortably and safely in their own homes and the district was revived.

John Winston and Frances made Blenheim a place of hospitality and welcome. The Visitors' Book reveals a stream of guests – family, friends and establishment figures, local and national. The dates of visits are significant and reflect the longer visits of groups of formal visitors as well as the less formal, shorter visits of friends at ease with their hosts. For over 20 years, the book is a roll call of the important and the influential: royal, aristocratic and political. It also includes regular family visiting by Frances' and her husband's families. Among the royal names are Prince Albert and Princess Alexandra (regularly), Princess of Schleswig-Holstein (Queen Victoria's daughter), Frederick William, Prince of Germany, Duc d'Orleans. The list of aristocratic names includes Dufferin, Northumberland, Caernarvon, Chelsea, Bute, Bath, Ranfurly, Grosvenor, Mitford, Walsingham, Buccleugh, Cavendish and many more. Among the politicians are Disraeli, Rosebery, Lansdowne, Curzon, Cecil, Balfour. Family names are frequent: Churchill, Portarlington, Vane, Stewart, Camden, Garlies, Roxburghe occur time and again, as well as Rothschild, a business acquaintance.

This was Frances' world. Although the names reflect the Duke's status, his political career and perhaps the interest and importance of Blenheim, they suggest Frances' superb skill as a social hostess. She had learnt well from her background.

The local gentry and notables seem to have benefited from regular invitations to the Palace. There are revealing, sometimes amusing, insights into the occasions hosted by Frances and the Duke. A Mrs Jeune, wife of an Oxford don, dined at Blenheim in November 1858, and observed rather resentfully in her diary that she was kept warm with furs and hot-water bottles. The following year Max Muller, of All Souls College, Oxford, did rather better: he describes the excellent meal he had in the Rubens room in a party of 24, and was allowed to wander through the rooms while music played. In particular he enjoyed a privilege which only private guests received:

The next day I saw the pictures in the private rooms, which one cannot see otherwise, the gems, the sketches, then more music.[2]

Mrs Jeune was back in November 1859 at a ball given for the Prince of Wales. The Palace looked very grand, well lighted and with a dozen footmen in the showy Marlborough livery drawn up at the entrance, and this time she provides a glimpse of one of the grand occasions. She followed the Prince into the Grand Cabinet Room where a large party had gathered, including the Earl of Portarlington and his wife (Frances' sister), Earl Vane (Frances' brother) and 'who not' in the county of Oxford. Despite her seriousness of character, Frances was vastly experienced in creating the grand occasion; she knew how to make the most of her fashionable guests and of the magnificent rooms of the Palace:

Dinner was in the Grand Saloon, brilliantly lit by candles and gas below, dark suggestive shadows in the vault above ... dazzled by the display of jewels round the table.

Such occasions needed a hostess who could organise and direct, and we are given a glimpse of Frances here on her own ground:

At ten the evening company began to arrive and they all proceeded to the ballroom. There was dancing in two of the tapestry rooms, too.[3]

It is true to say the Duke and Duchess were characterised by steadiness, responsibility and seriousness, but this does not tell the whole story. Frances in particular, had polished social skills of a very high order. Of all visitors, the Prince of Wales, later Edward VII, was the most frequent; he was at Blenheim in 1859, 1870, 1873 and 1896. An undated newspaper in the Bodleian Library gives an account of an even grander party given for the Prince:

After the shoot there was a banquet 'a la russe' in the Grand Saloon, with a vast bill of French fare. There was an evening party for three hundred; the display of diamonds and jewellery was dazzling in the extreme. All the apartments along the whole south front of the Palace were illuminated and thrown open to the autumn night and the gaze of hundreds of spectators gathered on the site of Henry Wise's vanished parterres. The first and second state drawing-rooms had been furnished anew for the occasion, the Prince's apartments fitted up in enamelled white and gold furniture ... Altogether it was the most brilliant spectacle in the county for a century.[4]

And thus Blenheim Palace began to emerge from its long sleep of over 50 years, from two generations of neglect both domestic and social. In 1861, however, there was a disastrous fire at Blenheim. For centuries the nature, size and location of the great country houses had made the threat of fire a nightmare for their owners. The corner of the north-east quadrangle, known as the Kitchen Courtyard, was completely destroyed, and the Titian Gallery with all its paintings was lost, including the series of paintings attributed to Titian and presented to the 1st Duke by Victor Amadeus II and an extremely valuable Rubens, 'The Rape of Proserpine'. These pictures had been removed from the main part of the Palace by the 4th Duke in 1796. John Winston had to make good the fire damage, which he did with exceptional good taste. In 1862 he rebuilt almost the whole south side of the Kitchen Courtyard with a conservatory of such quality that in recent years it has been converted into a gracious venue for corporate entertaining. Anyone who is a guest in the Orangery today has only to glance up at the glass roof, with its elegant tracery of wrought iron, to be impressed by the good taste of the 7th Duke, and probably his Duchess.

In spite of his elevation from the Commons to the House of Lords, compulsory for any MP who became a peer, the 7th Duke's career in politics continued to flourish. By 1866 he had become Lord Steward of the Royal Household and the following year he was Lord President of the Council. Given the commitment to education he shared with Frances, this was a welcome appointment. In the nineteenth century there was no Department of Education. It was part of the responsibility of the Lord President, an opportunity which John Winston exploited to the full, undoubtedly with Frances' support and influence. The initiatives he took are revealing. He introduced an Education Bill which proposed extending state aid to non-denominational schools and making state support for schools, based on results, dependent on results achieved solely in secular teaching. He advocated a complete survey of education provision in Britain which, three years later, a Royal Commission was set up to perform. He proposed a conscience clause, allowing withdrawal from lessons on religious grounds in single school parishes. For his time he was an enlightened man and he was in a position to provoke national debate and action on the issues and ambitions Frances shared with him. In February 1868 Disraeli became Prime Minister. He invited John Winston to lead the House of Lords but the Duke scrupulously told him that that honour belonged to Lord Malmesbury, who had often deputised for Lord Derby during his frequent absences.

In April 1868 the Conservatives fell from power and remained in opposition for six years. By now John Winston's mind and interests were considerably enlarged, church and education matters becoming the focus of his attention. In 1874, when the Conservatives returned to power, Disraeli proposed the Duke to Queen Victoria as Lord Lieutenant of Ireland. He thought the Duke had 'initiative, intellectual grasp and moral energy', and regarded him as one of the most competent Tories in the Lords. John Winston has been described as 'a serious, honourable and industrious man'. The impression created by these words is of a man that a woman such as Frances would be totally comfortable with. His qualities reflect and complement hers; they were happy together and in understanding and appreciating him we understand and appreciate her more readily. The public and official appreciation and regard he had achieved by this stage are impressive. He had fought several elections successfully, he was a Knight of the Garter (1868), a Cabinet Minister and a Privy Counsellor, and he was now deemed suitable to be the Queen's representative as Lord Lieutenant, Viceroy of Ireland. The post carried considerable status and significance but it was an expensive one to maintain: official receptions, regular courts at Dublin Castle, weekend parties and endless hospitality, not to mention the host of staff needed to support it all. Official financial support for the post covered only about fifty per cent of the cost, the holder of the office being expected to bear the remainder, which would amount to about £20,000, over £1,000,000 in today's values. John Winston was a prudent man and, knowing it would strain his resources, declined the offer.

As Blenheim began to revive, restored by the energy of the Duke and Duchess, the Duchess's mother Frances Anne picked up the threads of her own life of widowhood in the north. Firstly she erected an impressive mausoleum at Wynyard for her husband Charles, designed by Lord Ravensworth. All his orders, insignia, uniforms and trophies were displayed, and inscribed on the walls were the names and dates of the 25 battles he had fought from 1796 to 1814. She built a church in Seaham in County Durham and placed a dramatic equestrian statue of Charles in his Hussar uniform in the market-place in Durham City, and these stand as evidence of her love and deep grief. It had been a very successful marriage, begun in disapproval but continued lovingly in spite of the 20 year gap in their ages; 30 years later Frances Anne had to come to terms with being alone.

Like her daughter she believed in action. Her husband's will returned to her the collieries, originally her own property, and Garron Tower, which she had built on her mother's Antrim estate. She had the use for life of Wynyard Hall, Londonderry House and Seaham Hall, in the last of which she chose to live in spite of the fact that each of her married children, and the Disraelis, warmly offered her a home. Mount Stewart and Londonderry's Irish properties passed to her stepson Viscount Castlereagh, who now became the 4th Marquess of Londonderry. At the same time, her own eldest son, Harry, Viscount Seaham, succeeded to his father's earldom of Vane and other English titles in accordance with the terms of the special creation. Charles, ever the devoted and caring husband and father, had provided well for his loved ones.

The Londonderry sense of commitment meant Frances Anne saw her duty in the continuation of his work. She wrote to the people of Seaham:

> Be assured that, whether it may please God to lengthen or shorten my days, whatever remains of life will be devoted to the accomplishment of all his plans and objects. Deeply do I feel the responsibility in succeeding to the management of these great concerns, and bitterly do I deplore my inferiority to the master mind that preceded me, but with God's help I will do my best, and I promise the inhabitants of Seaham that my humble efforts shall never be wanting to advance and promote the prosperity of the town and harbour.[5]

She fulfilled her promise!

She had formed the annual routine of spending the summer and early autumn at Garron Tower, and she would go to Wynyard for Christmas. With the exception of a short visit to London during the season, the rest of the year saw her installed at Seaham, where she had built an imposing office overlooking the harbour her husband had built. Disraeli, her faithful admirer, stayed with her there in 1861, leaving us a vivid account not only of Seaham but also of Frances Anne's character and quality:

This is a remarkable place, and our hostess is a remarkable woman. Twenty miles hence she has a palace (Wynyard) in a vast park, with forest rides and antlered deer, and all the splendid accessories of feudal life. But she prefers living in a hall on the shores of the German Ocean, surrounded by her collieries and her blast furnaces and her railroads and the unceasing telegraphs, with a port hewn out of the solid rock, screw steamers and four thousand pitmen under her control. One day she dined the whole four thousand in one of the factories. In the town of Seaham Harbour, a mile off, she has a regular office, a fine stone building with her name and arms on the front, and her flag flying above; and here she transacts, with innumerable agents, immense business – and I remember her five-and-twenty years ago a mere fine lady; nay, the finest in London! But one must find excitement if one has brains.[6]

The dinner to which Disraeli referred took place in 1856 in a large factory at Chilton Moor and the numbers were indeed close to 4,000. The walls were decorated with the banners of the respective collieries, while at centre table stood a baron of beef weighing 130 pounds. Harry, Lord Vane, took the chair and grace was sung by the choristers of Durham Cathedral. Frances Anne knew her miners, and she spoke to them warmly and with commitment, urging them to educate their children in the schools she had provided and concentrate on good practice both inside and outside the pit. She was enthusiastically received by her audience, for she had continued her husband's caring practices and the Londonderry reputation stood high.

It was one of the last duties she carried out. She died peacefully at Seaham Hall in 1865, leaving five sons and daughters and 18 grandchildren, eight of whom were Spencer-Churchills. Her greatest gifts were a formidable intelligence and a feisty sense of humour, which carried her safely through an eventful and intensely public life. Brian Masters later pays her eloquent tribute, calling her a competent business woman who always spoke to the point and handled her workforce with respect and sympathy, a tall and elegant figure whose face communicated character and humour. She was more than this, however. She had also a strong will, confidence, a sense of purpose, social poise and accomplishment and, in particular, a compassion for and sensitivity to the needy and a true feeling of responsibility towards the vulnerable. There was much of her in her daughter.

Even after her death she proved to have a very long arm, as was discovered in a copy of her will in the Churchill Archives in Cambridge. Through her daughter she reached out to her unborn great grandson, Winston Churchill. After a fairly predictable distribution of her fortune, she bequeathed Garron Tower and its estate, the spectacular building she had built on her mother's property in Antrim, in such a way that the technicalities are worth repeating verbatim:

> … upon trust for her four grandsons Herbert Lionel Vane Tempest, Henry John Vane Tempest [the third and second sons of her son Earl Vane], Randolph Henry Spencer Churchill [Frances' and John Winston's second surviving son and Winston's father] and Francis Adolphus Vane Tempest [son of her late son Lord Adolphus Vane Tempest] and their respective issue male, so that her said four grandsons respectively with their respective issue male should take in succession in the order named, and so that each grandson should take an estate for life with remainder to his first and other sons successively, according to seniority in tail male with certain remainders over.[7]

Since Henry died in 1905 and Herbert in 1921, both without issue, and Randolph, Frances' son, died in 1895, this bequest actually came through to Randolph's son, Winston Churchill, in 1922. At a period of great sadness in his life, after his mother had died in 1921 and his three-year-old daughter Marigold just three months later, when he himself was in hospital with appendicitis during the General Election in which he subsequently lost his seat, this unexpected turn of fortune from the distant past brought him a generous income of £4,000 to £5,000 a year. The income from the Garron Tower Estate was his first taste of financial security and it enabled him to buy Chartwell, the home in Kent which he and Clementine loved and lived in for over 40 years. Surely, across the generations, his great-grandmother Frances Anne had heard him and had made her own substantial contribution to his future.

Chapter Ten

A BELOVED SON

L ike most mothers, Frances was careful not to favour one child above another. What she could not avoid, and what was growing in her as the days went by, was an anxiety about Randolph which possessed her whenever he took a risk or ventured forth on some boyish expedition. In her more reflective moments she connected this with the early death of Frederick, which had left Randolph in the unenviable position of the second son of two. It was customary in titled families to speak of the 'heir' and the 'spare', the latter attracting nothing but sympathy. For the second son there was often no inheritance, and yet he had to be prepared to step into his brother's shoes if it became necessary. In the mother observing this situation there was some appreciation of her lively, intelligent second son and a painful awareness of what lay ahead of him. In some ways his love for Blenheim, far more passionate than his elder brother George's, marked him out as ducal material; nevertheless, he had a recklessness which was not his father's and which possibly reflected the waywardness of previous members of the family, of which Frances must have been painfully aware. In her own position of marital and economic security, she had had plenty of time to study all this. She and John had recently had two more sons, Charles and Augustus, but both of them had died, and so Randolph carried the 'spare's' responsibility alone.

Randolph Henry Spencer-Churchill, second surviving son of John Winston and Frances, was born on 13 February 1849. Although he was not the heir to the title and dukedom, he was nevertheless to become a very significant figure, both in the family and in the country as a whole. Industrial England was beginning to assert itself: prosperity was spreading through the social system, and although the Chartist movement was still alive it was being submerged by the rising tide of universal comfort. The same conditions allowed the English aristocracy to survive unchallenged, although the Marlboroughs were facing the financial problems which had been created by the irresponsible behaviour of the 5th and, perhaps, the 6th Dukes.

Randolph's first years were spent with his elder brother George and his six sisters at Hensington House, east of the Palace and across the road from the Hensington Gate. They were a close and affectionate family, a luxury which does not always belong to that level of society, but reflected the stability and security of their parents' marriage and philosophy of life, in particular the warmth and caring instinct in Frances.

Randolph enjoyed a wonderfully happy childhood. For the rest of his life he loved Blenheim with passion and commitment; he was never happier than within the sturdy walls of that huge Palace and the old stone walls of that great estate. His enthusiasm for the open air extended to whatever he could find in the neighbourhood or, alternatively, at Wynyard Hall, his mother's family home in the north of England. Very much at home on horseback, he begged his parents to buy him a small pony called 'Mousey' from the local telegraph boy and on this he first rode to hounds with the nearby Heythrop hunt.

In 1857, at eight years old, Randolph was sent to Mr Tabor's school at Cheam, where he was happy and made steady progress; he was remembered by a fellow schoolboy as being rapid and vigorous in speech, ready to read and recite impressively. Lord Redesdale, writing later, described him as the most delightful of boys, bubbling over with fun and the 'sweetest devilry', devoted to his father and idolising his mother.

At Eton from 1863 he seems to have developed a rather different attitude, one which has been described as cheerful arrogance. By this time he was observed as having a degree of petulance and impetuousness which his parents no doubt expected the formality and discipline of the public school system to eradicate. There was no doubt about his ability to charm and he made friends very easily; he was 'all things to all men'.[1] The talent and charm which were such characteristics of Randolph's adulthood were beginning to reveal themselves but so were two of his fatal flaws.

He wrote to his mother on 11 March 1863 a letter in which he demonstrated how hugely self-oriented he was, as his neglect of his son Winston was later to show. He could not accept being in the wrong: why should he be punished just for cutting his name on a table or for sitting with his feet on the form?

He was ready to find an excuse for his inadequacies, telling his mother that he wrote one letter to her 'and I cannot find it anywhere' and, of a set of lines which could not be found, 'Somebody must have taken them.' The letter contains two entertaining examples of the penetrating wit which was to be so much part of his power as a public speaker later (as it was to become, too, of Winston). The school was being vaccinated but he 'declined' to let them 'perform' on him. Queen Victoria came to Windsor from Osborne one night and rushed off to Balmoral the next morning, which struck him as being 'rather eccentric'. Everybody had to re-enlist in the Corps, take an oath and sign their names 'to a lot of nonsense'.

His time at Eton was littered with escapades, not always to his credit. Mr Frewer, his housemaster, did not discipline him when he used his spoon to batter the table when his meal was late, but cherished the spoon as a memento instead; Randolph seems to have expressed his gratitude by locking Frewer's son in the cellar. His 'dandy' period was marked by a hideously violet waistcoat. As a lofty senior he controlled a team of 15 'fags' (junior pupils who ran errands for a senior), one of whom was ordered to fry an egg in marmalade when he reported there was no butter. Over his study mantelpiece was painted the Spencer coat of arms, and he was followed everywhere by his favourite bulldog, specially imported from home. A legend has been handed down about how one afternoon a fag came to him with a familiar problem: he faced a test on a piece of work he had not prepared and wanted to contract a sudden illness to avoid the consequences. Randolph sent him to lie at the foot of the stairs outside Matron's room, and then jumped over him with a pile of text books. Her attention attracted by the fuss and noise, Matron found Randolph sprawled under a pile of books with his fag apparently senseless at the bottom of the stairs.

It is difficult not to be entertained by all this. Every group can benefit from such independence by an individual with a flair for mischief. The Duke must have been weary of the serious complaints that were reported back to him, but he persevered with his son and threatened to take him away from Eton. The letter John Winston wrote to Randolph is as characteristic of him as it is of his errant son. His distress is moving, as he points out that Randolph was repaying all the kindness his mother and father had shown by giving them anxiety. He reveals his own innate decency, telling his son that there is nothing in the world 'which is so low and contemptible', and it makes a boy and 'subsequently a man so justly detestable'.

Randolph's first tutor was Mr Warre, later to become headmaster of Eton; the two did not get on well together, but the Duke left his son in no doubt that he supported the master. His letter throws considerable light on both father and son: he reminds Randolph that he had begged not to be taken away from Eton and yet continued his bad behaviour, a kind of wilfulness which pursued the boy into his adult life. The Duke is fair to the school: he would not accept Randolph's complaint that Warre discriminated against him and recognised his son's weak self-justification, noting that he seemed inclined to justify himself and to think Mr Warre harsh. He listed aspects of his son's undisciplined behaviour: impertinence to the staff, breaking of windows, bullying, and would not accept Randolph's attempts to justify himself: 'Why have there been only complaints about you?'

The letter is direct and uncompromising but shows John Winston was a loving and caring father. He was willing to hope his son was genuinely sorry and would try to regain his teacher's good opinion. He pointed out that if he were forced to take his son away from Eton, the only option would be to have a private tutor, 'not nearly so agreeable'; he wanted his son to be happy. His letter ends on a note of genuine Christian fatherly love and concern: 'My dearest boy, God bless you.'

Although the Duke was the voice of parental disapproval, the bad behaviour of their son clearly worried both parents. The fact that Frances was concerned about Randolph's misconduct, and had reproached her son about it, and that her husband was expressing her concern as well as his own, is revealed in a later letter in which the Duke speaks for the Duchess as well as himself, reminding Randolph of the promises he made so solemnly before he left home.

The Duke was under no illusions about his son Randolph and was quite firm in his support of the master who had disciplined him, but there is in both letters a patience and affection which warms his stern attitude and gives the lie to those biographers who have judged him as harsh and unfeeling. Furthermore, Randolph's undoubted charm could sometimes carry the day and the few friends he made at school were devoted to him. Chief among these was Lord Dalmeny, later Lord Rosebery, who became a lifelong friend. Randolph's natural cleverness and a remarkable memory, which his son Winston inherited, served him well academically, and the outstanding quality which his peers remember is his generosity.

A letter written by the Duke some time later, after a particularly poor report, is perhaps the most significant of all. By this time the lack of self-control was a noticeable feature of Randolph's personality and both parents were thoroughly worried. Randolph's greatest weakness was, despite his talent and charm, in time to bring him from the heights of success to the total ruin of his ambition and achievement. The Duke points it out to him uncompromisingly, bringing home to his son his impatience and resentment of any control, his inclination to stand on any imagined slight, his inability to see his duty, and his tendency to be uncontrolled in bad language and manner. He points out that if his temper causes him to quarrel with every tutor, as he has with his current one, Mr Pugh, even though Pugh had tried hard to be friendly, then he has no chance of succeeding at Balliol, or even of getting into Oxford. Despairingly he asks Randolph if in fact his temper can be controlled by anybody or under any circumstances.

Winston Churchill, writing his father's biography in 1906, confirmed that the letters written to Randolph by the Duke were affectionate and tolerant and intended to influence his son's education and attitudes. There was local news, varied and interesting, and he was encouraged to confide in his father, who always reasoned with him patiently and sensibly. John Winston appealed to his son's high principles and common sense. Both Blandford and Lord Randolph sustained respect for their father throughout their lives, although both of them challenged authority and convention in other ways. His parents neglected nothing that would stimulate Randolph's ambition, for they foresaw a promising career ahead: Oxford, a degree in History and Law, and finally politics, with Woodstock the obvious borough, traditionally the province of the Marlboroughs.

The family side of Randolph was more attractive. The most moving insight into his positive and endearing aspect, although it admits his weaknesses, was written by his mother after his early death. Over a hundred years later, one can feel a mother's anguish and distress as she expresses her grief and speaks of her memories of him, referring to 'one who was so dear to me that he is never out of my thoughts and for whom I go mourning to the grave'.[2] She painfully acknowledges the destructive side of his character, shown early in his life, and concedes that he was not particularly clever as a boy, with no interest in study, although he had an excellent memory and was very fond of reading, especially history, biography or adventure. She gives a vivid account of how Randolph loved sport and animals, recounting the story of 'Mousey' and Randolph aged just ten. Mousey was a ragged, skinny and tough little pony which belonged to a boy in the village. Randolph desperately wanted to have the pony and pestered his parents relentlessly until eventually they yielded and let him have it. He then trained it, apparently, called it his hunter and actually managed to follow the hounds with it. When he outgrew it, Mousey was passed on to his sisters and became quite famous in the locality.

A similar situation occurred when Randolph was 14, and Frances recalls the episode with love and affection. He managed to collect some beagles, which he trained into harriers, and was allowed to keep the dogs at the back of the Gardens, cared for by Jim, a disreputable little boy whom Randolph nevertheless called his whipper-in. He began with a few dogs, which he trained and walked out himself, but finally had enough for a pack, which Frances said 'will never be forgotten in the memory of this generation'.[3]

There is no doubt about his popularity at Blenheim, among his own family and also among the local people who were later to vote him into the House of Commons. One of them later wrote that he always found Lord Randolph a generous, friendly, cheerful personality, with strong likes and dislikes, but one of the staunchest and most amiable of friends. As for the borough of Woodstock, an interesting situation was developing. The retiring MP was the Duke's brother, Lord Alfred, who leaned more towards the Liberals than the Duke would like, and in 1864 John Winston had withdrawn his substantial support from him. The Marlboroughs had always hoped that their younger son, who would remain unclaimed by the House of Lords because he was not in the direct line of the title, would find his career as a politician. At this moment, therefore, it was 15-year-old Randolph who rose to his feet at a dinner given by the constituents of Woodstock to express thanks to Lord Alfred for his services in a carefully prepared and delivered speech. And so Randolph the public speaker was on his way and his future was taking shape.

1 *A miniature of Frances, 7th Duchess of Marlborough, aged about 12.*

2 *Wynyard Hall and Park, 'The finest 19th-century house in the country' (Pevsner). This was Frances' home in County Durham until she married. Her background prepared her perfectly for the grandeur of Blenheim.*

3 & 4   *Charles and Frances Anne, the 3rd Marquess and Marchioness of Londonderry, Frances' parents, 1819. Portraits by Sir Thomas Lawrence.*

5 & 6 *John Winston and Frances, 7th Duke and Duchess of Marlborough. The sculptures were made by Lawrence MacDonald in Rome in 1843, soon after the couple were married.*

7 *Londonderry House, Park Lane, London. Frances' family house in Mayfair, the focal point of her mother's pre-eminence as the social and political hostess of her day. Frances learned much from her mother, vital later to her success as hostess at Blenheim and as Vicereine in Ireland.*

8 *Frances as a young woman at around the time of her marriage to John Winston. Poise and self-confidence were amongst her strongest characteristics. Portrait by Buckner, 1840s.*

9 *The silver centrepiece (1845) in the state dining room at Blenheim Palace, showing the 1st Duke of Marlborough at the moment of victory at the Battle of Blenheim, 1704.*

10 *The 3rd Marquess of Londonderry, 10th Hussars, Frances' father and Wellington's Adjutant General. A gallant soldier, he was known as 'Fighting Charlie'. Frances possessed the same forceful character. Bronze sculpture in the city of Durham.*

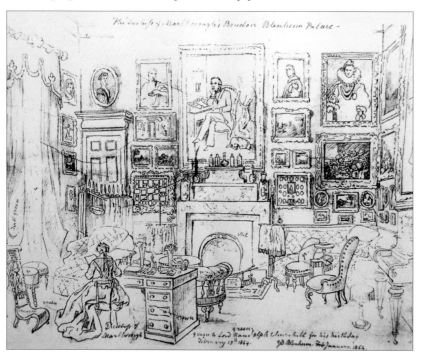

11 *Frances, 7th Duchess in her boudoir at Blenheim Palace. Running the household at Blenheim was a good preparation for the talents she later demonstrated at an international level with her relief committee during the Irish Famine of 1879.*

12 *Frances, 7th Duchess at Blenheim. The photograph suggests her sense of discipline and self-control, which she endeavoured to impart to young Winston. These qualities balanced the sensitivity with which she responded to his deep emotional need.*

13 *John Winston, 7th Duke of Marlborough. Lady Randolph (Jennie Churchill), by her own account never very happy with the old-fashioned formality at Blenheim, nevertheless wrote generously that it was partly relieved by the innate courtesy and kindliness of the Duke.*

14 *Frances, John Winston and members of the Spencer-Churchill family c.1860. Left to right, John Winston, Cornelia, Rosamund, Anne, Clementina, Fanny, Frances and Georgiana.*

15 *Lord and Lady Randolph Churchill, Winston Churchill's parents, in 1874, the year of their marriage and of Winston's birth (30 November).*

16 & 17 *Two pages from the Visitors' Book at Blenheim. Frances had a great commitment to her family. Twelve of the 17 guests on these pages are family members: Tweedmouth, Roxburghe, Fellowes, Marjoribanks and Wimborne as well as Churchill.*

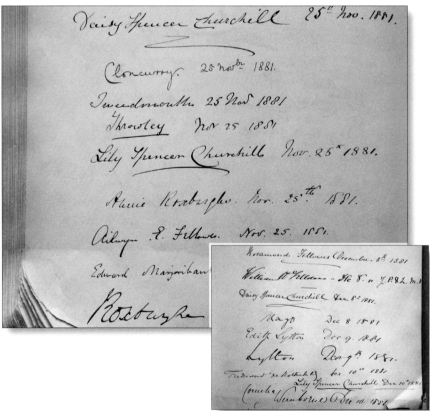

18 *Royal Yacht Squadron yacht* Wyvern, *1876. This was one of several yachts owned by John Winston. He and Frances went on cruises regularly and had to return home from the Aegean when the Aylsford scandal erupted.*

19 *Winston Churchill aged seven. The pose and expression suggest a strong personality and independent character even at this young age.*

20 *Frances, Duchess of Marlborough in 1880, aged 58.*

21 *Frances (right) in the chair of her Famine Relief Committee, Dublin Castle, 1879. Lord Randolph Churchill, secretary of the committee, is seen in the foreground second from right.*

22 *The Irish Famine Memorial, Toronto. In the 1843 famine 30,000 Irish immigrants were welcomed to Canada via Toronto, then a town of only 20,000 inhabitants. The figure, foreground, is 'Jubilant Man'. Inset: 'Orphan Boy'.*

23 *The Fourth Party, by Spy in Vanity Fair, 1880. Lord Randolph (standing) with (seated, left to right) Arthur Balfour, Henry Wolff and John Gorst, leaders of the ginger group which was such a problem for the Conservative Party leadership in the early 1880s.*

24 *Subscribers to Frances' Famine Relief Fund. Donations large and small came from individuals and churches, from Britain and abroad, from collections and special events.*

The Castle, Dublin, 23rd March.

The Irish Times

DUBLIN, THURSDAY, MARCH 25, 1890.

THE DUCHESS OF MARLBOROUGH'S RELIEF FUND.

The undermentioned additional subscriptions have been received:—

	£	s	D
Offertory of Longbridge Deverell Church, per Rev. J. D. Morrice	2	4	2
Offertory of Hartwith Church, Ripley, per Rev. J. Lucas	1	12	0
Offertory of Branhope Chapel, Otley, per Rev. T. R. Bruce	9	2	0
Offertory of Thornton Church, Bradford, per Rev. R. H. Heap	2	10	0
Offertory of Hawes Church, Bedale, per Rev. G. P. Harris	3	0	0
Messrs. Alberdingh and Zonew, Amsterdam (second donation), per T. G. White, Esq.	1	0	0
Offertory of Thornton-in-Craven, per Rev. L. S. Morris	5	0	0
M. K. Kinton, Esq., Liverpool	0	5	0
From Amoy, China	200	0	0
Mayor of New Brunswick	700	0	0
Contributed by a few gentlemen of Montreal, per W. D. Russell, Esq.	24	13	0
Old Globe Lodge of Freemasons	10	10	0
Proceeds of entertainment, per Post Office, Canada	7	6	0
Offertory of Norton Church, per Rev. Geo. J. Kinyer	0	14	4
Collection in Stamford, Ontario, per G. C. Leicester Inglis	5	0	0
Second collection from India, by Mr Maycott, per H. A. Dillon, Esq.	105	0	0
Proceeds of concert at Woodstock, Ontario, per T. D. Watson, Esq.	20	7	10
Entertainment at New Westminster, per Society of Sons of Temperance, British Columbia	13	10	3
Collection at Nice, per Mrs W. Miller and P. R. Pigott	8	0	0
Collection in poor parish in Durham, per G. P. Wilkinson, Esq.	2	5	0
O. Farder Smith, Esq.	2	10	0
Collection at Port Hope, Toronto, per Bank of Toronto	12	0	0
From Paris	197	8	8
Mrs A. M. Tottenham (second donation) per C. D. Fox, Esq.	20	0	0

E. A. FITZGERALD, Assist. Sec.

The Castle, Dublin, 24th March.

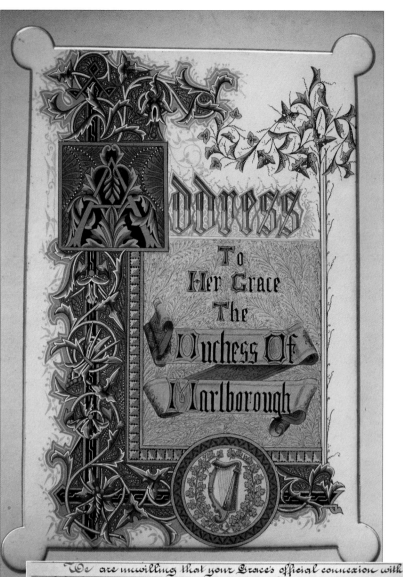

Address

To
Her Grace
The
Duchess Of
Marlborough

We are unwilling that your Grace's official connexion with our beloved Country should be terminated without some expression of the deep sense entertained by the City of Dublin of the interest in the educational and charitable institutions of the Country shewn by Her Grace the Duchess of Marlborough and of the efforts made by Her Grace in this time of dire distress to mitigate the horrors of famine and we beg to express our cordial satisfaction at the recognition of Her Grace's noble work by Her Majesty the Queen

25 & 26 *An illuminated address of thanks (1877) from a Dublin school and lines from the text of a citation (1880) from the City of Dublin. Frances' support, as Vicereine in Ireland, for those in need drew many sincere expressions of thanks, often beautifully expressed.*

27 *Frances, Duchess of Marlborough reading the letter received from Queen Victoria in which she is awarded the Order of Victoria and Albert. This was a special honour, dear to the queen's own heart, and she often wore it herself on state occasions in memory of her beloved husband.*

28 *The letter Frances received from Queen Victoria in 1880 after her work to avert the Irish famine.*

29 *Memorial of Lord Randolph Churchill in the Chapel at Blenheim. Frances' five sons and her husband all predeceased her. She erected impressive monuments to her husband and her son in the Chapel.*

IN MEMORY OF
RANDOLPH HENRY SPENCER CHURCHILL
BRILLIANT ORATOR AND STATESMAN
SOMETIME SECRETARY OF STATE FOR INDIA CHANCELLOR OF THE EXCHEQUER
AND LEADER OF THE HOUSE OF COMMONS
WHOSE REMARKABLE CAREER
WAS PREMATURELY CLOSED BY DEATH AT THE EARLY AGE OF 45
AFTER A LINGERING ILLNESS PATIENTLY BORNE
IN HIS PRIVATE LIFE HE WAS DEARLY LOVED
HIS POLITICAL CAREER WAS ONE OF RARE ACHIEVEMENT
HE PASSED AWAY LAMENTED BY HIS COUNTRY
BORN FEB 13 1849 DIED JAN 24 1895
THE THIRD SON OF JOHN WINSTON VII DUKE OF MARLBOROUGH K G
AND FRANCES ANNE VANE HIS WIFE
THIS MONUMENT WAS ERECTED   BY HIS MOTHER AND FAMILY
AS A MEMORIAL   OF DEEP DEVOTION

30 *Memorial plaque for Lord Randolph Churchill in the Chapel at Blenheim showing the inscription from his mother, to whom his early death at 45 was a crushing blow.*

31 *Winston Churchill, 4th Hussars, 1895. At 20, Winston's military career took him abroad and his period of closest contact with his grandmother was now coming to an end.*

32 *Blenheim Palace. The palace was originally built for John Churchill, 1st Duke of Marlborough, to honour his victory at the Battle of Blenheim, 1704.*

33 *Winston Churchill in 1900, on the threshold of a political career.*

Chapter Eleven

RANDOLPH AT OXFORD

W hen John and Frances' second son moved on from Eton, they agreed that now was the moment to plan for the future. His behaviour had improved considerably but the next hurdle awaiting him was a high one. The Reverend Lionel Damer was engaged to prepare him for entry into Oxford, and he left the Marlboroughs in no doubt about the enormity of his task. He tells the Duke that Randolph did not care for scholarship, that he was 'horribly inaccurate', and that he guessed at truth instead of applying his mind.

However, in 1867, after one unsuccessful attempt to pass the entrance examination, Randolph took up residence at Merton College, Oxford. Here he was assigned to Dr Creighton, a wise choice. The open and free atmosphere of the university opened up his life considerably. In the mid-nineteenth century Merton's reputation was one of social superiority, catering as it did largely for old Etonians, particularly aristocratic ones like Randolph. He soon forgot his disappointment at not getting into Balliol, where many of his friends were, and continued to spend a great deal of his time with his two closest companions at Christ Church, Lord Dalmeny and Edward Marjoribanks, who later married Randolph's sister Fanny and became the 2nd Baron Tweedmouth. The proximity of Blenheim brought him back regularly to his devoted family and the pleasures of a landed estate. Always a bold and skilful horseman, he took up hunting again with renewed vigour and these were the golden years of the Blenheim Harriers, which lasted for three years and demonstrated his good qualities. He built affectionate relationships with huntsmen and farmers. As a horseman he was courteous and composed, ready to take his tumbles with the best. He also took a keen interest in his sisters' lives, as by 1870 three of them were already launched socially. He was a good brother and a considerate son in this period, endearing himself to his mother and the other women in his life. His friendship with Lord Dalmeny, which lasted a lifetime, ripened now and the two young men were encouraged towards politics by Disraeli.

Randolph continued to worry Frances, however, for he had not lost his taste for social disruption. At Oxford he was a founder member of the 'Myrmidons', a dining club exclusive to Merton men and a few carefully selected guests, which met regularly at the city's *Mitre* and *Randolph* hotels, and soon attracted the attention of the college and university authorities. Although he may not have become particularly outrageous, nevertheless the legends have survived, and he was a familiar target for the university's proctors and 'bulldogs'; there was concealment in coal cellars, imprisonment of waiters in pantries and ice safes, and a general level of high spirits which often went out of control. Further, there was conflict with the city police, to whom students were a permanent problem. On one occasion Lord Randolph was charged with drunkenness, and he was so incensed that he brought an action for perjury against a police witness. The college authorities wanted him to withdraw the charge and appealed to the Duke for his support, but on this occasion, interestingly enough, the Duke supported Randolph. There were fines, however, for smoking in academic dress in the street; severe reprimands for breaking windows at the *Randolph Hotel*, an occupation which was later imitated by his son Winston at Harrow; and loud and forceful expressions of his opinions which would have been better expressed in the more formal surroundings of the Oxford Union Debating Chamber.

There was a brush with the Dean of Christ Church, H.G. Liddell, father of Alice, the inspiration for Lewis Carroll's famous 'Alice', and a regular guest at Blenheim, who accused him of acting outrageously in the college precincts and, more seriously, of denying the offence. The latter was the real issue, as it ran completely counter to the principles John Winston and Frances valued and had tried to instil. Dr Liddell wrote angrily:

> I was taught when I was young and I have always clung to the belief, that the first quality of an English Gentleman was to speak the truth without fear, or if unhappily he was compelled to tell an untruth, to feel shame at what he had done and to own his fault frankly … However, I have no

wish to prolong this correspondence. We shall accept your second note as an apology and shall hope that the expression of sorrow for what you did implies a promise that such an act will not be repeated.[1]

It is possible that the misdemeanours of the sons of public figures receive more attention than others and are more frequently thrust into the public eye than those from more ordinary backgrounds. Randolph was possibly no worse than his peers: no better, either. But he was the son of the Duke and Duchess of Marlborough, both public figures in their own right, and subsequent events have meant his childhood and adolescence have been researched carefully. Whether he had more than most to cringe about later is a matter of opinion.

What is more significant is the fact that, at the time of Randolph's student days, Oxford was alive with all the vigour and intellectual debate which characterised this period nationally. It seems to have taken place over his head. Immersed as he was in his own activities, both in Oxford and at home at Blenheim, there is no reference to the activity going on around him. The scene was dominated by the Oxford Movement and the Pre-Raphaelite artists; in 1859 Charles Darwin published his *On the Origin of Species*, although it was to be some time before the book became significant. From the proceeds of the Great Exhibition of 1851 were built in London the Science Museum, the Natural History Museum and the Victoria and Albert Museum. Prince Albert had died in 1861 from typhoid fever and Queen Victoria in her grief had withdrawn from public life. In Edinburgh Joseph Lister was revolutionising modern surgery with his introduction of antiseptic techniques; in 1867 Dr Barnardo founded his first home for destitute children. The London Underground was established in 1862, driven by steam with open carriages. Closer to home, the Dean of Christ Church, Henry Liddell, the father of three girls, had confronted his mathematics don, C.L. Dodgson, in June 1862 and forbidden him to have any further contact with his daughters. In 1865 Dodgson published *Alice's Adventures in Wonderland* under the pseudonym of Lewis Carroll and thus began the genre of children's literature. At Blenheim both Duke and Duchess were keenly active locally.

In the General Election of 1868 the Liberal candidate for Woodstock was one of the Merton dons, a Mr Brodrick. The seat was normally occupied by a Marlborough member, but because of the disagreement between the Duke and his brother, Lord Alfred, the contest was more exciting than usual and some of Brodrick's supporters waxed more enthusiastic than was acceptable. Lord Randolph took exception to the language used by these gentlemen, particularly when they accused his father of bribery, intimidation and dishonest interference with the suffrage. He showed his usual lack of restraint by proceeding to cut Brodrick's lectures, which in those days were compulsory. Accused by the Warden of Merton, he replied that he could not in all conscience attend the lectures of a man who had called his father a scoundrel. Nothing further was said but, typically, Randolph was unable to leave it there. He prepared a letter for the press, but before posting showed it to Dr Creighton, his tutor, a shrewd, competent man who later became Bishop of London. Creighton's comment was that if he were going to send a letter at all, he could not send a better one. He advised Randolph not to send it, however, telling him to keep out of politics at his age. Sensible for once, Randolph followed this advice, but he was not to be so wise 20 years later.

After the Conservative defeat in 1868 Disraeli was a frequent visitor at Blenheim. Even though his life-long friend and supporter Frances Anne was dead, he was still a welcome and honoured guest and he held a high opinion of Randolph and young Lord Dalmeny, who also was frequently at the Palace. Disraeli was greatly disappointed when Dalmeny, later Rosebery, was drawn by Gladstone's oratory and joined the Liberals, but his interest in Lord Randolph was more than mere politeness to the son of an influential colleague: he respected his talent, remarking to Frances that it lay with her younger son to make a distinguished political career for himself.

By 1869 Randolph, aged 20, was showing a maturity and sense of responsibility which can only have brought a sense of relief to his long-suffering parents. His reading had advanced from R.S. Surtees' *Jorrocks*, inspiration for *Pickwick Papers*, to Gibbon's *Decline and Fall of the Roman Empire*, for his knowledge of which he became well known. He suddenly disbanded his Blenheim Harriers, much to the members' disappointment, and announced his determination to work for his finals, in his case in History and Law. He was going to add industry to talent and, aided by the admirable Creighton, he worked long hours to try to repair the effects of years of idleness. A letter from Dr Creighton to the Duchess at this time shows the quality of his tutorial skills. She and the Duke were unfailing in concern and support for their son, and this particular letter must have been a welcome occasion for the Marlboroughs for it made clear that after long years spent causing worry and disappointment Randolph had at last come to his senses. Creighton began by acknowledging that Randolph had done well in his studies, the only question now being whether he would reach an appreciably higher standard if he deferred his examination for six months. At the moment Randolph was working very well and in general was up to a second class degree, in some cases a first. Dr Creighton wrote that if the exam could be postponed for six months Randolph might improve his prospects, but to wait six months could mean he would peak too early; therefore, better to take it now.

Then Dr Creighton made a remarkable offer. He told the grateful mother that he would require Randolph to give him a rigorous account of what he had done in the examination and if Creighton thought he had not done himself justice he would advise him to remove his name before the end and wait a further six months. Wisely, however, he asked Frances not to let her son know of this possibility. He wanted Randolph to make his best effort at the first attempt without knowing of the alternative plan.

A second letter a month later shows how well Dr Creighton had judged and acted. Admitting his own disappointment at hearing how narrowly Lord Randolph had missed the first class, he said he had been told by the examiners that his tutee was the best man to be placed in the second class. He found it tantalising that Randolph had come so near to a first, but the decision not to delay had been the correct one: Randolph would have peaked too early. The final words of Creighton's letter must have been balm to the parents who had had so many years of disappointment and anxiety: 'I am sorry to lose him.' It is tempting to compare this degree of parental involvement with the dismissive attitude of Randolph himself, when it came to the question of his own son's career. In spite of Frances' insistence that Winston was a clever boy, the future prime minister was never given the chance to go to university.

Obviously Randolph was difficult to handle and unused to the sort of consistent application that brings the best results; most academics would agree he was fortunate in his tutor and in his result. Two years later, after a lengthy and light-hearted tour of Europe, he emerged self-confident, elegantly dressed, socially accomplished and well-educated.

Chapter Twelve

RANDOLPH AND JENNIE

I n August 1873, as in every August, exhausted by their efforts at the end
of the London season, the English upper classes repaired to Cowes on
the Isle of Wight, where entertainment consisted of racing boats in
the Solent, the stretch of water between the island and Britain's south coast.
Cowes was in 1873, as it still is today, the centre of Britain's yachting world.
Close beside the walls of Osborne, the house which Queen Victoria and
Prince Albert had built together, the parties, the gossip and the flirting went
on with a privacy and anonymity which London could not afford. The leader
in all this activity, both the yachting and the socialising, was Albert Edward,
Prince of Wales. At the age of 32 his reputation for fast and loose living was
already established and he led a life devoid of commitment, either personal
or political, spending his time, as it were, waiting to be king and indulging
himself in every manner possible.

He had gathered around himself some of the country's younger aristocrats and
others who had become known as the Marlborough House set. Marlborough
House, originally built by Sarah, 1st Duchess of Marlborough next to St James's
Palace on the Mall, had reverted to the Crown in 1817 and been given to the
Prince of Wales on his marriage to Princess Alexandra. Included in the elite,
privileged group were George, Marquess of Blandford, aged 29, eldest son and
heir to Blenheim and the Marlborough dukedom, and Lord Randolph, second
son, aged 25 and fresh from Oxford and the Grand Tour of Europe. George's
personality seems by this time to have been set in the mould of the 'fast set';
nor is it surprising that Randolph, whose own capacity for self-indulgence and
self-justification had been amply demonstrated at school and university, was

gravitating in this direction, despite the fact that others were more experienced in the ways of the world than he was. Blandford's reputation was one of self-centredness and marital infidelity, but Lord Randolph was known to be much closer to his parents and sisters and less cynical.

At a ball given on 12 August by the officers of the cruiser *Ariadne*, the guard ship of the Royal Regatta, in honour of the Tsarevitch and Tsarevna of Russia, Randolph Spencer-Churchill met Jennie Jerome, a pretty ninteen-year-old American girl who was to play an important role in his life. Randolph's emotional volatility, however, which had so distressed his parents, dominated him again. The following evening he dined with her family, the day afterwards they went for a walk, and on that third evening, under a pattern of stars, as the moonlight danced above the yachts in the harbour, the ever-impetuous Randolph proposed marriage. Jennie accepted. It had taken him only three days to come to a momentous decision, which the contemporary observer would have thought highly impractical.

It had been a most romantic setting. The ball, the highlight of the Regatta, was held in the afternoon on the deck of the *Ariadne*, and guests were ferried across the harbour in crowded boats. The ship's ladder had to be negotiated by women in their full skirts, causing much hilarity and contributing to the excitement of the occasion. The deck, draped with the national colours of Britain and Imperial Russia, was lit by bobbing lanterns and a Royal Marine Band played in the background. Jennie and her two sisters, brought from America to Paris by their ambitious mother, had found life in the French capital very dull, but in Cowes the summer heat, the exuberant dancing and the freedom from social restraint worked its magic on them all. The invitation to the ball was a direct consequence of Jennie being presented to the Prince and Princess of Wales, and that was largely the consequence of Mrs Jerome's previous diligent work in Paris, where she negotiated the social scene tirelessly on behalf of her daughters. By the time the Jerome sisters reached the deck of the *Ariadne*, they were fully established in the social set in Cowes. Jennie was an accomplished dancer and her natural vivacity responded to the situation; her dark hair and sparkling eyes made her a magnet for dancing partners. Randolph, on the other hand, did not dance because it made him dizzy, but he made the most of the opportunities to converse and to display his own sartorial elegance.

He was introduced to Jennie at his own request by Frank Bertie, an old friend. What she saw before her was a pale young man of average height, with a large head and a walrus moustache, attractive but not handsome. He was immaculately dressed, however, with all the elegant polish of his class, and the fact that he belonged to the Marlborough set intrigued Jennie immediately. They lost no time in becoming more closely acquainted. Randolph always spoke with great rapidity and vehemence, occasionally with a compelling intensity; he could be charming and witty and was capable of captivating a woman for whom he felt a profound attraction. Soon they had both lost interest in everyone else and sat on the open deck, talking happily and sipping champagne. A souvenir of the occasion was kept by Jennie for the rest of her life: the invitation to the ball, ostensibly to meet the Russian royal couple, had Randolph's name inserted above theirs in Jennie's handwriting.

Mrs Jerome, who had rented Rosetta Cottage, a small house with pretty gardens facing the sea near the village of Cowes, was persuaded to invite Randolph and his friend, Colonel Edgcumbe, to dine with the family the next evening. There Jennie and her sisters demonstrated their prowess on the piano, and she later confided in her sister Clara, demanding that she should not be critical of Randolph because she was intuitively drawn to him and might marry him. Interestingly, the colonel was taken into confidence at almost exactly the same moment by Randolph, who joked that he would endeavour to marry the dark-haired Miss Jerome.

There seems no doubt about the strength of this attachment, even though they had known each other for only three days. However, in a social circle such as the Marlborough set, the idea of love being the basis for marriage was regarded with the greatest cynicism. Almost always, marriage was an 'arrangement' for practical reasons, usually to do with money. A girl's mother would find her a husband who could provide her with status and security for life; to love or be loved was usually irrelevant. An impoverished man could look to marriage to a rich girl to restore his and his family's fortune. This, in fact, was the usual pathway into the British aristocracy for rich young American girls, the 'Dollar Princesses'. Amazingly, here was Randolph, deeply in love and expressing his passion, and proposing marriage. He was due to leave the Isle of Wight that weekend, but of course he postponed his departure. Nothing was to be said to Mrs Jerome, and so his note to Jennie on Saturday from the local hotel was carefully worded: he had missed the boat that morning and would not now leave until Monday; he hoped to see her after church on Sunday.

After two more idyllic days together, Jennie broke the news to her mother, who refused to entertain it as serious; Randolph received Jennie's reply on Monday morning, before he boarded the boat, which said she could hardly bear his leaving and she hoped to see him again soon. And so a most affectionate relationship began, which was, in time, to have the most significant consequences. Their love was ablaze with all the passion of youth and impetuousness and one would imagine that the situation was settled. There were, however, other players in this game and soon they were all involved. Mrs Jerome, playing for time, forbade her daughter to write to Randolph and he was left to carry on a one-sided correspondence. He returned to Blenheim completely and utterly in love. He told his mother everything and, like Jennie's mother, she was shocked at the speed with which the situation had developed. Loving Randolph as she did and fearing for his happiness, she warned her son of how hostile his father's reaction was likely to be: this was a sudden attachment and an American connection was not the most desirable, she told him. Randolph knew, young as he was, that he would have to play his cards carefully. This story is best told through the letters which were written at the time, and which are so revealing.

Randolph wrote a letter to Jennie the following week full of tenderness and devotion: he could not let another day pass without writing; he did not think she had realised how much he loved her. He had told his mother everything, but did not tell Jennie of Frances' warning about the undesirability of an American connection. He wrote that the short time they had had together would decide his whole future. His language was extravagant and self-indulgent. His next letter protested, even though he had received no reply from her, that she had hardly been out of his thoughts, that the last week seemed like an eternity and he would give his soul for another day together. He called her his first and only love. Then, presumably calling forth all his resources, he wrote to his father in Scotland:

Blenheim. Wednesday, 20 August 1873

I must not any longer keep you in ignorance of a very important step I have taken – one which will undoubtedly influence very strongly all my future life.

I met, soon after my arrival in Cowes, a Miss Jeannette Jerome ... and before leaving asked her if she loved me well enough to marry me; and she told me she did.

He insisted to his father that, although this was bound to come as a surprise, his feelings were completely genuine and devoid of exaggeration: 'I love her more than life itself...'. He continued, 'You have always been very good to me, and done as much and more for me always than I had any right to expect,' and protested that now, with Jennie beside him to take an interest in his career, 'if I were married to her, if I had a companion such as she would be, I feel sure, to take an interest in one's prospects and career ... I think that I might become, with the help of Providence, all and perhaps more than you had ever wished and hoped for me.'[1]

He penned a depressing picture of how dreary and uninteresting life without Jennie would become for him, and how unmotivated he would be, his energies and hopes blunted and deadened. The letter was characteristic of Randolph, written with the same genuine openness with which he would often speak. However, it suffered from the character defect which marked him always. His capacity to feel was marred by a lack of reason and self-control or the sense of realism which would bring restraint, and he rushed ahead into a situation which, at the very least, was unusual and impractical.

Furthermore, he was so consumed by the need to have his own way that he did not hesitate to manipulate his caring father in order to achieve his own ends. The mention of his prospects and career, which he claimed would interest his father, reflected his parents' wish to have him settled and in a career, perhaps in politics, in the family seat at Woodstock. His letter is designed to force his father's hand, and to play on the care and feeling his parents had for him. What he is really saying is that he sees no difficulty in standing as MP for Woodstock if he has Jennie by his side. Without her, his motivation would be low. This was emotional blackmail; he was attacking his parents on what he knew was their weakest point. Worse still, he had so little self-awareness that he did not even realise how inexcusable was the course of action he was openly proposing.

Chapter Thirteen

A PARENTAL DILEMMA

_____

For the Marlboroughs, the news caused consternation. To meet and to propose marriage in a matter of days was not a Marlborough habit. Moreover, any hopes Frances and John might have entertained of Randolph solving his financial problems by finding himself a rich heiress now seemed extremely remote. Frances in particular felt her fears for Randolph increase as she contemplated this hasty proposal of marriage. Where would it lead? It ran counter to all the practical common sense that governed the steady and orthodox Duke and Duchess, practised in and familiar with the ways of the world.

The first reaction seems to have come from his eldest sister. Cornelia, who was in Scotland with her father and married by this time to Ivor Guest, later 1st Baron Wimborne, a member of a hugely rich family with whom Cornelia's future was safe and secure, wrote affectionately but cautiously that she could not help feeling he had chosen hastily. His elder brother Blandford, foolish and self-indulgent at the best of times, surpassed himself with a poem of 15 stanzas which likened Randolph to one who tarried near a funeral pyre, the fatuous effort serving only to aggravate Randolph's ill temper.

He returned to Cowes for two days. Mrs Jerome did nothing to hinder the development of the relationship, even though neither family had agreed to an engagement. The Prince of Wales was still at Cowes, and when Jennie was presented to him as the girl whom Lord Randolph hoped to marry, the Prince encouraged both of them to persevere with their parents.

Back at Blenheim, Randolph's passion continued unabated, as did the letters. He expressed his hopes that everything 'will come right', as if some great and distant power were in charge of the situation, rather than himself. He now believed for certain that Jennie loved him, and he wished he was great and very rich in order to be more worthy of her. The romantic side of the situation prevailed over the practical details, as he enjoyed being in love: he was going to London to purchase a locket in which to keep the photograph and 'little bit of hair' she gave him, the reaction of a teenager rather than a man of 24. In the next sentence he told Jennie that on Monday he was going out to shoot partridges as it was the first of September, a curious and unfortunate train of thought. Randolph was pleased the Prince of Wales approved of her and had expressed pleasure at making her acquaintance, but was presumably unaware of the Prince's taste, especially for American women.

The issue obviously lay between the Duke and his impulsive son; Frances was always sympathetic to Randolph in particular, but was clearly disappointed at his impulsive choice. The Duke, always cautious and thoughtful, took counsel before he replied to his son's letter, seeking information about Jennie's father, Leonard Jerome, which was mixed. He was told that Jennie's father had been financially successful in New York and was highly regarded among his friends and acquaintances but that he almost certainly lived beyond his means. On 31 August he wrote back to Randolph that, although it was unlikely his son could see anything but his own point of view, anyone from the outside 'cannot but be struck with the unwisdom of your proceedings, and the uncontrolled state of your feelings, which completely paralyses your judgement … You seem blind to all consequences in order that you may pursue your passion.'

The Duke understood his son extremely well by this stage and did not hesitate to point out the consequences of his impetuosity. He went on to give Randolph the benefit of the information that he had received about Jerome: the latter seemed to be 'a sporting and I should think vulgar' kind of man, and such a connection something which 'no man in his senses could think respectable'.

So this shrewd man had assessed the situation for himself, and of course he was to be proved right. He told his son how sorry he was that his affections were so deeply engaged but he had no intention of supporting Randolph's decision. He concluded by assuring him of his continued affection and care: 'May God bless and keep you straight is my earnest prayer. Ever your affectionate father Marlborough.'[1]

This letter has often been quoted, not always in full, by those who support a recently expressed opinion of the 7th Duke as a 'complete full-blown Victorian prig'. This ill-considered criticism, always too absolute, sits undeservedly on a man who had inherited nothing but family debt and had already gone some way towards repairing the devastation of the last two generations of his family. John Winston was a wise man, full of practical good sense. Everything he says in the letter is well judged. John Winston and Frances had had to deal with the consequences of Randolph's behaviour at school and university and there was no reason to think that in this latest episode he had behaved in a way which was not characteristic. They must have feared the worst, and rightly so.

Nevertheless, the Jeromes were a family of considerable significance both in New York and Paris. Leonard, Jennie's father, was a lawyer educated at Princeton and her mother was one of three orphaned heiresses. He had made a fortune on the Stock Exchange in New York, but his lifestyle and attitudes made it difficult for him to retain it, and his wife Clara took her three daughters to Paris to escape the embarrassment of his collection of mistresses. There they received a sound education and were socially accepted into the group around the Emperor Napoleon III and the Empress Eugenie, where wealth rather than birth brought status. In 1870, when Paris was besieged by the Germans in the Franco-Prussian war, the Jeromes had fled to London, where people were more aloof, as they were in post-war Paris, the Emperor having been deposed and his palace reduced to ruins. In 1873 they attended the Cowes regatta on the Isle of Wight and came to the attention of Randolph, younger son of a premier English Duke.

Unsurprisingly, opposition only served to inflame the impetuous Randolph's passion. He wrote again to Jennie on 7 September, beginning by saying there was no chance of going to Cowes again, since he did not wish to cross his father when there was no necessity for it. Soon, however, he was lapsing into self-pity. He began to question Jennie's love:

A love that is ready to go through any trials to surmount any difficulties, to wait if necessary almost a lifetime that looks only to one end and to one goal, that is resolved to look at no other and to be content with no other. Have you that, my darling?

and he added, 'They are as enduring as life itself and, I believe fully, last and receive their reward beyond the grave.'[2]

Mrs Jerome had forbidden Jennie to write to Randolph and he had had no news of her at all; he was becoming more idealistic simply because she was so remote. His expressions were born of frustration and the results of his too hasty proposal: he could not move forward into practical considerations, even if he wished to. It is possible to understand the stress of such emotion, and even admire the fact that in the face of a lack of response, his passion never declined but intensified; he agonised that he could not do more to love and protect his beloved Jennie. One wonders whether his mother Frances ever read these letters, and if she was moved by them.

Next there came a formal letter from Mrs Jerome to Randolph, written from Rosetta Cottage on 9 September, perhaps with a wider audience in mind. She assured him that whatever the outcome, he had won her heart by his frank and honourable manner and that she would always look on him with the kindest remembrance. She concluded by advising him to remember that his first duty was to his father, who only had his happiness at heart.

Randolph, meanwhile, still incandescent from his brother Blandford's clumsy attempts to get involved, showed the latter's letter to the Prince of Wales, who made an attempt to calm the situation and passed it on to Francis Knollys, his private secretary and close friend to Randolph. Knollys wrote from Abergeldie, the Prince's estate near Balmoral, sympathising but advising him not to reply to Blandford in the heat of the moment for fear of creating a more serious breach between them. In a later letter he reminded Randolph that Sir E. Thornton, the British envoy in Washington consulted by the Duke about Leonard Jerome, had not yet reported back.

Heartened by all this support and rekindled by a brief meeting with Jennie in London on 15 September, as the Jeromes made their way back to Paris at the end of the summer, Randolph thought he had reason to be optimistic. On the evening of the same day, on his return to Blenheim, he addressed an agricultural dinner in Woodstock and the next day wrote to Jennie, entreating her to lift her spirits and to have hope: he insisted she should use all her influence and powers of persuasion to support his arguments against delay so they could be married in December.

The Marlboroughs continued to worry about their second son, but found themselves increasingly impotent in the face of Randolph's passion and determination. It is very tempting to talk of young love in all its various forms and to applaud spontaneously when it triumphs over all obstacles, particularly those put forward by parents. But it is advisable to look at situations, even the most romantic ones, with a clear unprejudiced eye before making judgements. The Duke, principled and committed to his family, working hard to recover the lost ground which faced him when he inherited, cared and indeed worried so much about Randolph that he went to the lengths of having Jennie's father investigated in case of disaster.

Given Randolph's impetuosity and impulsive behaviour, is it any wonder his parents feared the consequences of this latest escapade? There was nothing to reassure them he was not heading for trouble again. Three days was insufficient time for him to consider making a proposal of marriage, particularly if he had not yet settled his own future; it seems almost as if he were driven by something outside himself. Even more worrying, the situation was fast developing into one where he was more intent on having his own way than on finding a solution to the dilemma he had created.

If Randolph followed his parents' wishes and managed to gain the Woodstock seat, and he seemed to have had no fear that he might not, then as an aristocrat he would not qualify for an MP's salary: he and his family would be dependent on John Winston for life. This would be another burden for his father; also, at some point in a discussion with Jennie, Leonard Jerome had warned her, 'You are no heiress!' There was even some hesitation on the part of Mrs Jerome, who appeared to believe at some point that Jennie could have done better.

Jennie's letter to Randolph on 16 September ventured similar concerns. She told him, 'Sometimes I almost wish I had listened a little more to Mama's advice … from the beginning she asked me not to think of it – and begged me to forget you.' And again, later in the same letter, she expressed a similar sentiment:

> Believe me, I consider you as free – as if nothing had passed between us
> – and as I told you last night if your father or mother object in the least to
> our marriage – why cross them? Is it not much wiser to end it all before
> it is too late?'[3]

This was partly due to her not being allowed by her mother to write to Randolph, though Mrs Jerome's motives were never given. It becomes evident towards the end of the letter, however, that two things had upset Jennie: Randolph had 'heard something against her father', and, secondly, she had read in the *Court Journal* a report over which she had wept and raged:

APPROACHING MARRIAGE IN HIGH LIFE

Miss Jerome, one of the prettiest young ladies that ever hailed from New York and landed at Cowes, is about to marry Lord Randolph Churchill, the third son of the Duke of Marlborough. The young lady, who has resided for some time in Paris, will receive a splendid dower on her marriage. Mr Jerome is one of the most inveterate of American yachtsmen.

The journal was obliged to print an apology the following week. Recent commentators are inclined to lay the responsibility for the indiscretion at the door of the Jeromes, largely because of the exaggeration of the dowry. Certainly the Marlboroughs would not be inclined to speak to the press; the Duke would obviously be furious at the unwelcome publicity. Whatever the truth of the matter, Jennie's letter received a sharp riposte from Randolph on 18 September; matters were coming to a head and feelings were running high. His biting sarcasm was well to the fore:

This is the first letter I have had from you and it certainly is an encouraging one. I can assure you that if I am to receive many like it, I can only say that at any rate I was a good deal happier when the letter-writing was only on my side, and when I could leave your answers to my foolish imagination. I am more pained and hurt than you can imagine and if that was your object in writing you may congratulate yourself on having fully attained it … If you cast me off tho' from your beauty and attractions you will have always admirers at your feet, but you will have trifled with and spurned the truest and most honest love and devotion that man is capable of feeling.

He concluded, still very emotionally:

I do entreat and implore you to have confidence in me if you really love me and never again to write so cruel and so painful a letter.

Yours as ever, Devoted but despairing, Randolph S. Churchill[4]

In this letter Randolph veers from one extreme state of mind to another, beginning with an onslaught on Jennie, full of sarcasm and bitterness, and accusing her of making heartless accusations against him. She mocked him, he insisted, and never intended to be led into a serious engagement. The

Victorians had several collections and deliveries of mail each day and several letters could be written in a very short space of time. But it was possible for letters to cross and thus promote misunderstanding. In this case, Jennie had obviously received the last letter, because she replied immediately and with equal warmth:

Paris, 18th September

This must be – and shall be the last misunderstanding between us – my own darling Randolph unless you wish to make it – if my letter pained you and gave you any anxiety – it has caused me a thousand times more – The moment it had gone – I'd repented and if I could have got it back then – you would never have received it – yet in a way I do not feel sorry – for it has given me a fresh proof of your love – and has made me discover the strength and depth of mine – I did not know how much I loved you – until I left England and felt that I was leaving all I love most on earth behind me – perhaps for ever – Darling I love your angry cross letter – it has done me more good – than twenty tender ones – I could leave Father, Mother – and the whole world for you – if it were necessary.[5]

Jennie's explosion of dashes can be easily forgiven, as can Randolph's abuse of the comma; they are both emotionally involved and completely open with each other. In the short term, this small crisis served to strengthen each of them and draw them closer together. They were so thoroughly engaged with this 'first and only love' that their sincerity cannot be doubted.

Randolph still wasn't finished, and replied in a most moving way. Indeed, he had never moved beyond this point. He began by asking forgiveness for his letter of the previous day but soon shifted the blame to Jennie, admitting that he was cross but that it was Jennie who made him so. All this was, of course, the result of Jennie not writing to him; a one-sided correspondence was bound to lead to misunderstanding. He continued to reassure her that he was still strong in his love and that he meant to marry her. He added significantly:

I can now assure you, dearest, that my father and mother will not oppose my marrying you; they will very probably try to insist on some delay in order that their incredulous minds may be fully persuaded that I am as fond of you and that I love you as dearly as I have continually dinned into their heads ever since I saw you that I do. But it won't be for very long. I know them so well, they always pretend to be very stern at first about everything, but they can never hold out long as they are really very kindhearted and very fond of me (strange to say). And I assure you that when you do marry me they will be as fond of you as of their own daughters and will be very proud of you indeed and you will never for a moment regret having come into my family.

There is a subtly different note here: have his parents, those two people who have shown him such love and forgiveness over and over again, done anything to deserve the phrase 'incredulous minds'? Is Randolph's attitude towards his parents what one expects? Here is the dark side of this charming, well-educated, articulate man. He seems very confident of his ground as he continues to make plans: things are now coming to a crisis and they are only waiting for the formal consent of their parents; Jennie must hold on. He wrote persuasively, asking Jennie for her support:

I call upon you most solemnly and seriously to write to me words of affection and encouragement such as you know how to write. I know you well enough to feel certain that you never would have spoken to me and talked to me as you have done without feeling everything you said or without being prepared to abide by it all. Talk of my giving you up!! Why, as long as I feel sure of your affection as I do now, thank God, you might just as well expect the earth to stop still from ever moving or the sun to cease to shine.[6]

Chapter Fourteen

RESOLUTION

The united ambition of Frances and John Winston to see Randolph represent Woodstock as its Member of Parliament had existed for a long time and had not diminished with the years. Up to this point Randolph had not established any clear way in which his future could develop – and he was now 24. A problem was that it was seen as inappropriate for a Duke's son to take up paid activity; he would certainly not have been paid as an MP, which seems unfair on a second son who would not have had the benefit of a ducal income.

Two acceptable options were the Army and the Church. Randolph showed no interest in either, wisely, in view of his lack of self-discipline. A third option was the House of Commons, which would give the necessary shape to his life and also maintain the family tradition: his father, grandfather and great-grandfather had all been Members of Parliament. Not being in the direct line of the dukedom, Randolph would not have to move later to the House of Lords. His father particularly wished him to take the Woodstock seat which he and the 6th Duke had occupied.

Randolph now relied on his parents' plan to help further his and Jennie's wishes. His elder brother Blandford, heir to the dukedom, had given nothing but trouble since his schooldays. He was highly intelligent and extremely talented in science, but he was wilful, wayward, unfaithful, and even violent towards his wife Albertha, daughter of an old friend, the Duke of Abercorn. John Winston and Frances had long ago given up all expectation of him, and all hope of a political career; their attention was focused on Randolph. The latter's suggestion in his letter that, if he were allowed to marry Jennie, he would stand as MP for Woodstock, was given the treatment it deserved and ignored for the moment, but he was certain that it would have its effect. Randolph's attitude towards his parents reflected his character: the son who had had love and affection given him so generously was blackmailing his father. He had changed greatly from the attractive personality he was as a child.

Towards the end of September 1873 the news he was after arrived: his father did not wish for a moment to prevent the young couple seeing each other as often as they could, and promised to give his consent to the marriage when he was sure they were fond of each other. His sister Cornelia agreed that their parents would not wait the year that they had earlier stipulated. Randolph's letters at this point suggest great jubilation; he was as 'happy as a lark', 'the clouds have all cleared away', and 'the sky is bluer than I have ever known it'.

However, he was volatile. He told Jennie there was a possibility of Parliament being dissolved and then, he wrote, he would be Member for Woodstock. A public life held no charms for him, he reflected, but that would change 'if I thought it would please you'. Was he saying that if he did not succeed it would be her fault? He added in this letter that it was exactly six weeks since their first meeting on board the *Ariadne*. He was over-confident and full of assertiveness. Jennie was radiant with youth, health and beauty. Randolph had all the confidence of his background and education but his attitude was childish and superficial. He seemed to have no grasp on reality, no understanding or insight.

The Duke's next letter was written from Cowes, where Frances had now joined him; there is a more gentle tone, reminiscent perhaps of Frances, who wrote, she said, at the dictation of her husband, who was a little tired:

> Your mother and I are only anxious for your happiness. I am quite willing, my dear boy, to give you credit for all you say, to make allowances for the state of mind in which you say you are. I only hope that it will not lead you to treat your mother and me ungratefully … You must imagine to yourself what must be our feelings at the prospect of this marriage of yours. You cannot regard yourself alone in the matter and disassociate yourself from the rest of your family … Under any circumstances, an American connection is not one that we would like. You must allow it is a slightly coming-down in pride for us to contemplate the connection.[1]

John Winston was making an enormous effort to be conciliatory. His reference to Frances was quite deliberate. What could she think of Randolph's actions? All her hopes and dreams of his future were threatened by this headlong leap into a marriage which had no practical base. Her hopes of a political career for him were fading. Jennie had no supporting fortune, which meant they would have no security beyond what their respective fathers could produce. What did they think they could live on? Randolph paid no heed to the advice he was being given: did he care? He did not seem to think beyond his own desires and emotions. His father was counselling him that he was not alone in this matter but that it would affect them all; Randolph seemed incapable of listening. Across the Atlantic, Leonard Jerome was beginning to raise corresponding objections. His opinions on the inbreeding of the British aristocracy had always been strong and his ambitious wife viewed this impending marriage as one on which their favourite daughter could improve. He wrote to Jennie that she had startled him, and made him anxious. He feared that if anything were to go wrong 'you will make a dreadful shipwreck of your affections'. He added, 'You were never born to love lightly.'

Here was a man who understood his daughter very well and at that moment was being very cautious. Despite his irregular and ostentatious lifestyle, Leonard Jerome had made and lost more than one fortune in the United States. He had founded the first two great racecourses – Jerome Park and Coney Island; he owned and edited the *New York Times* and was said to have subscribed nearly half his fortune to the Federal War funds. He was at the time on the verge of a crisis and could only promise Jennie £2,000 a year. On the other hand, his wife had succeeded in bringing up their three daughters to be sophisticated and fashionable. Jennie's good looks and musical skills took her into a level of society which encouraged her mother to be ambitious about marriage. When the Jeromes heard about the Marlboroughs' reactions, they withdrew their original consent.

Jennie, however, was just as determined as Randolph when it came to getting what she wanted and she enjoyed a battle. She had chosen her husband and she would not give him up. They loved each other wholeheartedly. She had no head for practical matters like money and she expected a high and stylish life which Randolph could not deliver. In the end, however, Leonard made what financial provision he could for his daughter and the Duke agreed to his son's suggestion: Randolph was to contest the Parliamentary seat at Woodstock. The blackmail had worked; he would, without any real commitment on his part, do what his father had wished for. Also, Randolph and Jennie were expected to wait a year to demonstrate the strength of their commitment. Knowing how mercurial Randolph's emotions were, the condition of a year's wait was the shrewdest thing the Duke could do: Randolph's emotional euphoria might deflate over time. It did, of course, but not within the year; only when the marriage was well under way. As always, John Winston had acted with clear knowledge of his son and the wisdom which characterised him; he saw the possibility of settling Randolph down into some regularity of life. In all, he had done his utmost to safeguard this volatile situation.

There were two major obstacles in the way before Randolph could return to Paris to be with his beloved Jennie. The first concerned a favourite aunt, Frances' sister Alexandrina, the Countess of Portarlington, who was desperately ill at her home in Ireland at the age of 51. Randolph managed to spend some time in London with the newly arrived Leonard Jerome, and passed the test with honours, then crossed to Ireland to join his mother at his aunt's bedside and do what he could to assuage considerable family grief. Lady Portarlington hovered between relapse and recovery for several weeks. Frances, anxious to let her future daughter-in-law know that she had not been forgotten, sent a telegraph to Jennie. She followed this up with a letter written from the Portarlington home:

Dear Miss Jerome,

Although in great anxiety and affliction, I write a line for dear Randolph to enclose as I feel grieved for his disappointment in not being able to start so as to spend your birthday with you.

(Randolph had been on the point of departure when his aunt had a dramatic relapse; he felt obliged to stay but clearly felt the disappointment.) Frances continued by saying that she hoped to meet Jennie soon under happier circumstances.[2]

Finally, a month after Randolph first arrived in Ireland, his aunt died. Following the funeral he set off across the Irish Sea with the intention of crossing to France from Dover. Fate intervened again, however, for the dissolution of Parliament, which had been so long awaited, finally arrived. In early 1874 Randolph turned back to Blenheim to begin his campaign to be returned as Member of Parliament for Woodstock.

The Liberal government had been limping along for five years and the tide of political opinion which had swept them into power in 1868 had now turned against them; Randolph had every chance of winning the seat, even though his experience and ability were bound to be called into question. Addressing an important meeting of local farmers in Woodstock's *Bear Hotel*, he was nervous and awkward in front of a critical audience; he had written out his speech on small pieces of paper and placed them in the bottom of his top hat, which was on the table in front of him. The audience was not unfriendly, fortunately for him, and as soon as they noticed what he was doing they shouted advice and encouragement: 'Take the things out of your hat!' There was little sign here of the skilled orator he was to become. He was helped through the questions by the skill of Edward Clarke, a rising young barrister and experienced campaigner from London. Randolph had excellent support from his father and friends, and struggled through the speech and answers to questions without disaster.

He longed for Jennie to be with him, painfully aware of the support and enthusiasm that she could have generated. As for Jennie, she was reading everything she could lay her hands on in an attempt to be informed about British politics. When his electoral victory was declared, the relief of the Marlboroughs was intense: the many years of dreaming and hoping were fulfilled and a rare sense of general well-being and collective affection pervaded the Palace. In Paris Jennie went wild with excitement. Randolph had fulfilled his part of the bargain.

Matters now began to move forward. The Duke and Duchess crossed to Paris to make the acquaintance of their future daughter-in-law and were charmed by her. Financially, however, the future was not radiant: the Duke had an income of £40,000 a year (two million pounds in today's values), out of which he had to meet the running costs of Blenheim and find allowances for his children. He had already sold the Marlborough Gems; nevertheless, he paid off Randolph's debts and bought them a lease on an elegant four-storey house at 48 Charles Street, Mayfair. Randolph was deeply grateful to his father and wrote immediately to thank him:

Indeed Papa, thanks to you this last difficulty is removed and I feel quite confident that Jennie and I will be very happy together, which I know will please you. Nor are we at all likely to forget to whom we chiefly owe our happiness.

The £2,000 a year that Leonard Jerome had promised Jennie was the best he could do in his circumstances, but he was appalled at the idea that an English husband should have control of his wife's money and insisted it should be entirely hers. Just as whatever money Frances had when she married John Winston in 1843 would have passed to him, so Jennie's £2,000 was expected by English law to go to Randolph.

Chapter Fifteen

FAMILY LIFE

From the British Ambassador in Paris, Lord Lyons, to the British Foreign Secretary Lord Derby, a certificate of a marriage solemnised at this Embassy ...

I hereby certify that Lord Randolph Henry Spencer Churchill, bachelor of the parish of Woodstock and the county of Oxford, now residing at Paris, Hotel d'Albe, and Jennie Jerome, spinster, of the city of Brooklyn, in the state of New York, USA, were duly married according to the rites of the Church of England in the House of Her Most Historic Majesty's Ambassador at Paris this 15th day of April in the year of our Lord one thousand eight hundred and seventy four ...

And so, after many trials and tribulations, the marriage went ahead, a simple service at the British Embassy in Paris on 15 April, Frances' birthday, in 1874, the year Benjamin Disraeli became Prime Minister once again at the age of 70. The best man was Francis Knollys, private secretary to the Prince of Wales, later Edward VII; the bridesmaid was Jennie's sister Clara. The bride wore a dress of white satin with a long tulle veil, a long train and flounces of Alencon lace. Present were Randolph's brother the Marquess of Blandford, three of Randolph's sisters and his aunt, Lady Camden, step-sister of John Winston. Leonard Jerome presented his daughter with a pearl necklace and her mother gave her a magnificent white lace parasol. The bride and groom ate their wedding breakfast separately from their guests in a small drawing-room and, after saying goodbye to their guests, changed and prepared to depart for a short continental honeymoon.

The Duke and Duchess did not attend, and no reason for this has ever been established, although it does not signify a lack of support for the marriage: the agreement had been made and the Marlboroughs were people of their word. There could have been a perfectly practical reason for their non-attendance, now lost in time. Certainly Randolph was well supported by his brother, three of his sisters and his aunt. There is uncertainty over why the marriage took place in Paris, but perhaps this was Mrs Jerome's natural base; it was to Paris that she brought Jennie and her sisters when they travelled to Europe. Nevertheless, to the modern eye the marriage does seem to have begun under a slight cloud.

On his wedding morning Randolph received a very carefully written letter from his father which, nominally expressing good wishes for the occasion, actually says much more. The text reads in full:

> I must send you a few lines to reach you tomorrow, one of the most important days of your life, and which I sincerely pray will be blessed to you, and be the commencement of a united existence of happiness for you and your wife. She is one that you have chosen with rather less than usual deliberation, but you have adhered to your love with unwavering constancy, and I cannot doubt the truth of your affection, and now I hope that, as time goes on, your two natures will prove to have been brought not accidentally together. May you both be 'lovely and pleasant in your lives' is my earnest prayer. I am very glad that harmony is again restored, and that no cloud obscures the day of sunshine; but what has happened will show that the severest faith is not without its throes, and I must say ought not to be without its lesson to you ... We shall look forward shortly to seeing you and Jeannette here, whom I need not say we shall welcome into her new family.[1]

This expresses support and welcome, but it is difficult to see wholehearted approval in it: Randolph is reminded bluntly that he acted with 'less than the usual deliberation'. John Winston avoids the word 'confidence' but uses the much more limited 'hope': 'which I sincerely pray will be blessed to you ... I hope that as time goes on ... is my earnest prayer ... not to be without its lesson to you.' Is responsibility rather than love behind the Duke's closing words: 'We shall welcome [her] into her new family.'

Randolph brought Jennie to Blenheim on a late spring day in May 1874. The villagers of Woodstock demonstrated their support in the traditional way by meeting them at the station, taking the horses from the carriage and dragging it themselves to the Palace. The first sight of Blenheim is always most impressive, its dramatic and powerful shape silhouetted against the skyline. As they entered the Park, Randolph drew his wife's attention to the view of the Palace, the Grand Bridge and the lake. 'This is the finest view in England,' he told her. Writing about the moment nearly 40 years later Jennie admitted how awed and impressed she had been, but confessed that her American pride forbade the admission and she tried to conceal her feelings.

She was welcomed by the 7th Duke and Duchess and the rest of the family. The Duchess of Marlborough was by 1874 showing a strong resemblance to her mother, which was enough in some eyes either to elevate or condemn her. She had grasped the nettle at Blenheim and pitted her strength against what Sarah, the 1st Duchess, called 'this wild and unmerciful house'. Certainly Frances had come a long way from that baby her glamorous and cavalier parents had rattled over the snow-covered Alps in the winter of 1822: she was still a tiny figure against her ducal background but those who underestimated her did so at their peril. Her grandson Winston Churchill was to write later that she was a 'woman of exceptional capacity, energy and decision'. At this point in time, she was enjoying the social and political success she and the Duke had planned and worked for. They nurtured hopes that Randolph and Jennie would become part of this, with Randolph at last settling down and applying himself to a Parliamentary career, and that the love and passion the two young people had declared for each other would develop into a successful and stable marriage. Jennie was welcomed into the family circle at Blenheim. She was in awe of the way in which Frances organised the household, but she saw the Duke as a man of grace, courtesy and kindness. She decided that Randolph's sisters were less beautiful than herself, though she was aware of her husband's affection for them. As a family they exuded warmth and humour. They did their best to make Jennie welcome, although there must have been concern for the future. Certainly Jennie, from her own account, was ill at ease at Blenheim.

Life at the Palace soon bored her. It was much more formal than she was used to: in her *Memoirs*, she later recounted how, after a leisurely breakfast, one read the newspapers with a view to being able to join in discussion at dinner. The afternoons meant visiting, both social and charitable. After dinner, which was a formal affair, everyone congregated in the Van Dyck room, perhaps playing whist, till 11 p.m., when they fetched their candles and dutifully kissed the parents good night. So tedious were the evenings that it was not unknown for a sleepy member of the family surreptitiously to advance the clocks a quarter of an hour. In between times Jennie read, painted and practised piano. Any inadequacies in the heating system were compensated for by furs and hot-water bottles.

His insistence that love was enough meant Randolph had given no consideration to how the youthful Jennie, with her vital and lively nature, would fit into his family's way of life. The strains soon appeared. Her letters back to her family carried scornful criticism: there was no knowledge of fashion, the tableware was 'frumpy' and she described the table water decanters as having thick tumblers on top, 'the kind we use in bedrooms'. The typically formal meals, when the Duke and Duchess presided over a large gathering consisting not only of family but also of staff, such as nannies, tutors and governesses, as well as the frequent guests, were something to endure. Jennie and her friends relieved the monotony by dressing up as tourists and giggling at the comments they overheard as they made their anonymous way round the Palace on open days. 'My, what poppy eyes these Churchills have got!' was one remark she enjoyed. She does not seem to have identified with the Marlboroughs or thought of herself in any way as part of the family; her attitude was objective and critical.

Anita Leslie, her niece, has written that Jennie had no small opinion of herself. However, she worked very hard at her music, practising for four or five hours every day, and, trained by her father, she was a skilful horsewoman. Randolph's sisters, on the other hand, had supported their brother over the last few months and were prepared to welcome and include her in their family circle. They lived simply and economically and were astonished by the 23 beautiful dresses from Paris with which Jennie arrived. Frances, who had been quiet but influential before the marriage, does not seem to have said much at this point. What all were agreed upon, however, was that Jennie was Randolph's choice, and now his wife, and so the sensible and proper thing to do was for everyone to be pleasant and to get on with each other as well as possible.

Randolph himself kept his part of the bargain and was elected to Parliament for the Woodstock seat. On 22 May 1874 he duly made his maiden speech in the House of Commons. This moment must have stood out as an occasion of great happiness and pride for Frances and John Winston, especially after the crisis Randolph had caused over his marriage. He spoke against a proposal that a new military centre should be built near Oxford, speaking passionately in defence of the peace of the city and his university. Disraeli, Prime Minister and leader of Randolph's party and friend of the family since the time of Frances' mother, was moved to write to Frances in praise: he told her the House was captivated by his energy and natural flow, and by his natural manner; he believed it was a speech of great promise. Whatever indignities Randolph's son Winston was to suffer at his father's hands, he was indebted to him for one major asset: an extraordinary talent with the spoken word. Eighty years later this was to be part of the citation awarding Winston the Nobel Prize for Literature. Disraeli gave some ominous warnings also, however. His letter drew attention to Randolph's need for self-control and warned that he 'said some imprudent things', a view endorsed by another member, Sir William Harcourt, who criticised Randolph for the intemperance of his language and attitude. So the Marlboroughs' pleasure was marred a little. The old problem remained: the lack of restraint was still there.

Disraeli had already given Randolph encouragement and support and was a powerful ally. Perhaps he saw in Randolph's oratorical power an echo of himself. Years earlier, 'this strange and brilliant man' had destroyed Peel's leadership of the Conservative party with a series of speeches 'that for concentrated invective have rarely been equalled' in the House of Commons. One of Disraeli's characteristics in Parliament for over 30 years had been the priority he gave to being in the House almost constantly while it was sitting; thus 'his acute perception of real Parliamentary talent' was the consequence of lengthy attendance on the front benches. The Duke and Duchess's pleasure was well founded. Here was an icon of their own political generation making a judgement on Randolph which could be respected.

One thing Randolph did not share with Disraeli was his debating chamber stance. Disraeli sat, impassive and sombre, arms folded, head bent on to his shirt front, seemingly asleep but actually acutely aware. His thoughts and likely response were difficult to predict. Randolph, on the other hand, indicative of his confidence, adopted a dominating and challenging sprawl on the bench, which, although hugely irritating to the Opposition, possibly made his likely reactions easier to predict.

As part of the Duke's settlement on his son, he had paid £10,000 for the 37-year lease on 48 Charles Street, Mayfair, the gracious four-storey house with balconies and window boxes. London was much more to Jennie's taste, and Frances was supremely well-equipped to guide Jennie into the highest levels of London society. The Duchess helped her pay the customary visits to those who were socially important; Jennie wrote to her mother that she and Frances set off in grand style in the family coach. She wore the pearls her father had given her, while the Duchess lent her diamonds and rubies for her hair. A bouquet of gardenias was also given her by Frances, and Jennie acknowledged her appreciation of all the characteristic thoughtfulness.

She was presented to Queen Victoria and introduced into the elite circle of friends surrounding the Prince of Wales. She moved quickly and easily into a hectic social life. At Ascot Races in 1874 she appeared, as fashion then dictated, in her slightly modified wedding dress of white satin, her exquisite white lace parasol held like a cobweb behind her head. She wrote to her family that dinners, balls and parties succeeded one another without intermission till the end of July. She found a natural place in the fashionable world that flocked to the Derby and Ascot and Goodwood races. She described how they used to drive down in coaches in Ascot frocks and feathered hats, and stay to dinner, driving back by moonlight. For Jennie, the social life that marriage had brought her was everything. Whereas Frances' priority had been to create a home for her husband and children, her new daughter-in-law had little time or inclination for anything but the social scene.

There was one family event, however, which interrupted Jennie's social whirl: the birth of her first son. In late November 1874, Randolph and Jennie were staying with his parents at Blenheim. Predictably, the fun-loving Jennie would go out into the Park with the shooting party, despite being over seven months pregnant. A combination of a fall and a bumpy carriage ride brought on her confinement some six weeks prematurely and so, on 30 November 1874, her first son, Winston Leonard Spencer-Churchill, was born.

This stroke of chance had huge consequences. Winston's birth at Blenheim began a relationship with that great house, and the achievements of his great ancestor which it represented, which were to become an essential part of Winston's inspiration and his belief in himself. The sense of his destiny, of being born to fulfil some great task which, against all the odds, carried his country and allies to victory in the Second World War, was centred on Blenheim. Energetic and precipitate as he was in all things, Winston was no less so in his birth. His early arrival meant there was no time to summon the obstetrician from London; the local doctor from

Woodstock delivered the baby, who was then dressed in a borrowed layette. As soon as the mother and baby were through their ordeal, Frances slipped away to send the news to Jennie's mother in Paris, reassuring her of her daughter's safety and that of the baby: 'We had neither cradle or baby linen nor anything ready,' she wrote, 'but fortunately everything went well and all difficulties were overcome.'[2]

The new baby was the second Spencer-Churchill grandson for John Winston and Frances and someone with whom Frances in particular would forge strong affections; she was to play a vital part in shaping him for the role he was called upon to play 66 years later, in 1940.

The year of 1874 was significant for people other than the Marlboroughs. On Christmas Eve, a bitterly cold day with snow falling, there occurred the worst railway disaster in Great Western Railway history. Because of extra Christmas traffic the 10 a.m. London to Birkenhead express had been forced to use extra carriages of out-dated design. Just outside the village of Hampton Gay, very near Blenheim, the express left the rails and tumbled down the embankment towards the frozen canal loaded with hundreds of passengers returning home for Christmas. The death toll finally came to 34, with over a hundred injured; many marvelled that the figures were not higher. Jackson's *Oxford Journal*, the local paper, gave a dramatic account of the scene:

The third class carriage was smashed to atoms in a meadow, some 16 to 20 feet below ... other carriages imitated with fatal precision the example set by the third class. One laid beyond it, wheels upward, and splintered into matchwood, parts of the fragments flying into the canal, whilst another, which had carried away the stone parapet of the bridge, had evidently glanced over the top of the woodwork and plunged to the foot of the embankment, and was so completely ruined that the roof and lamps lay mixed up with the wheels and bottom of the carriage in dire confusion. Two other carriages lay next, on their side, both of course greatly shattered, and the next was a first class carriage which had found its way across the up line and was pitched down the embankment, and then three other carriages on the down side of the line, all lying on their side. One end of the first class was crumpled up, and the ghastly stains of blood on the yellow roof, the cushions and the floor testify to the terrible tragedy which was enacted therein.

Among the helpers who quickly arrived on the scene was Lord Randolph Churchill and a party from Blenheim Palace; his strong instinct for immediate action was to his advantage for once. He and his party worked hard to do what they could; the wounded were carried to the house nearby and given food and blankets to protect them against the severe cold. Randolph, taking his position as MP very seriously, did not restrict his work to these practical measures; he spoke at length to the train crew at the scene of the accident and wrote a detailed letter to *The Times* newspaper, explaining the technical nature of the accident to the public at large.

This was already an eventful winter for the Churchills, but more trouble was to come for Frances and John Winston. Randolph's elder brother Blandford, the heir to the dukedom, was a highly intelligent and talented man but wayward and self-indulgent. He had married Bertha, daughter of the 1st Duke of Abercorn, a pleasant girl but not too intelligent, with a penchant for practical jokes of the bucket-above-the-door variety. Not surprisingly he had tired of her and his infidelity was common knowledge. On the other hand, he was very taken with Jennie and gave her a ring in October 1875 which she showed to the Duchess and Randolph's sister Rosamund. They recognised it as Bertha's, and this was just the kind of cynical action of which Blandford was capable. Randolph, in conciliatory fashion, wrote to his brother asking him to sort out the matter, pointing out that if the ring were indeed Bertha's then Jennie could not accept it. It was a pleasant enough letter, but as usual Randolph did not guard his tongue completely, referring to his mother and sister 'giving several vicious looks and insinuations' concerning Blandford's action.

Blandford's behaviour had for years caused serious tension between himself and his parents. He seemed to seize the opportunity to cause trouble and maliciously forwarded Randolph's letter to their mother, adding a harsh note of his own which accused her of 'the intense jealousy which you often display' and 'the mischief which you so often make'. He ended by saying that if this was to be her behaviour then 'you need not expect to hear very often from me'.

All that is known of Frances' family loyalty, her warmth and kindness, her affection and care for Blandford, as for all her children, makes it easy to understand how wounded she was. The letter hurt her dreadfully, as it was meant to, especially as she was sharply aware of how badly Blandford was treating Bertha, for whose vulnerability she had much sympathy. Knowing of Blandford's attitude towards women, she could not completely dismiss the thought that he might have designs on his sister-in-law. But the problem was caused in the first place by Randolph's typically careless language about his mother in his first letter.

Tempers and feelings were becoming increasingly overwrought, when John Winston became involved, springing to Frances' defence. Writing from London to Randolph, he accused him of provoking Blandford and made it abundantly clear that he saw his younger son as demonstrating once again the thoughtlessness and insensitive attitude with which he had plagued his parents for most of his life. In the context of the Duke's hopes and prayers that Randolph might have begun a promising political career, his expression of disappointment in the letter is moving. He attacked Randolph on several fronts, pointing out to him that while he, Jennie and the baby had been received with kindness, he had 'dishonourably and treacherously' abused the confidence which he himself pretended he shared with his mother. The uncompromising language demonstrates the measure of the Duke's (and Frances') hurt.

Predictably, Randolph's deep-seated weaknesses, self-justification and emotional extravagance, re-emerged to govern his response. He refused to accept his father's criticism and did not even seem to be aware (or care about) the hurt he caused his mother. He told his father that if this was his attitude then further communications between them were not only 'useless but impossible'.

Thus both sons were alienated from their parents. Jennie emerges out of the matter quite well. Appalled at the storm she had occasioned, she wrote next day to Frances, tactfully attempting to smooth things over, and expressing her concern about 'being the unintentional cause' of the dispute. But one might question the vanity or naivety of a young bride taking a gift as personal as a ring from another man, albeit her brother-in-law. She tried to defend Randolph, but failed to explain his use of 'vicious looks and insinuations' ascribed to his mother. Her letter seems to be a genuine attempt to heal the breach and restore good relations and was therefore most commendable.

Frances was too upset and worried to respond graciously to this; the long letter she wrote to Jennie in reply is revealing. Normally so self-contained and self-disciplined, she was so upset that she could not help but pour out just how deeply she had been hurt. When she bursts out, 'It is a bitter sorrow to find both our sons turn against us and reward our affection and kindness by insult and abuse,' we sympathise readily, and we feel her hurt when she comments on how Randolph and Blandford have got into a way of 'abusing and ridiculing us'. She made it clear that Randolph's accusation of 'vicious looks and insinuations' was completely untrue, and when she claimed that Randolph was deliberately rousing Blandford's angry temper, it is difficult to question her. The claim that 'He has got himself so into the habit of abusing people' also has a ring of truth. Frances was a caring, loving and warm-hearted parent, and she could not refrain from an outpouring of her feelings: 'never was so upset … such a blow … could not control my emotions … I feel too cut up … cuts me to the heart … trampled on my affections … God forgive'. Such an outburst is so uncharacteristic of Frances that it is completely convincing.

Her distress is made all the more poignant by the contrast in the second half of her letter, where she declares her love and affection for Jennie and the baby: 'I love you and your dear little child and I shall never cease to take a loving interest in you.' She is totally honest and all the more compelling for being so.

We are fortunate that this letter has survived. There could be no better insight into the sensitive, caring nature of this often undervalued woman. It is obvious that she had been deeply wounded. Blandford's insulting letter is completely lacking in the courtesy and consideration one would expect; Randolph enjoyed his mother's confidence and should have been sensitive to her feelings, as his father observed; and the language of Frances' letter to Jennie is highly personal. Randolph and Jennie had been married only 18 months and already there were cracks appearing in the family; unfortunately they involved Jennie. Perhaps these were 'teething troubles', the tensions of any family settling into its adult relationships, but they do not come as a surprise. It was several months before this family quarrel was made up and there are almost prophetic tones in the last letter of the Duchess. Blandford and Randolph were indeed unrestrained in language and behaviour, as their mother well knew, and both seemed strangely unaware of the extent of the present damage. Soon those same faults would cause more trouble on a larger scale.

Chapter Sixteen

DISAPPOINTED HOPES

There were some warning signals of trouble ahead. Jennie was a beautiful young woman, with very dark hair and flashing eyes; she was radiant with health and when stimulated socially became vivacious and amusing. Sometimes there were unfortunate repercussions. The story is told of how, when Lord Falmouth was visiting, Jennie's attention was caught by an old lady stepping out of a four-wheeler carriage in St James's Place. 'Who on earth is that old demon?' she demanded. 'Why, it's my mother,' replied Lord Falmouth courteously. On another occasion, at a masked ball in Holland House, her sister Clara had been walking in the garden with an eligible young man who was the target for designing mothers with marriageable daughters. Later in the evening, disguised in a painted mask and yellow wig, Jennie pretended to be Clara's mother and approached him, saying that her daughter had just confided that he had proposed to her and she had accepted him. The sight of his horrified face must have amused the pair of them but it was unlikely to bring them friends. It gradually became obvious that her lovely face and figure were not allied to other desirable qualities, such as sensitivity to others' feelings.

Jennie's financial settlement, which supplemented what the Duke gave the couple, should have made comfortable provision for them, but Jennie's deep-rooted inclination to gratify any fashionable whim took them far beyond their means. The Duke's hopes that Randolph might be governed by Jennie's competence in financial matters were not fulfilled. They lived far beyond their income and it was not long before creditors appeared.

Her extravagance plunged them deeply into debt and this set Jennie in a role opposed to the two women on either side of her in the family. Her mother-in-law, Frances, and later her daughter-in-law, Clementine, were both excellent managers and effective complements to their respective husbands. In aristocratic terms John Winston was not a hugely rich man; his income of about £40,000 was scarcely adequate for the huge cost of running Blenheim and his large family. Despite being the daughter of one of the richest families in the country, Frances adjusted well to the management of the Blenheim household in an effective, non-extravagant way. There was never any question of Frances running her husband into debt, even though hospitality to the many guests welcomed at the Palace was, as we have seen, generous. There is, of course, one famous entry in the Visitors' Book during Frances' time: Sir Alexander Cockburn, the Lord Chief Justice, complained that while he was prepared to share almost everything in life, he drew the line at half a snipe for dinner. This is more likely to have been due to a temporary lack of supply rather than to any lack of generosity. Cockburn would hardly have been so abominably rude in all seriousness, particularly if he wished for a further invitation. Jennie herself describes the generosity of the usual lunch provision:

> rows of entree dishes adorned the table, joints beneath silver covers being placed before the Duke and Duchess, who each carved for the whole company, and as this included governesses, tutors and children it was no sinecure. Before leaving the dining-room the children filled with food small baskets kept for the purpose for poor cottagers or any who might be sick or sorry in Woodstock. These they distributed in the course of their afternoon walks.[1]

Frances was her mother's daughter. Frances Anne had managed not just the domestic households of her various magnificent homes, Wynyard Hall, Mount Stewart, Seaham Hall and Londonderry House, but also, after her husband's death, the business affairs of the huge Londonderry estates and coal-mining interests. Jennie's genetic inheritance was different. Her father had had the acumen to build several large fortunes but had been extravagant and dissipated every one in turn. One more burden that Randolph imposed on his mother as well as his father was the stress of having to watch as an extravagant wife ran their son into debt.

This trait of Jennie's seems to have passed to Winston who, for much of his earlier life, lived well beyond his means. However, unlike his father he acquired a wife who was a restraining factor. Although of aristocratic descent, Clementine had grown up in a household in straitened circumstances, where every penny had to be accounted for. Famously, after her marriage, her trousseau contained underwear of cotton, carefully mended; Winston's underwear, on the other hand, was of silk for, as he himself put it, he could bear no other 'against his tegument [skin]'. Clementine was the counter to Winston's extravagance. Jennie, on the other hand, was incorrigible; after Randolph's death she frequently needed Winston to bail her out of the consequences of her extravagance, even though his income must have been very restricted at the time. Jennie had none of the character, the self-denial, the dedication and commitment possessed by Clementine, which made her such a powerful helpmate to Winston.

Jennie's behaviour seemed superficial. Randolph's biographer, Robert Rhodes James makes it clear that at the time she was having little influence on Randolph's political career apart from the important one of being a very successful hostess. There is little evidence of Randolph seeking her advice. Perhaps it is unreasonable to expect a young American girl to become conversant with the ideas and attitudes of British politics – but that, of course, is exactly what Randolph's mother did. From her earliest years Frances had been exposed to the political world, internationally as well as nationally. Her father, after a brilliant military career, had become a diplomat, the British Ambassador to Vienna, an influential and successful representative at the post-Napoleonic Congresses of Vienna and Verona; Castlereagh, British Foreign Secretary, was her uncle; Wellington, soon to be Prime Minister, was her godfather. In character, background and experience she was ideally placed to provide a stable base, first for her husband's political career and later for his diplomatic success as Viceroy of Ireland. Jennie had none of her advantages.

Randolph's sisters, too, were politically interested and informed, but the circumstances leading up to Randolph and Jennie's marriage had been difficult and their early years did not suggest the kind of stability that Frances and her husband had always known in their own marriage. Jennie's lack of familiarity with the political system was a concern. Was she going to be able to give Randolph the motivation and support in the career which his parents hoped would be his future? They would not wish there to be an area of family interest from which she might feel excluded.

Although the early years of the marriage were happy, this was based on the excitement of their social lifestyle and not on any commitment to

Randolph's political career. It was probably this more than anything which caused the coolness between Jennie and Frances, although it is difficult to establish this exactly. Only a deeper commitment to the serious development of Randolph's career, instead of the superficiality of the social whirl, would have satisfied his parents.

Rhodes James gives us a detailed description of Randolph, regarded at this time as one of the most fashionable figures of the day. He dressed immaculately although he tended to wear far too much jewellery for a man, including a large ring shaped like a Maltese cross set with diamonds, given to him by Jennie; he smoked heavily, using a holder. He became one of the dandies of the day, often wearing a dark blue frock coat and coloured shirts. The ostentation was possibly a compensation for his lack of height, as he was slightly built. He was alert, with large, bright, protuberant eyes, his nickname having been 'Gooseberry' Churchill at Eton. He had a heavy moustache and a rather unhealthy mahogany brown complexion. Altogether, he appeared like a young man more at home in the stalls of the Gaiety theatre than in the councils of the state.

His was a figure which lent itself readily to caricature but that if anything enhanced his image in the eyes of the electorate. We have the example of his son Winston to indicate how aspects of appearance and manner can fix a politician endearingly in the public imagination. Who can forget Winston's V-sign, his cigar or his lisp? But there has to be substance behind the appearance: with Winston this was there in abundance; with his father, so far, there was nothing. What distressed Frances and her husband was that Randolph's reputation was not being built on solid Parliamentary performances but on a superficiality with which they associated Jennie. The promised commitment to politics, which Randolph had used to force his father's agreement to his marriage, did not seem to be happening. Instead, he seemed satisfied at a level of social accomplishment which was distasteful to both parents.

His admitted dislike of a public career now seemed evident and his attendance to Parliamentary duties was fitful. It took him several months to make his maiden speech, although Disraeli found it quite promising. What his parents had become accustomed to regard as normal in Randolph, his rashness and lack of considered and responsible thought, surfaced once again when he managed to alienate Disraeli, Prime Minister and leader of his party, by cutting him at a social function. Disraeli believed this was because he had not given Randolph the vacant Lordship of the Treasury, and such a petulant response would certainly have been characteristic. His tactlessness compounded the resentment Disraeli already felt because of a letter in *The Times* signed 'by a Conservative MP', attacking the arrangements made by his government for the forthcoming visit to India by the Prince of Wales; Disraeli was convinced it was written by Randolph.

Randolph's lifestyle could only bring disappointment and pain to his long-suffering parents; and this state of affairs could have continued indefinitely if there had not taken place an event that was to alter dramatically the career and character of this talented but flawed personality. Randolph was to reach the heights of achievement, but not before he had caused even more pain and frustration than he had so far inflicted.

Chapter Seventeen

THE PRINCE'S REVENGE

Frances and her husband were soon to be confronted with a crisis which was to surpass by far any of the previous excesses of either son. On this occasion, however, the degree of Frances' pain was revealed through no less a person than Queen Victoria herself. The Queen and Frances were contemporaries and friends, the Queen only three years older, and their lives had run parallel in several respects. They had shared anxieties and commiserations over the years, particularly about their children, and Victoria felt great compassion for her friend. When the traumatic experience was over, the Queen invited Frances and John Winston to Windsor. In writing later of the meeting, the Queen noted the anguish Frances had suffered, singling her out particularly. She was much grieved, she recorded in her Journal, to see them look so distressed and unhappy and noted that Frances, especially, 'could scarcely restrain her tears'. So intense was Frances' grief that she was unable to control it, even among the formality and protocol of the Court; nothing could reveal the depth of her pain more.

The trouble did not actually begin with Randolph. Fashionable social life in London revolved around the Marlborough House set. The splendid house, built by the 1st Duke and Duchess of Marlborough in the early eighteenth century as their London home, was on land leased from Queen Anne for four generations which had reverted to the Crown on the death of the 4th Duke. It was now the home of Edward and Alexandra, the Prince and Princess of Wales. The unwritten rules of this small but exclusive social set, to which both Randolph and Blandford belonged, were dictated by the portly Prince, who was notorious for his marital infidelity and the looseness of his living generally. He was renowned for his demands on the wives of friends and he had a particular fondness for American women. His attentions to Jennie were, of course, noticeable and could have been responsible, in part, for Randolph's actions in the dramatic events which were to follow. The Prince's behaviour was seen as acceptable among his set, on the condition it was discreet. Any public scandal resulted in immediate expulsion from the set and from society in general. The London Season ran from spring to the end of July, and included Henley Regatta, Ascot Races, and yachting at Cowes; it was followed by the round of country house shooting-parties. These gave plenty of opportunity for what came to be regarded as a kind of sexual open season. Country house hostesses were expected to accommodate clandestine relationships by tacitly providing adjacent rooms where required; staff maintained a diplomatic silence.

The year 1876 was to bring trouble and heartache to the Marlboroughs, felt as usual more by Frances and John Winston, in their decency and integrity, than by the careless and self-willed perpetrators of the events. It began unexpectedly. Lord Blandford, a womaniser with little scruple about marital fidelity, set the disaster in motion. The Prince of Wales had arranged for himself and some friends a Grand Tour of India, financed by Parliament (£112,000) and the Indian government (£100,000). Since it consisted of shooting wild animals, especially tigers, and enjoying extravagant entertainment, in particular state banquets, its excesses were greatly disapproved of by Queen Victoria, as were most of the raffish friends the Prince took with him. Among them was Lord Aylesford, popularly known as 'Sporting Joe'. As soon as he was gone to India Blandford moved himself and his horses to an inn near Packington Hall, the Aylesfords' home near Coventry. He and Lady Aylesford were conducting what they thought was a secret affair; he was there to hunt, he said, but it became common knowledge that he had a key to her house and used it to visit her as soon as darkness fell.

Edith, Lady Aylesford, wrote to her husband in India that she and Blandford were in love and intended to elope; she asked him for a divorce so they could marry, and told him that Blandford intended to divorce the Marchioness, Albertha. Aylesford set off for home amid great consternation while, back in England, Randolph tried to restrain his brother from doing anything irrevocable. He was well aware of the disaster that divorce would bring for Blandford, understanding perfectly well the cynical code on social licentiousness and divorce which prevailed among the Victorian aristocratic class. Commentators on the Victorian age and its social propriety have pointed out the apparent paradox between the horror of adultery, if made public, and the lack of private morality which prevailed among the upper classes. The guiding principle was to prevent revelation and scandal. Not only was divorce destructive of the family structure and a disgrace in itself, but to have adultery disclosed was a serious social error, especially among the upper classes. The French Revolution and its dreadful warning to aristocrats had not yet passed into historical obscurity, and the Russian Revolution was still to come. Those few families, including the royal family, which belonged to the privileged class were acutely aware of the need to set an example to those less fortunate: to provide the moral leadership of the time. Thus there emerged an attitude that the public face of society must be preserved at all costs.

The Duke and Duchess were cruising in the Aegean at the time, and so Randolph flung himself into the crisis with characteristic impetuosity. Once more, he was about to heap pain and anguish on his father and mother. In his defence, however, it must be said that this time his motive was altruistic: he was trying to protect his brother. This is all the more admirable as in his letters he discloses just how foolish and irritating he found Blandford's conduct. The true offender, of course, was Blandford. He knew how sexual misconduct would strike deep into Frances' and John Winston's strong Christian conviction, and how much pain it would cause them. For it to become public was a double betrayal.

For a time Randolph was able to prevent his brother from taking the matter any further and he telegraphed the Prince of Wales in India, asking him to influence Aylesford against divorce. When the Prince refused to intervene, Randolph typically rushed into precipitate, ill-considered action. His next move changed what was a private matter, albeit subject to the public gaze and criticism, into a constitutional crisis involving the heir to the throne. He counselled Blandford to do nothing precipitate, but failed to follow his own advice. Edith Aylesford numbered the Prince of Wales among her former admirers, probably lovers, and she showed Blandford and Randolph personal letters which the Prince had written her. Randolph was convinced the Prince had encouraged Blandford in his affair, and possibly connived at it by deliberately taking Aylesford to India, and he knew full well the attention the Prince had been paying to Jennie. Randolph had unscrupulously used pressure to further his own wishes before, when threatening his father that he would not enter Parliament unless his marriage to Jennie was agreed to, and now he resorted to blackmail to force the Prince of Wales' hand. The unpleasantness he had forced on his parents earlier was nothing compared to the distress he was to inflict on them now. He armed himself with the incriminating letters and went to Alexandra, the Princess of Wales, and threatened that if Aylesford sued his wife for divorce the letters would be produced in court. If this happened, he went on recklessly, the Solicitor General, no less, was of the opinion the Prince of Wales would never sit upon the throne of England.

It was vital the licentiousness of the Prince of Wales and his associates should not reach the newspapers or the courts. He had already attracted public attention to himself by being involved in the Mordaunt divorce case of 1870 and another scandal would destroy him. The careers of such men as Charles Stewart Parnell and Oscar Wilde were ruined by their failure to keep their immorality out of the public eye; any divorced woman, innocent or guilty, was ostracised for life. Publicity for the Prince could be fatal: the whole royal succession would be threatened. It would be a constitutional crisis!

The Prince of Wales, in India, was furious at being dragged into this scandal. He was desperate to avoid any further personal disgrace. He returned to England and appointed his Master of the Buckhounds, Lord Hardwicke, to demand an apology and negotiate some kind of settlement. Randolph considered his brother a fool and a bore but stayed local to him; he did, however, attract considerable resentment to himself. According to his son, Winston, he boasted that he 'had the crown of England in his pocket'. The Prince, of course, was furious.

At this point, however, the quarrel came to the ears of Queen Victoria and she arranged an approach to both parties: to Randolph she sent the best emissary she could, the distinguished Lord Hartington, later to become the Duke of Devonshire. Hartington told Randolph he would do nothing for either side until he saw the letters to Lady Aylesford, which Randolph produced. He then asked Randolph for his authority to make such use of them as he himself thought best. Having received this, he walked to the fireplace and burned the letters in the grate, saying that he did not think it would be necessary to carry the situation any further. Randolph's respect and trust of the man was sufficient to make him believe this had ended the affair. But he was mistaken.

On their return home from the Aegean, the Duke and Duchess had once more to shoulder a burden their sons had created and did their best to effect a reconciliation. Randolph and Jennie wrote individually to John Winston and Frances seeking their help. There is no evidence that Blandford sought any kind of mitigation in the crisis he had provoked. In his heedless and self-oriented way, he cared nothing for the distress he was causing, least of all to his loyal mother and father. Even his formal expulsion from the officers' mess of his former regiment, the 'Blues' (Royal Horseguards), a social disgrace, failed to move him.

The correspondence between Randolph and Jennie shows that Frances and John Winston acted together to cope with the burden placed upon them. The Duke went to see the Prince of Wales and Frances thought the meeting had gone well, although Randolph's letters show him to have been less sure. He wrote to Jennie, telling her about the interview, in which he gathered the Prince had shown great animosity towards him. He believed his father had stood up to the Prince well. The Prince demanded an apology, which the Duke advised Randolph to give, and he duly did so.

The most recent letters between Randolph and Jennie are a mixture. On the one hand they demonstrate signs of maturity and of a developing intimacy between the couple. A vein of family information runs through them, in spite of the problems they face: the suggestion of a smaller house, complete with price; the reassurance of baby Winston's good health. They give an insight into Randolph's movements during Jennie's absence: he spent some time at Broxmouth Park, the home of sister Annie and her husband, the Marquess of Bowmont, eldest son of the Duke of Roxburghe; he is eating three meals a day in St James's Square, the home of the Duke and Duchess, to whom he turned when on his own. On the other hand, there is all manner of superficial gossip, indicating how oblivious they seem to have been to the seriousness of the situation. A friend has gone abroad wine-tasting; Randolph has bought four plates, 'very nice for a mutton chop'; Jennie is going to the opera; Jennie is in Paris and has bought some gloves and silk hairnets 'which I think look very pretty sur mes cheveux noirs', and so on.

Despite the lack of seriousness which Randolph and Jennie were affording the matter, its importance was being addressed in more significant quarters. Because of the serious threat to the monarchy, matters had reached the Queen and the Lord Chancellor, both of whom were fully aware of the danger should the matter develop and threaten the position of the Prince. Another letter of apology to the Prince had been drawn up for Randolph to endorse, a letter contrite enough to ensure her son's acceptance and allow 'the matter' to blow over. There it could have ended, except Randolph could not resist having his own way, and added a sentence of his own to the words the Queen had devised. It referred to his existing apology and stated very formally that 'as a gentleman he was bound to accept the words of the Lord Chancellor for that apology'.

On 13 September the Duke wrote to Francis Knollys, the Prince's Private Secretary, informing him of his son's acceptance of the terms of the apology and making it clear that he believed his son to have behaved correctly but, since the Queen and the Lord Chancellor were now involved, Randolph had no alternative but to sign the apology. There is no doubt about the Duke's opinion of the whole escapade.

Without knowing the whole content of this letter, it is impossible to understand the position fully. The Prince of Wales was unable to appreciate the subtlety of the apologies, and was not used to making reconciliations. He gloried in the position he held and, though he had no political power, exploited his social position. He made it clear he would not visit any house which entertained the Spencer-Churchills, and this was dramatically effective as people feared to cross him. This is what Blandford and Randolph had brought upon their parents; the family became virtual social outcasts. Disraeli, commenting on the Prince, called him 'a thoroughly spoilt child'.

Randolph and Jennie took ten years to recover from this blow. The betrayed Aylesford went to America, where he died of alcoholism at the age of 36. Blandford and Edith fled to Paris, where they lived together for several years and had a child. True to form he then deserted them, leaving them penniless. Later, after the Marchioness had divorced him in 1883, he married Lillian Hammersley, a rich American widow. Frances is said to have given the unfortunate Edith a pension.

Disraeli had been asked to intervene in the situation but had found the storm of petulance on the Prince's side and the intransigence on Randolph and Blandford's allowed no room for effective action. Now, however, at a stroke, the consummate politician found a solution to the problem. He offered the Duke the position of Viceroy of Ireland, the Queen's representative. This would remove Frances and John from the embarrassing social situation in England and give them a position of dignity, away from the Prince's influence. Randolph, too, would be removed: he was to go as the Duke's secretary. It benefited Disraeli as he judged, rightly as it turned out, that John Winston and Frances, with their personal skills, would perform the duties of the role successfully, at what was becoming a critical time in Irish politics. He would assume the Duke had enough wealth to subsidise the costs of the position, as was the custom.

So a new chapter in John Winston's and Frances' lives unfolded. For John Winston, who saw that his absence from England would probably bring one political career to an end, it would bring a higher status and the opportunity to take his talent and reputation to new ground; for Frances, although it removed her from her home and friends, it was to be a period in her life that she looked back on with great satisfaction. What was to follow was without doubt her greatest achievement.

Chapter Eighteen
IRELAND, 1877-80

For over 20 years Frances and her husband had struggled with the two sons whose self-centredness and lack of judgement had instilled a capacity for self-destruction. A sense of responsibility and genuine care and affection had resolved the parents again and again to rescue their sons from themselves: finally, it seemed now, to little avail. Their exile to Ireland is a measure of their commitment. For the down-to-earth and sensible Frances there was no lure in any social prestige the position might carry; far more important was the fact that she had three daughters for whom to find husbands. And for how long was the posting to be? No time limit had been set. Fortunately it was not in Frances' nature to dwell too long upon disaster. That tremendous resilience, born perhaps during her early years, was to stand her in good stead in the years ahead. Before the boat docked at Dublin, she would have carefully reviewed their position and steadfastly begun again to count their blessings.

Their six daughters were happy and healthy: Cornelia had married Ivor Guest, from an established and very wealthy family, who was later to become the 1st Baron Wimborne; Fanny had married Randolph's university friend, Edward Marjoribanks, later the 2nd Baron Tweedmouth; Annie had married James Innes-Ker, Marquess of Bowmont, heir to the Duke of Roxburghe and she would become chatelaine of the magnificent Floors Castle. Moreover, the orphaned Clementina, John's step-sister, whom Frances had taken into her care, was now the Marchioness of Camden. Any Victorian mother would be satisfied with such progress in the marriage market. From what little is recorded of them, Frances' daughters seem to have presented a phalanx of unity and support. Like their mother and grandmother before them, their virtues were intelligence and humour rather than beauty, each one contentedly playing her part in this large Victorian family. They conjure an image of those sweeping choruses in Gilbert and Sullivan's operettas, crinolines dancing rhythmically to the lively music. Three daughters, Rosamund, Georgiana and Sarah, remained unmarried and travelled to Dublin with their parents. The two surviving sons were undeniably the biggest problem. Blandford had long ago gone his own way, without regard for the consequences for himself or other people; Frances could only pray that he would learn something from this last experience. She believed Randolph was different: he had the capacity for regret and recovery which, coupled with his abilities, could be the means of his personal salvation.

The respect that the office of Viceroy of Ireland commanded cannot be over-estimated. As the Queen's representative the Duke was welcomed to Dublin in royal style. He was met with a guard of honour and a 21-gun salute. The streets, decorated with flags and banners, were packed with spectators and lined with troops; His Grace, dressed as Viceroy and wearing the ribbon of the Order of the Garter, was mounted on a fine white charger. At Dublin Castle, the official residence, he was received officially by the Irish dignitaries; the ceremonial was dignified and impressive. He was presented with the keys to the city by the Lord Mayor and formally returned them, as was the custom.

This was the normal panoply but neither John Winston nor Frances was the kind of person to welcome or enjoy such ostentation. It was a part of the position they had accepted and both of them had the background, character, social experience and poise to perform the role which the actions of Blandford and Randolph had forced upon them. Disraeli had chosen well in appointing the new Viceroy. Ireland was entering a tense period in its history with the emergence of the Home Rule lobby under Charles Stewart Parnell. The Queen's representative needed to be more than a figurehead. Nor would he be effective alone: so much of the contact with people would depend on the social arrangements of the official 'season' and on the informal day-to-day contacts with ordinary people. In these the Vicereine was vital, and in this role Frances was supremely successful. She received both admiration and respect for the way she handled her official duties. Deep appreciation of her work was soon being expressed. At his official banquet in 1878 the Lord Mayor of Dublin summed up her special qualities: her innate thoughtfulness, kindness and compassion. Her concern for the vulnerable, the commitment and integrity which had characterised her all her life, were felt and appreciated now that she had a public role:

> Her Grace the Duchess of Marlborough, by her kindly interest and generous munificence in every district of the country, sustained our charitable and benevolent institutions … the magnificent hospitality over which the Duchess so naturally presides in the Castle and Vice-Regal Lodge.[1]

The Times newspaper linked Frances to her husband in similar vein. Although they had come to Ireland as comparative strangers:

> They have won the confidence and esteem of all parties by their impartiality, consideration and kindness … in the promotion of useful works and in acts of generous benevolence.

The newspaper appreciated that Frances had dispensed hospitality at Dublin Castle with a generosity and style which recalled the Castle at its best. To use a modern expression, this was 'part of the job description', what she was expected to do.

A genuine difficulty in her position as Vicereine was the danger of the limited social circle surrounding Dublin Castle and her husband's position. Many a woman of her class would have been content to relax and enjoy the privileges of the position; others might have wished to reach out beyond its limits but lacked the personality and skill to do so. From the example of her parents, and from her experience with the household workers and their families at Blenheim, on the estate and in the surrounding communities, Frances had a well-developed instinct and natural talent for crossing the class boundaries.

Where she really endeared herself to the hearts of people was in the way she spent her unofficial time: she sought out the needy, the defenceless, the deprived. She gave much of her time to visiting and supporting schools, particularly charity schools and those for the poor and for girls. Frances had been mother to a family of 11; relating to children was natural to her. It seems hardly surprising, therefore, that by all accounts her visits to schools were made with genuine warmth and interest. She appears to have prompted happy responses from the pupils and given the staff who worked in these schools, often in difficult conditions, a sense of being valued and appreciated. Her visits were not stilted, formal affairs. She asked the children about their work, admired and praised it; they sang for her, gave her flowers, acted plays.

One of her first visits was to a school for poor girls who were either blind or deaf and dumb and it was typical of many that were to follow. An account of it in the press at the time describes how some of the girls performed a representation of scenes from the life of Joan of Arc in action and sign language while one of the teachers spoke the text. Frances was moved by what she saw:

> Most sad as was the picture, one could not but be delighted with the marvellous expressiveness of every gesture, the perfect grace with which the representation was enacted.

The young faces then looked at her expectantly, but how was she to respond? They could not hear. Without hesitation, Frances asked for a blackboard and wrote a few words indicating the deep pleasure they had given her. The school was run by Dominican nuns and the Duchess was meticulous in dealing with both Catholic and Protestant sides of the community impartially. The whole community responded to her awareness of such matters.

Her second commitment was to hospitals and orphanages caring for those with the greatest needs: the insane, blind, deaf and dumb, incurables, the dying, crippled, the poor and the children. A visit to St Vincent's orphanage for poor girls in Dublin was characteristic of her. The children laid out a large exhibition of their work in artificial flower-making. Frances was impressed and delighted with this and pleased the children by purchasing a large number of their specimens, an example followed by the other ladies in the party. The Medical Officer attending a visit by the Duchess to St Clare's orphanage, also in Dublin, expressed his admiration for 'Her Grace's large-hearted benevolence in patronising the many works of charity in our city'.

The Duchess's priorities were clear. On 18 February 1878, when the Duke elected to visit the establishment of a Mr J.W. Edmundson, 'with regard to his inventions in electric lights', Frances visited High Park Reformatory in Drumcondra. Her concern for the needy and the impartial division of her time between institutions run by both Catholic and Protestant communities won her wide acclaim. Public awareness of her work was aptly summed up:

There is scarcely an institution of public utility, scarcely a charity deserving patronage that she has not visited or encouraged. Religious differences, heretofore so adverse to Irish prosperity, are no longer thought of. The poor and suffering, be they Catholic, Protestant or Dissenter, be their creed what it may, are objects alike of her Grace's solicitude. In distant Mayo or lonely Donegal, the little village school or the little local hospital feels the beneficial influence of the Duchess's genial encouragement.

Respect and affection arose from the Irish people's awareness that these commitments were those Frances chose to make in her own time, prompted by a genuine concern for hardship and a wish to help and improve where she could.

Frances also recognised that the Irish manufacturing industry had been in recession for some time, and her response was a practical one. She took every opportunity to promote Irish materials, particularly Irish poplin and silk, to the extent that the chairman and secretary of the Dublin Weavers' Association thanked her publicly:

We appreciate the voluntary action of Your Grace in bestowing your kind attention and favour upon our poplins as a sincere desire to promote the welfare and domestic happiness of the artisans of this country.

A cartoon drawing of the time shows symbolically how her support for the poplin industry was noted and appreciated. A very maternal, caring image of Frances, wearing a dress labelled 'Irish Poplin', comforts a poplin weaver kneeling in despair in front of his empty loom. To the side are figures of women labelled to represent poplin weaving in other countries, such as France and Germany, in retreat in the face of Frances's concern. The caption reads:

Her Grace of Marlborough: 'Do not give up, my friend. I will induce, or shame, every Irish lady into having at least one dress of your beautiful national fabric. Believe me, your countrywomen are not heartless but only thoughtless.'

Frances' innate thoughtfulness was part of her strength in Ireland as it was in her life as a whole. Her sincerity, another strong instinct, was to make a difference to ordinary people.

Part of Frances' charm and success with the people was her lack of pretence and her honest modesty. In a letter of reply she pointed out that the thanks were not due to her but to the ladies of Ireland. She was referring to one of her early initiatives: within weeks of her arrival in Dublin she had requested that all ladies attending Court functions should wear dresses made from or incorporating Irish materials. If there is one thing that can endear a person to the Irish, it is sharing with them their deep love of horses and racing. It was one of Frances' pleasures, particularly at the popular Punchestown. She also had an instinct for a gesture which could strike a chord. With a stroke of genius, when she attended the Punchestown races soon after receiving the thanks of the Dublin weavers, she wore a dress 'of sky terry Irish poplin … richly trimmed with Irish guipure lace'.

Her wedding present to Queen Victoria's daughter, the Duchess of Connaught, was a 'parasol of exquisite Irish point lace'; it had been worked by children of a school at Youghal. The ladies of the Court had responded cheerfully to her request that they wore Irish poplin, silk, lace and ornamental work at all Court functions. The response was typical of the warm atmosphere Frances created at the social functions of the Court. The *Freeman's Journal* acknowledged that 'the gaiety of which the Vice-Regal Court is the centre radiates through various circles of Dublin society'. Frances was having as much influence on the Irish national scene as she had hitherto been able to exercise only in her family and neighbourhood.

A large family to care for, the household affairs of Blenheim Palace to supervise, and the support needed in her husband's political career meant Frances was no stranger to hard work. Nevertheless, now in her later fifties, she must have found the pressure of events during the official Court Season at Dublin Castle a tax on her stamina. Their kindness and consideration for others meant she and John Winston actually made things more difficult for themselves. The Season had normally been over at the end of February. In 1878, however, she and her husband moved it forward three weeks, so that members of Irish society who had responsibilities in the London Season, or who simply wished to participate, could now take part in the Irish Season beforehand. This significantly increased the numbers in Dublin with which she and the Duke had to contend.

Another of Frances' kindnesses, warmly welcomed, was to ensure the dates of official events were published well in advance so that people could plan other engagements around them.

The Season consisted of 15 formal events spread over 35 days, based around the most important events of two Levees and two Drawing-rooms. In 1878 the details of the Court Season were:

8 January	Tuesday	1st Levee
9	Wednesday	1st Drawing-room
10	Thursday	Dinner and Dance
11	Friday	Dinner and Dance
16	Wednesday	Official dinner
23	Wednesday	State Ball (Irish Manufacture to be worn)
26	Saturday	Command Night at Theatre Royal
29	Tuesday	2nd Levee
30	Wednesday	2nd Drawing-room
31	Thursday	Dinner and Dance
1 February	Friday	Official Dinner
6	Wednesday	Dinner and Dance
20	Wednesday	Dinner and Dance
26	Tuesday	Dinner and Dance
28	Thursday	State Ball

These were occasions when everyone in Irish society of rank, importance or achievement (and those who aspired to be part), were recognised by the Court. They were highly formal gatherings subject to rigid protocol on matters such as invitation, dress, precedence, conduct and demeanour, seating, location and so on. Frances and John Winston, as members of the aristocracy, would have endorsed the need for such functions as part of the social structure surrounding the monarchy. The events themselves would certainly have tired them, permanently on show on these long-drawn-out social occasions. *The World* magazine, in March 1878, describes a 'Drawing-room' in the Throne Room of Dublin Castle where the Duke, as the Viceroy, stood at the centre, the Duchess at his side and the Household in a rather forbidding semi-circle around them. It described the 'rites' of Presentation, implying with that word that this was something already rather old-fashioned:

The fair debutante comes to the door, her train is let down and she advances alone to His Grace, while her card is passed rapidly up a file of aides ... Then, as she bends before the Viceroy, he takes her ungloved hand, draws her towards him and gracefully kisses her on the right cheek. She then, after another curtsy to both their Graces, retires backwards, joins her chaperon who has preceded her and sweeps on to St. Patrick's Hall.

In the two Drawing-rooms of that season there were some 140 girls to be presented, each with a sponsor. Frances had to stand throughout with nothing to do but smile at each girl as she passed. Afterwards she would have to circulate among some several hundred guests gathered outside the Throne Room. Drawing-rooms began at nine o'clock in the evening, so tiredness compounded the tedium. Her appearance would be scrutinised by every other lady, huge importance being attached to dress. Newspaper reports on the two Drawing-rooms of that season devoted no fewer than 14 columns to describing in detail the dresses of the highest-ranking ladies.

Frances' ideal was always to be useful: here she was merely decorative, although she was wise enough not to fall short of what was expected and dutifully played her part. Just how she was expected to present herself is worth describing in full, because the extravagance is at odds with her natural inclination. At the first Drawing-room she wore:

a cream-coloured train of Irish poplin (expressly manufactured for Her Grace), magnificently brocaded in cream floss with sprays of stephanotis and lily of the valley, bouquets of roses raised in crimson silk and gold lined with cream satin, trimmed with cordons of gold cord and edged with double plaiting of cream satin and gold bullion fringe; corsage, fronce berthe of crimson satin and face of Irish point lace, petticoat of the richest satin cuit, trimmed biases and revere of satin; fronce tablier trimmed with two volants of Irish point lace (made by special order of Her Grace at the Convent schools at Youghal); agraffed with crimson-shaded roses and foliage. Headdress – tuft of shaded coral roses and foliage; Court plume and Youghal lace lappets; tiara of diamonds.

The other ladies were described in similar detail, providing welcome publicity to national fabrics and products and thus benefiting a whole range of people who had an interest in Irish crafts and artisanship.

None of this would have given pleasure to Frances, apart from the Irish poplin and Irish point lace 'made in a school in Youghal', which reflected her true interests. Nevertheless, the dress she wore for the second Drawing-room three weeks later was entirely different and equally magnificent. The multitude of guests among whom she would have to circulate, never allowing her poise to slip, would be taxing in itself. Each Drawing-room had over 700 guests; formal Dinners and Dances were usually for 300 at a time; the State Ball was for 600, and the St Patrick's Ball, with which the season culminated, was for over a thousand. Frances had some responsibility in making up the guest lists.

There were other commitments during the same period: the Royal Hospital Ball; an official visit to the Bishop at Tuam; an official welcome to the Crown Prince of Austria; attendance at Divine Service each Sunday and, of course, Frances' visits to schools and hospitals. During the official Season the Viceroy and his family had to move into Dublin Castle, so Frances lost the use of her own pleasant and more comfortable and convenient Vice-Regal Lodge. Now the official home of the President of Ireland, this is a pleasant and dignified house idyllically set in the 1,800 acre Phoenix Park. After a lifetime spent in gracious houses, Frances would have had no difficulty in meeting the style, either here or at the Castle.

Unsurprisingly, one of the main supports Frances received during the Irish years was from her family. Her daughters had been central to her hospitality at Blenheim, and now they were regular visitors at Vice-Regal Lodge. Cornelia and her husband Ivor, Baron Wimborne, took a house in Ireland and were regularly with Frances, as were Rosamund, married in 1877 to William Fellowes, 2nd Baron de Ramsey, Fanny and Annie and their husbands. Georgiana, her unmarried daughter, lived with her, as did Sarah, the youngest daughter and not yet a teenager. The wider family too – her sister-in-law, the Dowager Marchioness of Londonderry, her dead sister's husband, usefully a Catholic peer, the Earl of Portarlington, and her brother-in-law and his wife, Lord and Lady Alfred Churchill – gave their support. The loyalty she had been at pains to forge all her life stood her in good stead now. Support in state duties also came from Bertha, the Marchioness of Blandford, although there was never any appearance from the Marquess himself, who had caused the exile to Ireland in the first place.

For Jennie and Randolph the move from London to Dublin meant simply replacing the enjoyment of English with Irish fashionable social life. Predictably Jennie became a centre of attraction. A well-known appreciation of her at the time brings out what she was best at: the display of vitality and an almost animal-like physical attraction in a social situation. At a Vice-Regal reception Lord d'Abernon observed her 'dark, lithe figure … radiant, translucent, intense'. It is ironic that Jennie excelled at this rather superficial, glittering level of society whereas Frances, who had qualities greater and deeper by far, found it only a duty and a responsibility.

Despite the crisis he had caused, and the consequences for John Winston and Frances, Randolph seemed unrepentant and unchanged. Yet there was some room for optimism. He and Jennie were spending time enjoying the pleasures of Ireland, particularly on the hunting field, and this, and his role accompanying his father as secretary to all parts of the country, gave Randolph an awareness of the appalling conditions under which the rural population was struggling. Also, a vital new force was emerging in the Home Rule movement, which had been moribund for years, and Randolph's sympathy for this new intellectual movement was alarming his father.

Within months of the arrival in Ireland Randolph was denouncing his party, who were in government, for the inadequacy of their policy in Ireland and drawing attention to years of inadequate British government of the country. Once again, in his self-willed way, he caused anxiety and distress to his mother and father. His trouble-making became so severe that the Chief Secretary of Ireland asked the Duke for an explanation of his son's behaviour. John Winston dissociated himself completely from Randolph's actions and actually suggested he be given an official rebuke. But Randolph showed no sign of remorse. By early 1878 he was openly attacking Conservative policy on major issues, on one occasion speaking in support of the Opposition and causing an important Bill on local government to fail. The move to Ireland had not yet alleviated his parents' anxieties.

John Winston was a popular and successful Viceroy of Ireland, partly thanks to his background but mainly because of the person he was. His conduct as the Queen's representative, and the public reaction he provoked, reveals how hopelessly wide of the mark was the dismissal of him in modern times. As a landowner and countryman and former President of the Royal Agricultural Society, he had a clear understanding of and familiarity with agriculture, the basis of the Irish economy. His first important public appearance, within three weeks of his arrival, was at the Lord Mayor's banquet: his background and Parliamentary experience enabled him to speak at length and with clarity and conviction on the Irish agricultural economy, which gained him immediate respect. He raised and discussed the threat to the Irish cattle exporting industry of the arrival of cheap American beef. He skilfully outlined and urged a move from live cattle to carcass meat for export.

The integrity and honesty which had been his distinguishing qualities all his life now equipped him well. He often had the task of proposing and defending government policy, whether he believed in it or not. At the Lord Mayor's banquet at the beginning of his second year, his speech brought him praise from the opposition press. He had claimed 'Prosperity to Ireland' in times clearly not prosperous. The *Freeman's Journal* praised 'the frankness, bona fides and moderation of a man who ... not only means well, but does well and tries to face the truth even when it is unpalatable ... If the facts were too strong for him ... the Duke was not more skilful but more candid.'

The reporter particularly welcomed the part of the Duke's speech in which 'he acknowledges the kindly feeling won for him and the Duchess ... by their honest anxiety to know and be of service to the country'. The writer described Frances' and her husband's aim as being 'to know and be of service'.

John Winston was unflagging in his commitment to official duties. He too had the strain and pressure of the official Seasons; additionally, he was meticulous in giving time and support to all those institutions which would look to the Queen's representative to endorse their activities. His official diaries show an unfailing round of attendance at organisations such as the Royal Irish Academy, the National Gallery of Ireland, the National Festival, the Royal Hibernian Academy, the Royal Institute of Architects of Ireland, the Irish School of Art, the Irish Drawing Society and many others.

Not all of these would have aroused his interest but he devoted endless evenings to them as a responsibility and a duty. He was unfailingly courteous and showed, too, an unexpected sense of humour. Speaking at Trinity College Historical Society, he was described as 'animated and humorous ... warmly received by the students'. One newspaper commented on his manner as rather quiet but 'quick at a rejoinder ... prompt at repartee'. These were valuable qualities, a sense of humour being dear to the Irish heart, as was his way of spending his leisure. He was a skilful and enthusiastic fisherman, loving particularly the Blackwater, the most famous of Irish fishing rivers. He shared Frances' enjoyment of racing, particularly at Punchestown.

He was perceptive and intelligent in ensuring his and Frances' presence across the whole community and throughout the whole of Ireland. They toured the country from Belfast to Cork, Stranraer to Killarney, Mallow to Mayo, Sligo to Limerick, Drogheda to Westport; Youghal, Clare, Tuam, Meath – all were visited. What was especially noted and appreciated was that they did their best to understand every aspect of Irish social and political life, inspecting the charities and institutions of the island, 'not perfunctorily but with interest and sympathy'. The Duke and Duchess established themselves unequivocally in the hearts of the Irish people, which was most fortunate as both of them, and Frances in particular, were about to be confronted with the possibility of a national disaster.

Chapter Nineteen

THE FAMINE FUND

T hirty-three years earlier Ireland had been in the grip of a terrifying famine which inflicted the most horrifying consequences on an already impoverished country. The fertile land contained a population trapped in poverty, for whom potatoes were the staple of their diet, and without which they starved. When the potato crops were ravaged in the 1840s by a fatal fungal disease, 'phytophthora infestens', a sentence of death was passed on those struggling in the wretched economy of the west and south west, and there was a great deal of suffering elsewhere. Cholera, typhus and dysentery were followed by starvation in the bitterly cold winter of 1846-7. Many parts of Ireland became a landscape of dying villages, hovels inhabited by poor wretches huddled in filthy straw who were too weak to bury their dead and, worse still, forced to watch the corpses of their loved ones devoured by dogs and rats.

Attempts by the British government to relieve this appalling tragedy were inadequate and incompetent. In the name of humanity, the greatest of help was required, but the aid was not forthcoming. The government in England seemed unable, either by inclination or by design, to take any effective action. Its attitudes were formed by a different agenda, its vision blurred by distance and unfamiliarity. It virtually stood by and did little that was effective; the view seemed to be that if the people were helped too much they would not help themselves. The Gregory Clause in the Poor Law ruled that no man could receive relief if he owned quarter of an acre of land or more. The government simply failed to grasp the magnitude of the problem and continued to allow huge exports of corn: throughout the famine Ireland was actually a net exporter of food! So, because of this, the Irish citizens themselves starved, often to death.

The results were far-reaching. The shocking statistics indicate a loss of population, from death or emigration, ranging from a cautious 2,500,000 to a possible 4,500,000, in a country comprising, according to the census of 1841, just over 8,000,000 people. The neglect by Britain is emphasised by the marked contrast in international awareness, reflected even today in the many commemorative monuments throughout the world. Toronto, where the population more than doubled as a result of Irish emigration, has a particularly moving one. An emotionally charged sculpture of five separate figures portrays the distress, the desperate emigration and the escape of the fortunate few: 'Apprehensive Man', 'Orphan Boy', 'Woman on Ground', 'Pregnant Woman' and, finally, 'Jubilant Man'.

Not surprisingly, therefore, when in 1879 the potato crop failed again and the spectre of famine reasserted itself in the regions which had previously suffered the most extreme deprivation, the Irish people trembled. Was there to be the same inadequacy of government help, and the same starvation and death? The stories of hardship had not even had time to pass into legend and were still fresh in the minds of the Irish poor.

This time, though, a major and vital difference was the Vicereine, Frances. She saw the danger instantly and, in contrast to the inefficiency with which the earlier situation had been met, she took immediate and effective action. This potential catastrophe provided the very occasion that allowed Frances to reveal her worth on an international level. Trapped within the Victorian limitations imposed on womanhood, especially within the aristocracy, it had only been at a family and local level that she had been able to demonstrate her compassion and humanity, her care for the vulnerable and her instinctive warmth. Now, with the weight of her constitutional power and influence behind her, these qualities were revealed on a large scale. On the wider stage her good judgement and insight, together with her energy and administrative and organisational skills, were displayed impressively and dramatically, revealing a hitherto unsuspected character.

It was an outstanding example of that best Victorian precept, that wealth was a responsibility, not a privilege. She had grown up with the precedent of her father, with his sense of honour and social responsibility, and of her mother, practised in the traditions of charity which she herself had inherited. Through her genuineness and warmth as Vicereine, Frances had already attracted the respect and affection of ordinary people, regardless of religion or politics. She now proved splendidly equipped to meet the famine hardship. Independently of the official government relief scheme, she set about remedying the dreadful situation and launched a famine relief campaign. She concentrated on two things: firstly, the collection of funds to finance what turned out to be a substantial operation; secondly the simple but effective distribution of the aid to where it was most desperately needed.

Frances was not normally a person to seek publicity, yet she had the acumen and insight to realise how important publicity was. So, on 16 December 1879, in a powerful letter to the editor of *The Times*, who was a close friend, she precisely and forcefully set out her aims, making clear how the tragic spectre of famine again threatened the west of Ireland. She stated her intention of establishing a famine fund and asked for support. She proposed to open an account in the Bank of Ireland in the name of her fund, which would receive the donations. Although not practised in the art of public communication, she proved articulate and lucid, beginning her letter with three clear points:

> In doing this I must explain: firstly the reasons that impel me to this step; secondly the channels through which I would propose the money should be spent; and thirdly the uses to which it should be applied.

She outlined her reasons succinctly, arguing that in spite of government initiatives and the attempts by landlords to stand by their people, there were parts of western Ireland which were sinking into crisis. Although the present distress was not yet comparable to that of the 1840s, there was, nevertheless, 'no doubt that in parts of Kerry, Galway, Sligo, Mayo, Roscommon, Donegal and the south of the county of Cork – in fact in most of the western districts of Ireland – there will be extreme misery and suffering among the poor, owing to want of employment, loss of turf, loss of cattle, and failure of potatoes unless a vigorous effort of private charity is got up to supplement the ordinary system of Poor Law Relief'.

She proposed organising a committee of 'influential and philanthropic persons to meet in Dublin once a week, or more if necessary, to receive applications from the distressed localities and to decide on the various claims for assistance. It will not be difficult to form local committees and agencies to work in conjunction with the Dublin committee and superintend the distribution of the money.'

In this she showed shrewd judgement and no little bravery. Although birth and class gave her a Tory background, where tradition and status quo were inherent, she bypassed the established Poor Law committees which had been so ineffective in the previous crisis and set up her own, thus ensuring that decisions were made by informed local people who were able to identify need accurately.

She indicated, in practical vein, that

as regards the expenditure of the fund it should be spent on food, fuel, clothing, especially for the aged and weak, and in small sums to keep the families of the able-bodied in temporary distress out of the workhouse.

She anticipated further questions by adding:

I should like to spend some of the money, while carefully guarding against proselytism of any kind, to give grants to schools to provide a meal of bread and potatoes, and, if possible, a little clothing where found necessary, for the little children attending them.[1]

Two further measures confirm the extent of the thought she had put into this project. The bank account was named 'The Duchess of Marlborough's Relief Fund', lending it strength and status and implying integrity, as well as safeguarding it from abuse and exploitation. Most importantly, she arranged with great common sense for new, high quality, Scottish potato seed to be provided so there would be seed for the next season; often in famine, those suffering had been forced to eat seed normally kept for the next season, thereby extending the consequences of the present disaster. This initiative gained her much praise later. A press report commented:

The Duchess of Marlborough's committee was second to none in the actual work of distributing seeds and potatoes for planting the cotters' denuded plots.

She emphasised the responsibilities and difficulties of the whole task, but stressed her own commitment. She undertook to see that all monies contributed would be judiciously expended and faithfully dispensed and accounted for without regard to creed or politics.

Her letter was very logical: the need for action was justified at the beginning, the extent of suffering was outlined with care and feeling but without sentimentality, and the intended method of fundraising was kept simple but effective.

The Times editor responded to her letter with one of his own, giving his whole-hearted support and urging the public to respond and not be misled by those who, for their own political purposes, might ignore or exaggerate the misery of the poor. Nor should they fail to realise that the Duchess's Fund would go straight to the heart of the problem, without 'what is always most mischievous and is too commonly suspected in Ireland, anything like favouritism to any class, creed or locality'.

Significant here was Frances' own background. She bridged the traditional Catholic-Nationalist/Protestant-Loyalist divide in Ireland. Her father's family was Scottish/Irish Protestant based in Londonderry (Mount Stewart), but her sister Alexandrina had become a Catholic and married the Earl of Portarlington, a leading Catholic member of the Irish nobility. Her awareness of the danger of any charge of proselytism was vital and her success at avoiding any trace of it was fundamental to the success of her campaign.

The response to her appeal was instant and effective. Throughout the following weeks lists of contributors were published, together with the amount given and the explanation of how it was distributed. It is obvious from these that money was flowing into the Fund from all over the world. In the short space of only four months it realised a total of £132,000, equivalent to almost £10,000,000 in today's values. True to her word, the Duchess withheld nothing from the public scrutiny. The Reports of the Relief Fund are still carefully preserved in the archives at Blenheim Palace, along with contemporary accounts and comments.

As one would expect, there was a warm reaction from the districts close to Blenheim, the parish church at Woodstock giving the Sunday collection, £1 3s. 2d., and the parochial school at Bladon collecting £1 13s. 6d. But the whole of the British Isles responded, the Lord Mayor of London's appeal generating more than £10,000. There is no doubt about the spontaneity and the extent of the response.

The skill and power of her campaign produced contributions on a worldwide basis. There was an immediate response from neighbouring France, where the Irish had always been held in high regard. Through the medium of two missionaries, Reverend and Mrs Twing, the Indians of Minnesota (only one step removed from want themselves, living as they did on boiled corn) gave all the money they had. Donations were forwarded from Canada via both Protestant and Catholic clergy. In India, collections were made among British residents but also among the Indians themselves. Hong Kong sent more than £4,000 and Penang £1,600; Cape Town raised £750 and the Falkland Islands £142. There seemed hardly a corner of the British Empire, or the world at large, that the Duchess did not reach with her appeal; the response was warm and generous.

There are some charming touches in the extensive lists of donors. In one report a letter was received from a young boy in Kent:

Madam, I send you a sovereign for those poor, starving people in Ireland. It is my pocket-money, and my brother's, and Violet's, and I hope it will give two or three of them a good tuck-out.
From George Francis Pittar

PS I think it would be best to buy Bath buns, but Vyvyan thinks chocolate.

A press report of 15 April 1880 revealed that just as the Duchess's Relief Fund executive committee was about to hold its meeting at Dublin Castle, two small boys arrived, half-naked, travel-stained and barefoot, to say they had walked over 200 miles to ask the Duchess for the sum of £2, which was the deficit on their father's rent on his land in the parish of Caharagh, near Skibbereen. They were brought straight into Her Grace's presence to tell their simple and pathetic story:

Their father had a bit of land but the times were so bad that he could not pay the rent and he now owed eight pounds. He had managed to raise six with the help of friends and neighbours, but he was desperate for the remaining two pounds.

The two boys asked 'the good Duchess' for this sum. The journey had taken them three weeks, begging their food and lodging on the way and asking directions from town to town.

Moved by the appearance of the two boys and impressed by the way they had faced up to their responsibility, and by the trust they had placed in her,

Frances immediately promised them the £2, commending them for their courage and persistence as well as their sense of family responsibility. One wonders how they had learned of the Famine Fund, considering the poor communications of those times; it demonstrates how quickly and effectively the campaign had penetrated even the most remote parts of Ireland. The boys hardly knew what to say, struck speechless at the success of their undertaking, but they managed the traditional 'God bless your ladyship'. She gave instructions they should be fitted with new tweed suits. When they had had a substantial dinner, their pockets were filled with silver by the ladies of the committee. Next morning they took their first ride on a train, thus covering their journey home in six hours, a contrast to their outward struggle. On that same day an order for £2 was sent from the committee to their father via the local parish priest.

A powerful illustration appeared in the press at the time showing Frances, formidable and determined, seated at the head of her committee in Dublin Castle. The strength of support she generated socially and politically is apparent in the names of the people seated at that table. Despite its size, the expenses of the appeal were minimal, largely because Frances shrewdly galvanized the members of her own family and her friends to work voluntarily. Among the 85 members of the executive and general committees, and the honorary secretaries, all of whom were active workers, are daughter Annie (the Duchess of Roxburghe), adopted daughter Clementina (the Marchioness of Camden), daughter-in-law Bertha (the Marchioness of Blandford), sister-in-law (the Marchioness of Londonderry), eldest daughter (Lady Cornelia Guest), another daughter (Lady Rosamund Fellowes), daughter-in-law Jennie (Lady Randolph Churchill), as well as many distinguished Irish titles and family names. Randolph was one of the honorary secretaries of the fund, a role which was to prove a significant experience for him later.

Unfortunately, however, in the General Election of 1880 Disraeli and the Tories fell from power and, since the Viceroy was appointed by the party in power, the Marlboroughs were recalled from Ireland. Frances finalised her efforts and self-imposed responsibilities with further letters to the press, typically warm and caring, thanking all concerned and publishing her accounts in the professional manner now expected of her. She ensured that a committee was established so the Fund could continue and be conscientiously wound up only when appropriate.

On 21 April 1880, Frances' final letter to the press from Vice-Regal Lodge bade farewell to those whose distress had concerned her over the last four months and expressed her gratitude at the way people of all ages, classes and countries had responded so immediately and so warmly. She made clear the present position of the Famine Fund:

> I have received a sum of about £112,000 so far, and I have thus been enabled, with the assistance of my committee, to supply food, clothes and potato-seed to those districts which were most in want. There remains an unexpended balance of nearly £15,000, which I propose to leave in good hands to be appropriated among the most destitute until the next harvest, which will, I trust with God's providence, bring you plenty and prosperity.[2]

The final total raised came to just over £130,000. Frances promised her prayers for their future plenty and prosperity and asked for their kindly remembrance. She ensured that this, her final letter, was printed in Gaelic as well as English; one of the foundations of her success had been the insistence that her relief was for the whole needy community, irrespective of political or religious affiliation.

And so Frances, at the age of almost 60, finally reached the highest levels of personal achievement and fulfilment. The charitable work she had undertaken, not just within the family, as previously, but on a far larger scale, brought her gratitude and recognition nationally and internationally. As Duchess of Marlborough she had enacted the formal Vice-Regal duties, official and social, with poise and confidence. But to be moved personally by the plight of the vulnerable to such an extent that she would break with convention and demonstrate such an electrifying capacity to act swiftly and decisively, is what made Frances special.

On Wednesday 28 April 1880 Frances and her husband took formal leave of Ireland, surrounded by all the ceremony due to the Queen's representative: eight regiments of troops lined the route to the station; their carriage had a Field Officers' escort; an artillery salute was fired; five different bands played, and there were two guards of honour. Yet, much dearer to Frances' heart, surely, was the thanks given her by the Irish people for alleviating their distress. The *Daily News* commented that in nearly every farewell address special allusion was made to the Duchess and her efforts for the relief of the famine.

The Times described her work:

In all its doings the pity of a kind heart and the method of a strong understanding are perceptible. Together they have created a model of what such a fund should be, than which whoever hereafter desires to relieve Irish scarcities will find none more humane and more honest.

Of the many personal thanks given her, particularly moving were the 20 young girls drawn up on the station platform from St Mary's Blind School, to which the Duchess of Marlborough 'has been a kind and consistent benefactress'.

Queen Victoria sent her friend a letter of personal thanks and commendation which carried considerable warmth and affection:

Windsor Castle
April 19th 1880

Dear Duchess
I, as everyone is, am filled with admiration at the indefatigable zeal and devotion with which you have so successfully laboured to relieve the distress in Ireland.

She added:

I am therefore anxious to mark my sense of your services at this moment when alas! they will so soon be lost to Ireland, and wish to confer on you the Third Class of the Victoria and Albert Order. I will wait till you come over to invest you with it.

Believe me always,
Yours affectionately

Victoria R.I.[3]

The Victoria and Albert was a rare tribute: worn by the Queen herself on state occasions, this is said to be the first instance of its being conferred on anyone outside the Royal Family.

Later Frances gave this letter, so highly prized, to her grandson Charles, by then the 9th Duke, to place in the archives at Blenheim. Her words on that occasion were:

I may seem a useless old woman now, but this letter will show you I was once of some importance and did good in my day.

Perhaps she foresaw the injustice history would impose upon her achievement. Charles, in many ways a sensitive and perceptive man, later presented the precious letter to the Congress Library in Washington.

Chapter Twenty

THE SAD AFTERMATH

On 1 May 1880 Frances and her husband returned to Blenheim. After the pressures, pains and stresses of recent years Frances, now 58, could look forward to the quiet pleasures of Palace life, with no more to trouble her than finding husbands for her two unmarried daughters, Georgiana and Sarah, now aged 20 and 15 respectively. There was to be happiness for her, now, in the emergence of Randolph as a major and popular political figure, although her daughter-in-law Jennie still caused anxiety, and errant son Blandford was not yet finished inflicting social humiliation on his parents. A major new responsibility, her grandson Winston, was also about to emerge, engaging once more her capacity to respond to the needs of the vulnerable. Her work with him was to bring unimaginable results.

Her most pressing concern, however, was to share with her husband his real anxiety about the future of Blenheim itself. Their income was based almost entirely on land revenue, which was steadily declining in the face of the Agricultural Depression. Even before they left for Ireland, the estate had been in financial difficulty; a crisis was looming and John Winston had to find extra revenue if Blenheim were to survive. The problem had been exacerbated by the fact that his steward, who had been entrusted with the running of the estate in his absence, had performed poorly and so high-handedly he had offended the tenants and local community. The consensus at present is to criticise the Duke, or even condemn him, for the steps he took, when in fact he had no alternative. Apart from land, his only resources were the Palace and its contents. He was a wise and steady man, supported by similar qualities in his wife; neither was given to rash or ill-founded decisions.

It was obvious, however, that the only choice was to sell some of Blenheim's treasures. John Winston did not have the option, available to his son and grandson when they met with the same financial problem, of a strategic marriage into American money. The choice of what was to go had to be subtle. He and Frances shared a strong sense of Blenheim's heritage and the great achievements of the 1st Duke, and he needed something of high value which could be disposed of without damaging this heritage. His choice was perfect.

The Marlborough Gems were not part of the principal Blenheim tradition. Collected by the 4th Duke, they had been his particular fascination and his special interest. Their sale would remove nothing integral to Blenheim. Man of principle that he was, John Winston took Counsel's opinion, to establish he had the right to sell, before he put the jewels up for sale in 1875, when they realised 35,000 guineas. Although the value of farmland was in decline, land for building was a different matter. In 1875 he was also able to sell 7,500 acres of land in Buckinghamshire to Ferdinand de Rothschild for £240,000, which became the site for Waddesdon Manor.

Yet, when John Winston and Frances returned from Ireland, the original problem remained. Official government funding of the post of Viceroy actually covered only about half the cost; the rest was traditionally borne by the appointee. The financial pressures on those who served as Viceroy were widely acknowledged. Thus John Winston and Frances' period of nearly three and a half years in Dublin had drained them of between £60–90,000. In addition, Palace records show that, from the mid-1860s, he was paying off the large loans his father had been forced to take out when he inherited a virtually bankrupt Blenheim.

The Duke was forced to sell again, this time the Sunderland Library. His friend Earl Cairns, the Lord Chancellor, enabled him to push through Parliament the Blenheim Settled Estates Act, which freed the Blenheim chattels from entail, and the sale became possible. So, the government disregarding *The Times* suggestion to buy the Library for the nation at a cost of £40,000, a sale on the open market raised £56,581. Eighteen thousand precious books were auctioned during 1881 and 1882. Historian A.L. Rowse commented that the Prince of Wales could have bought it with a fraction of what he spent on his vulgar social life, or the Queen from what she saved for her family.

The splendid collection of books, monument to the scholarly tastes of the 3rd Earl of Sunderland, passed under the hammer. It contained early editions of the classics; a large selection of Bibles and Testaments in various languages from early presses; a large collection of Renaissance authors, including a volume of the Valdarfur Boccaccio; a greater number of early books printed on vellum than any private library in Europe; large collections of English county histories, medieval chronicles and Americana. There was an extraordinary full section of English pamphlets and tracts ranging from the reigns of Elizabeth I to Queen Anne, a large number of books on canon and civil law, and a unique collection of French controversial tracts of the sixteenth and seventeenth centuries.

All that now remains in the Long Library at Blenheim are the original handwritten catalogue of the Library and the auction catalogue of Puttick and Simpson, who sold the Sunderland Library. It is sad to read through this and think of the precious books being scattered throughout the world; the Duke's anxiety at having to do this was possibly one of the factors contributing to his early death. Modern criticism of the Duke for this desperate act amounts almost to vituperation. It is seen as opening the floodgates to his self-willed and self-indulgent heir, who used the breaking of the entail to justify massive sales of the Blenheim picture collection, one of the finest in the land. The criticism is ill-informed and pays no heed to the stark financial reality facing John Winston, nor to the fact that had the Duke lived a normal life span it would have been many years before the 8th Duke inherited. John Winston certainly did not foresee, and would not have tolerated, the lengths to which his son was to go.

Magnificent though the Library was, one of the finest collections in private hands in Europe, it was not integral to Blenheim. It arrived as a consequence of an unpaid mortgage the 1st Duke made to the 3rd Earl Spencer, father of the 3rd Duke. A subsequent minor sale of enamels from the collection realised £8,226. Again, these were a specialist interest, peripheral to the main history of the Palace, having arrived almost by accident as a gift in the 4th Duke's time. John Winston had again targeted a non-essential area of Blenheim.

Frances' return to Blenheim was overshadowed by the powerful anxieties and decisions weighing down her husband. The problem of marriage for her next daughter, Georgiana, was comfortably solved quite soon with a very suitable match to George Curzon, later Earl Howe. They were married in the January of 1883. At Blenheim the Palace continued to receive attention; this time parquet was being laid in their drawing-room.

Within a month, however, Frances had the hardest of all blows to bear: the sudden death of her steadfast and caring husband on 5 July 1883. He had resumed his Parliamentary career and spoken in the Lords only a week earlier, typically on a matter of moral principle, opposing the Deceased Wife's Sister's Bill. Frances was a woman of sensitivity and feeling, allied to which qualities was an inner strength she seemed able to draw on in the face of pain and distress. She needed this now. The depth of her grief on her husband's sudden and untimely death can only be imagined. She had suffered family losses earlier; now, at the time of her husband's death, her brother Harry, the 5th Marquess of Londonderry, and her youngest sister Adelaide both died at a young age. She had recently lost her step-brother Frederick, the 4th Marquess of Londonderry, and her sister Alexandrina, Countess of Portarlington, who had been only 51. She was the only one left of her generation, always a pitiful and unenviable position.

The Duke's body, after lying in state in the Great Hall at Blenheim, where 3,000 of the tenantry, staff and local population filed past his coffin, was laid to rest in the vault beneath the Blenheim Chapel. Two memorials bear witness to the love and regard for this 'serious, honourable and industrious' Christian gentleman: the esteem in which he was held locally is represented by the lovely stained-glass east window above the altar in the parish church at Woodstock, installed by the subscription of his friends and fellow-parishioners. Frances interrupted the simplicity ordained by Sarah, the 1st Duchess for the family place of worship in the Blenheim Chapel, and erected a gracious memorial statue by Sir Joseph Boehm. The statue is poignantly telling in its combination of strength and gentleness. She chose the moving inscription:

> eminent for his public and private virtues ... true son of the Church of England, ever anxious to broaden and deepen her foundations in the hearts of the people ... wisdom, courtesy and liberality,

concluding with her own grief:

> a sorrow only to end with life itself to his mourning, loving and devoted wife ... fond remembrance of forty years of devoted wedlock.

The Duke died of angina pectoris at the age of 61. Without doubt, the years of anxiety over his sons, the struggle of maintaining financial stability at Blenheim and the unceasing round of duties and engagements as Viceroy had all played a part.

Modern history takes at best a dismissive view of John Winston, but the unworthiness of this judgement is made clear by the high regard in which he was held in his own time. A *Figaro* cartoon emphasises succinctly how his contemporaries judged him: underneath a figure of the Duke a caption borrows from Shakespeare's *Twelfth Night*, quoting the sea captain's reply to Viola's challenge, 'Who governs here?' 'A noble Duke in nature as in name.'

To set against her great loss Frances had some recompense: success for Randolph. For the first time, she could relax and enjoy her son's achievements. He now began to fulfil the potential which she and John Winston had long dreamed of but, even more satisfying for her, others were aware of his success. In the early 1880s he enjoyed a meteoric rise in the House of Commons, revealing a new sense of purpose as soon as the new Parliamentary session opened. The Duke and Duchess's deferred and often disappointed hopes began to be realised. He invited Lord Salisbury, one of the most influential men in the Conservative party and a future Prime Minister, to speak in his Woodstock constituency. Salisbury stayed at Blenheim, of course.

The impact Randolph made in a matter of months was remarkable. His recent experience in Ireland had given him a sensitive awareness of the complex issues in that neglected country. His depth of knowledge was far superior to that of his fellow MPs who had had little contact with Ireland. Unbelievably, Gladstone had only visited Ireland once, Disraeli never. In other matters, however, Randolph was ill-prepared: he had a poor grasp of domestic political issues and knew little about foreign affairs. Fortunately, he had the luxury of being in Opposition, which suited his natural inclination to attack, and of being in a party demoralised by its recent landslide defeat; the Liberals sweeping into power in the 1880 election by turning a deficit of 151 votes into a majority of 146.

The House of Commons was ripe for the impact Randolph made. The Conservatives had no one to stand up in debate to Prime Minister Gladstone and the talented team he led. The great orator Disraeli was now in the Lords and the Opposition was led by Sir Stafford Northcote, who lacked the devilry that Randolph was to bring. Experienced, well-informed and always well-prepared, Northcote was held in respect but that was not enough. He lacked the fire to rouse his recently defeated members and left a gap into which Randolph was to step.

It would not have mattered which issue gave Randolph his opportunity but, again, he was lucky. Charles Bradlaugh had refused to swear the Oath of Allegiance, demanding the right to affirm loyalty instead. When the matter was tested in the House of Commons, Gladstone and his Cabinet were absent, needing to seek re-election to Parliament, as those obtaining office were obliged to do. Lord Northcote supported the line the government was taking on this quite minor issue but there was opposition led by, among others, Sir Henry Wolff, MP for Portsmouth, and John Gorst, MP for Chatham, both Conservatives. Randolph joined them, and the wit and style with which they peppered the government and their own leader with objections and arguments made the latter look ridiculous. Members stood and cheered. The drama of Randolph's style was established when he threw a pamphlet Bradlaugh had written on the floor and jumped on it, causing uproar.

Randolph, Wolff and Gorst took over the Opposition front bench below the gangway and were soon joined by Arthur Balfour, forming a pressure group with powerful debating skills; Northcote was no match for them. The story goes that when a member said there were two great political parties, Parnell shouted 'Three!', only for Randolph to stand up and call 'Four!' Thus was born the Fourth Party, which was to be a vital part of Randolph's political life and success.

The four men made a formidable team, their qualities complementing each other. Wolff, with whom Randolph formed a lasting friendship, was steady, supplying the diplomacy that did not come easily to Randolph. Gorst was experienced, with a seriousness and calculation which tempered the impetuosity that bedevilled Randolph all his life. Balfour had the advantage of being Lord Salisbury's nephew and the independence of private wealth. Although seeming indolent, he was actually very able, and his ambition and ruthlessness were useful spurs to Randolph. It was useful for Randolph to have the support of such a team, rather than plough an individual furrow.

The confidence and style with which they imposed themselves on the House was splendidly brought to life by 'Spy's (Leslie Ward's) cartoon of the quartet in *Vanity Fair*. They are shown seated on the Opposition front bench, where Gorst and Balfour sprawl with total confidence; the tall, thin Balfour, who joked that he had to sit on the bench to find room for his long legs, balances himself on the base of his spine and neck and gazes disdainfully at the ceiling. Wolff sits upright, a figure of confidence and determination; Randolph stands beside them in a pose he made his own, partly copied years later by his son Winston: hands on hips, slightly stooped, one foot forward, he stares at his listeners, demanding their attention and challenging them to contradict him. Within two months Disraeli expressed support, referring to 'the light cavalry' and refuting their lack of intelligence.[1]

Disraeli saw Randolph and his group as a healthy force, and handled their disruptiveness very well, ensuring Randolph did not go too far and precipitate himself into the wilderness by abandoning his official party leader. He was well aware of their effectiveness and popularity and, before his death in 1881, commented that when the Conservative party came into power they would have to give Randolph anything he asked for.

The Parliamentary method practised by Randolph and his friends was supremely successful. Having seen how Parnell and his allies had drawn attention to their cause in the previous Parliament by the system of obstruction, they adopted the same technique. In Opposition they did not need to present policies, only oppose them, and Randolph used the delaying tactics of repeated questioning, interruption and over-lengthy speech-making to impede Gladstone's programme of policies, cheered on by his party in the face of a frustrated government.

Randolph was a master at reading the mood of the House. When it was light-hearted he made it laugh; when it was angry he made the flames spread. The group exuded gaiety and youth, even in their non-Parliamentary lives, and when the merry quartet and a few companions found themselves one evening on Westminster Bridge, someone wagered that it was impossible to run across the bridge and back again while Big Ben was striking midnight. Randolph promptly accepted the challenge, set off across the bridge on the first stroke accompanied by cheers, and returned breathless but exultant, his coat-tails fluttering behind him, just as the twelfth stroke was booming out across the river.

In the first three years of the Parliament, he not only established a commanding personal position but also contributed significantly to the development of policy. In particular, he was effective on the question of Home Rule for Ireland, his informed and enlightened opinion limiting the Liberal tendency to move headlong into Home Rule and revitalising the Conservative position, which was not really facing up to the problems in Ireland at all. He was also developing two initiatives which took the Conservative party into the future. The first was the concept of Tory democracy. His mother and her parents had shown a fine awareness all their lives of the need to protect the vulnerable. As a result of what he had seen in Ireland, Randolph too was sensitive to the condition of the working classes who, with the Labour party in Parliament still decades away, had no political representation. He was also aware that a party based on the landed classes was going to become less and less electable as the franchise broadened. His message of Tory democracy was rejected by the leadership well into the twentieth century, but its common sense and justice ultimately prevailed. One notable consequence was the priority his son Winston gave to measures of social justice – pensions, limits on the working day, arbitration, labour exchanges – in his early years in Parliament.

Randolph's second important contribution to the future was triggered by Disraeli, his admirer and supporter, who died in 1881. On the anniversary of his death, Sir Henry Wolff noticed how many Members were wearing primroses, Disraeli's favourite flower, and suggested a Primrose League, an idea immediately adopted and promoted by Randolph. The League was hugely successful, developing as a political-social organisation where Conservatives of all classes met to discuss ideas and assist in elections. It soon had two million members and flourished into the 1990s, finally winding up in 2004; Winston Churchill was Grand Master from 1944 to 1965. It put women into politics with the formation of its Ladies Grand Council, which was given a very cautious welcome in some quarters. Lady Salisbury, however, was an enthusiastic member. When they were discussing election tactics and she was asked, 'But is it not vulgar?' 'Vulgar?' she replied robustly. 'Of course it is. That is why we have got on so well!'

Frances was the first President of the Ladies' Grand Council. Jennie had also worked hard with Randolph, especially with the Fourth Party, frequently hosting the group in her home and travelling widely with her husband. But the now forceful Frances was clear about her own role with regard to her son, retorting brusquely to Cecil Spring-Rice, who enquired about Jennie's influence on Randolph, that the only real influence on his career was herself. Certainly, after the Duke's death she focused on Randolph's career, frequently hosting Fourth Party meetings at Blenheim.

Chapter Twenty-One

RANDOLPH ASCENDANT

These were good years for Frances, the only period she experienced that was free of anxiety about Randolph. With pleasure and pride, she saw him mature and become the political focal point of his time. John Winston's death was hard to bear, but there was consolation in the flood of genuine tributes that poured in, reflecting the high esteem in which her husband had been held nationally. Stafford Northcote and William Gladstone led their parties in the avalanche of letters of condolence she received.

Frances remained at Blenheim after her husband's death because of her commitment to the care of yet another grandson in need, Blandford's son Charles, now 12. Her pleasure increased when Randolph began to form a better relationship with his brother, and when, diminished a little by his father's death, he returned with his family to Blenheim, she derived satisfaction at the comfort he found in its familiar walls and acres. He also visited her more frequently in her London home in Grosvenor Square.

At last, in March 1883, the Prince of Wales came to dinner with Randolph and Jennie. The breach had finally been healed, and after several years in the social wilderness they were again welcome in fashionable society. One of Frances' concerns had always been with her son's impetuosity and rashness; now she would see a more mature Randolph. The Prince let it be known that Randolph Churchill's manner 'was just what it ought to have been'. Forgiveness for Randolph meant renewed contact for the Prince with Jennie, a cause for concern, and he was soon giving her presents of expensive jewellery.

A mixture of hard work, a phenomenal memory (passed on to his son Winston) and the extrovert, confident nature of his personality equipped Randolph to become the principal speaker in the House. As happened later with Winston, the chamber filled to hear him, and even today, over 120 years later, his speeches impress in their vigour, power and their expression. Caspar Weinberger, US Foreign Secretary, described Winston Churchill's oratory as not prose but poetry; there was a poetic quality in Randolph's delivery, too. A major element in his speeches was humour, but his first impressive speech at this time struck a serious note.

He spoke persuasively and constructively on his concept of Tory democracy, pointing out that the Conservative party was still not heeding an important lesson: they would never exercise power without the confidence of the working classes, who were determined to govern themselves and would not be forced or tricked by other class interests. The way forward should be in trust, not opposition, he declared:

> The Conservative party will never exercise power until it has gained the confidence of the working classes; and the working classes are quite determined to govern themselves and will not be either driven or hoodwinked by any class or class interests. Our interests are perfectly safe if we trust them fully, frankly and freely; but if we oppose them and endeavour to drive them and hoodwink them, our interests, our Constitution and all we love and revere will go down. If you want to gain the confidence of the working class, let them have a share and a large share – a real share and not a sham share – in your Party councils and in your Party government.[1]

By the time he spoke in Blackpool three months later he was developing the withering wit, the feigned disbelief and the skill with the telling image ('[he] has studied politics about as much as Barnum's new white elephant') which became such a characteristic of his son. Gladstone had criticised Salisbury, the Conservative party leader who was a marquess, for representing a class 'who toil not, neither do they spin'. Randolph demolished him mercilessly:

> Just look, however, at what Mr Chamberlain himself does. He goes to Newcastle and is entertained at a banquet there, and procures for the president of the feast a live earl, no less a person than the Earl of Durham.

Now Lord Durham is a young gentleman who has just come of age, who is in the possession of immense hereditary estates, who is well known on Newmarket Heath and prominent among the gilded men who throng the corridors of the Gaiety Theatre, but who has studied politics about as much as Barnum's white elephant, and upon whose ingenuous mind even the idea of rendering service to the State has not yet commenced to dawn. If by any means it is legitimate, and I hold that it is illegitimate, to stigmatise any individual as enjoying great riches for which he has neither toiled nor spun, such a case would be the case of the Earl of Durham; and yet it is under the patronage of the Earl of Durham and basking in the smiles of the Earl of Durham, that this stern patriot, this rigid moralist, this unbending censor the Right Honourable Joseph Chamberlain, flaunts his Radical and levelling doctrines before the astounded democrats of Newcastle.[2]

Here is the effective use of repetition ('who ...'), the disbelief ('ingenuous') and the final mounting climax ('this stern ... censor') so familiar to modern ears.

Randolph's greatest delight, in which he showed considerable skill, was baiting Gladstone. His searing attacks were not personal, an attitude very much in harmony with his parents' innate decency and integrity, as he actually had the highest personal regard for Gladstone: 'the most worthy man I ever knew', he once commented. On a memorable occasion he launched an attack on Gladstone, for self-advertisement, which calls to mind the contemporary vocabulary of 'spin', 'pretence' and 'dissimulation'; its message is as relevant to politicians today as the day he uttered it:

Gentlemen, we live in an age of advertisement, the age of Holloway's Pills, of Colman's Mustard, and of Horniman's Pure Tea; and the policy of lavish advertisement has been so successful in commerce that the Liberal party, with its usual enterprise, has adapted it to politics. The Prime Minister is the greatest living master of the art of personal political advertisement. Holloway, Colman and Horniman are nothing compared with him. Every act of his, whether it be for the purposes of health, or of recreation, or of religious devotion, is spread before the eyes of every man, woman and child in the United Kingdom on large and glaring placards. For the purposes of an autumn holiday a large transatlantic steamer is specially engaged, the Poet Laureate adorns the suite and receives a peerage as his reward, and the incidents of the voyage are luncheon with the Emperor of Russia and tea with the Queen of Denmark. For the purposes of recreation he has selected the felling of trees; and we may usefully remark that his amusements, like his politics, are essentially destructive. Every afternoon the whole world is invited to assist at the crashing fall of some beech or elm or oak. The forest laments, in order that Mr Gladstone may perspire.[3]

The influence on Winston is clear: the amused tone which conceals a deadly seriousness, the ability to demolish an opponent by making him seem ludicrous or ridiculous, the biting irony, all became important weapons for Winston. Even the force gained by investing an inanimate object with human qualities is a trick Winston modelled on his father: '… the forest laments so that Mr Gladstone may perspire.'

Winston seems to have echoed his father's physical stance, too. The political cartoons reveal that Randolph had a slightly forward leaning posture, jacket open, hand on hip, not given to expansive gesture. Winston adopted all of these. In early days Randolph was thought not to have an attractive speaking voice, which was sometimes described as guttural. It became a trademark, distinguishing and identifying him in the way that Winston's delivery did too.

Following the example of Disraeli, he seized upon an occasion when Gladstone had recently received a deputation of working men at Hawarden to heap ridicule upon him:

It has always appeared to me somewhat incongruous and inappropriate that the great chief of the Radical party should reside in a castle. But to proceed. One would have thought that the deputation would have been received in the house, in the study, in the drawing-room, or even in the dining-room. Not at all. That would have been out of harmony with the advertisement 'boom'. Another scene had been arranged. The working-men were guided through the ornamental grounds, into the wide-spreading park, strewn with the wreckage and the ruin of the Prime Minister's sport. All around them, we may suppose, lay the rotting trunks of once umbrageous trees; all around them, tossed by the winds, were boughs and bark and withered shoots. They come suddenly on the Prime Minister and Master Herbert, in scanty attire and profuse perspiration, engaged in the destruction of a gigantic oak, just giving its last dying groan. They are permitted to gaze and to worship and adore and, having conducted themselves with exemplary propriety, are each of them presented with a few chips as a memorial of that memorable scene.[4]

The self-confidence which, in excess, had so marred Randolph's early years now became one of his greatest assets, very much part of his ebullient style. Although Jennie was a regular visitor to the Commons Visitors' Gallery, it was some years later before Frances was to hear her son speak in Parliament. Frances certainly heard Randolph speaking on the political platform outside Parliament, possibly encouraged by the Primrose League whose ladies were more overtly active politically.

Randolph's biographer, Robert Rhodes James, remarked on the broadness of Randolph's appeal. Ordinary Tories wanted a leader who would be blunt and, if possible, rude about Gladstone and the Liberals, and in Randolph they found exactly what they wanted. In contrast to his restrained style in Parliament, in the country his style was dramatic and demonstrative, which was enjoyed coming as it did from the small, not particularly attractive, figure. He delighted partisan audiences by hurling abuse at the Liberal leaders until he was exhausted. They would urge him on: 'Give it 'em hot, Randy!'

His speeches still make entertaining reading today. A speech on 'laissez-faire' and the need for tariff reform was a classic masterpiece, showing many of the skills of rhetoric that Winston was to master:

Your iron industry is dead; dead as mutton. Your coal industries, which depend greatly on the iron industries, are languishing. Your silk industry is dead, assassinated by the foreigner. Your woollen industry is 'in articulo mortis', gasping, struggling. Your cotton industry is seriously sick. The ship building industry, which held out longest of all, is come to a standstill. Turn your eyes where you like, survey any branch of British industry you like, you will find signs of mortal disease. The self-satisfied Radical philosophers will tell you it is nothing; they point to the great volume of British trade. Yes, the volume of British trade is still large, but it is a volume which is no longer profitable; it is working and struggling. So do the muscles and nerves of the body of a man who has been hanged twitch and work violently for a short time after the operation. But death is there all the same, life has utterly departed, and suddenly comes the rigor mortis … But what has produced this state of things? Free imports? I am not sure; I should like an inquiry; but I suspect free imports of the murder of our industries much in the same way as if I found a man standing over a corpse and plunging his knife into it I should suspect that man of homicide, and I should recommend a coroner's inquest and a trial by jury.[5]

The rhetorical skills came naturally to both father and son and were convincing; they never obtruded. Both used repetition, Randolph employing the word 'your' six times in the first six lines here. The withering irony in the last few lines is characteristic of both men.

The status and admiration Randolph had acquired, though not in all quarters, made it virtually certain he would be given office in a Conservative government. He could still be troublesome but Salisbury's view was that it would be safer to have him in the party than outside it. Probably in anticipation of the office he would be given, Randolph made a four-month trip to India, taking in Egypt on the way. So, when he addressed the Primrose League at their banquet in April 1885, he spoke on India with some knowledge and authority. He had come a long way from the ignorance of foreign affairs with which he had begun his Commons career ten years earlier. Frances, as President of the Ladies Grand Council, was there to enjoy a truly dignified speech in the tradition of the best of Victorian statesmen, principled, articulate and sensitive:

My lords and gentlemen, our task of governing India, which we have been carrying on now for more than a hundred years, is a task of great difficulty and danger, the difficulties and dangers of which do not diminish as time goes on. Our rule in India is, as it were, a sheet of oil spread over the surface of, and keeping calm and quiet and unruffled by storms, an immense and profound ocean of humanity. Underneath that rule lie hidden all the memories of fallen dynasties, all the traditions of vanquished races, all the pride of insulted creeds; and it is our task, our most difficult business, to give peace, individual security, and general prosperity to the two hundred and fifty millions of people who are affected by those powerful forces; to bind them and to weld them by the influence of our knowledge, our law, and our higher civilisation, in process of time, into one great, united people; and to offer to all the nations of the west the advantages of tranquillity and progress in the east. That is our task for India. That is our raison d'etre in India. That is our title to India.[6]

There are premonitions of Winston here: the considered pace, the repetition of key words and phrases, the short sentences as he approaches his climax and particularly the apt image of 'sheet of oil'. The responsibility to give peace, security and unity to India, and in time to bring back to the West the advantages that India would then enjoy, indicate his imperial attitude.

By April 1885, in spite of its huge majority, Gladstone's government was in a perilous state. There was trouble in Ireland, in the Sudan, and on the Afghan border. Randolph's return from India was looked forward to by the press and the Conservative party's confidence was growing substantially. Randolph had a firm grip on the House of Commons and indeed on the country, as witnessed by the political cartoons that appeared everywhere, showing him with large moustache and bulging eyes. The texts of his speeches, whether in the House of Commons or in public, were familiar throughout the country. Parnell came to Connaught Place, Randolph and Jennie's home, to inquire after Tory attitudes towards Ireland if they came into power, and promised him the Irish vote at the election. On the adverse side, Arthur Balfour had withdrawn from the Fourth Party and was in the habit of keeping his uncle, Lord Salisbury, informed of what was happening. Salisbury, however, was warmer towards Randolph than formerly and the letters between them suggest a more cordial relationship.

In June 1885 the Liberals were defeated on a Budget issue and Queen Victoria asked Salisbury, not Northcote, to form a government. Randolph then began a period of intense bargaining, refusing to serve with Northcote. The self-destructive determination to have his own way, which had dogged his past, now almost lost him his political future. Frances wrote him a long, sensible letter, to no effect. He was saved only by Salisbury, the experienced and skilful politician, who reconciled conflicting interests and ambitions among those involved. Northcote agreed to go to the Lords and on 16 July 1885 Randolph became Secretary of State for India, a worthwhile first post for a rising politician. At last he had achieved something worthwhile; after all the anxiety and effort Frances could at last see her own and John Winston's hopes fulfilled. His later admission that he had acted foolishly gave some indication of maturity.

Randolph was at a crossroads. He was in huge favour with many but he had enemies who saw the situation differently. Chamberlain had inflamed the lobby against him before he actually took office: 'We now know who is master. Goliath has surrendered to David and Lord Randolph Churchill has his foot on Lord Salisbury's neck.' Randolph, and indeed the whole Conservative party, was holding a poisoned chalice. No matter what his gifts or powers of application, the parameters of progress were laid down by the circumstances in which Randolph found himself.

To make matters worse, one last by-election had to be fought on home ground, even though the Woodstock constituency was scheduled for extinction and Randolph was looking to Birmingham for a future seat. Inundated by the workload from his new post in the India Office, he was depending on Jennie and his sister Georgiana (Curzon) to carry the responsibility of the campaign. He was also without the support of his elder brother, now the 8th Duke, who had caused acrimony in the family by selling a major part of the collection from Blenheim: over 200 magnificent paintings. This showed a blatant disregard for a major and important part of the Palace heritage, a sale neither the 7th Duke nor Frances would have contemplated for a moment. It so appalled Frances, whose love and respect for Blenheim was deeply ingrained, that she refused to continue living at the Palace. Jennie and her supporters had to make their headquarters at the local hotel, the *Bear*. Theirs was not an easy task, but a flamboyant and determined campaign led by the flamboyant Jennie carried the day and Randolph was re-elected.

Meanwhile the India Office was settling to its new Minister. Contrary to expectation, Randolph was successful, both in listening to his advisers and in making decisions. The notion of a shallow, if articulate, Randolph had to be discarded in favour of an able administrator with charm and a natural manner. It suited him to have such a powerful position; his better self prevailed and he flourished. He improved his relations with Salisbury and the letters between them show a marked cordiality; they moved into place for the General Election of 1885 with some confidence.

For the first time, Frances had the pleasure and satisfaction of taking part, actively and publicly, in Randolph's political life. Both she and Jennie canvassed for him in his new constituency in Birmingham, Woodstock having been abolished in 1885, in what must have been very contrasting styles. But these intelligent women could not carry the day and Randolph lost, and had to be found another seat, South Paddington.

The Liberals won the 1885 election and Randolph was back in Opposition. The Irish party and Parnell had enough votes to make things awkward for the Liberals and so debate inevitably raged around the Home Rule issue. Despite his sympathy for the Irish people, Randolph totally opposed Home Rule. Like his father he saw improvement coming from better education and better living conditions. This was another opportunity to bait Gladstone, accusing him of 'the ambition of an old man in a hurry'; Randolph delivered the 'most severe verbal lambasting' since the days of Disraeli in order to remind everyone of the failures of Gladstone's policies:

> The negotiator of the Alabama arbitration, the hero of the Transvaal surrender, the perpetrator of the bombardment of Alexandria, the decimator of the struggling Sudan tribes, the betrayer of Khartoum, the person guilty of the death of Gordon, the patentee of the Penjdeh shame, now stands before the country all alone, rejected by a democratic House of Commons … He demands a vote of confidence from the constituencies … confidence in what? In the Liberal Party? No! The Liberal Party, as we know it, exists no longer. In his Irish project? No! It is dead … In himself? Yes! At this moment, so critical, we have not got to deal with a Government, or a party, or a policy. We have to deal with a man; with a man who makes the most unparalleled claim for dictatorial power which can be conceived by free men.[7]

Even without the aid of Randolph's voice and the inflection of his words, we can appreciate the effect of this pointed, stinging speech, the crescendo of accusation relentlessly building to its climax, and the final note of incredulity: 'He demands a vote of confidence!!!'

The Liberal Home Rule Bill failed, producing yet another election. Again Frances and Jennie campaigned for Randolph, their high point being a meeting in the Royal Military School near Hyde Park. As Randolph, Frances and Jennie entered the hall, the audience rose and sang *Rule Britannia*, applauded their candidate with warmth and approval, and concluded the proceedings with the National Anthem. This time the Conservatives won the election, Gladstone resigned and Lord Salisbury was invited to form his second administration. This time he could not ignore Randolph for a Cabinet post.

Chapter Twenty-Two
A Caring Grandmother

Apart from the Irish Famine Fund, there was virtually no public awareness in Frances' lifetime of her personal qualities or of anything else she accomplished. It is only when family letters (particularly Winston's) became readily accessible, over 50 years after her death, that the vital part she played in the formation of her grandson Winston's character begin to emerge.

Neither Randolph nor Jennie was equipped to be adequate parents to Winston. He was preoccupied with his career and she threw herself back into the whirl of London society. They reflected the attitudes to parenting of their social class at that time: parents played little direct part in bringing up their children, which tended to be left first to servants and then to schools. Even so, Randolph and Jennie did not give Winston much of the parental support he still needed. Jennie was young, attractive and extrovert. Her world was dominated by the superficiality of fashionable society. Randolph's life had been a rather impetuous pursuit of whatever he enjoyed, with little self-discipline or self-criticism. He joined Jennie in high society and public life, led by what Frances described as the 'fast set', and threw himself headlong into his political career. Neither he nor Jennie found much time to devote to Winston. Despite this Winston idolised both parents, writing of Jennie that 'she shone for me like the Evening Star', and making a biography of his father his first publication.

His parents passed Winston on to his grandmother at Blenheim, where he spent his formative years. At 52, Frances might have been looking forward to a quieter life. She had worked hard to create a happy family home at Blenheim and her daughters were comfortably embarked on life, but once again her sense of responsibility and duty, her 'warm heart particularly for members of her family', as Jennie was later to describe it, and her sensitivity to the needs of the vulnerable responded to a new demand. On a basic level her help was practical: Blenheim or her London house provided Winston with somewhere safe, and soon familiar, for him to stay when it was inconvenient for his parents to have him. Winston, however, had a far greater need than simply for this 'bed and board', as it might be termed. The huge importance of Frances' contribution lay in providing him with the security he cherished, his desperately longed-for love and affection.

This period of Winston's life consisted of being shuttled between Blenheim and London at the convenience of his parents. It was a great help socially and financially that he and his younger brother Jack, born in Dublin before they left, could stay at Blenheim, supervised by grandmother Frances. After lessons had been attended to, sometimes with his grandmother and sometimes with the governess, Jack and he, cousin Charles and later Guy were free to roam the Park, which was better, Winston assured his parents, than the London parks. Since Charles, the eldest, was lacking in confidence, and Jack and Guy were the youngest, the leadership fell to Winston, who was eager to rise to the challenge. All these juvenile 'military operations' were led by him with enthusiasm, and it was Winston who usually needed the discipline that Frances was known to insist on. With the golden stone of the Palace glowing in the evening sun, the serene beauty of the lake and trees, the occasional splash of a leaping fish, the wind in his face as he rode swiftly across the Park; this must have been the time when he laid the foundations of his great love of Blenheim. The busier Randolph and Jennie were, the more time he had to enjoy his grandparents' home and the happier and more secure he became. He wrote later that he made two fortunate decisions at Blenheim: to be born and to marry. He never regretted either. During the whole of his lifetime the lovely home of his grandparents was his refuge and sanctuary, and at the very end it was in the nearby village of Bladon that he chose to be buried.

Winston's earliest letters from Blenheim to his mother, at Christmas 1881, reveal an almost urgent longing to be loved. The pattern of emotional need was to be repeated and became the norm. After thanking Jennie for his presents, Winston devotes the rest of his first short letter to declaring the strength of his affection: 'I send you my love and a great many kisses, Your loving Winston.' As a goodbye the emphasis is not surprising, but it dominates such a short letter: he needs his parents and he fears they will not come. His next two letters, written within days, begin to fill out the picture of his insecurity and vulnerability. Much of one letter is devoted to his lengthy and almost impassioned declaration of love, kisses and affection; the other introduces a significant new note, being a blunt request for Jennie to come to Blenheim to see him. Virtually every subsequent letter for years contains the same two forceful expressions of emotional intensity: he pours out his love and begs for his parents to come and see him. They rarely responded.

Within months Winston had been left at Blenheim once more and wrote again to his parents. Only in one letter does he conclude in a way that would be normal for a seven-year-old, restricting himself to 'I am your loving son'. The other three, written in close succession, reveal his need to express deeper feelings: 'With best love, Your ever loving son', 'With many kisses, Your loving son', 'With best love and kisses, Your ever loving son'. In another short letter, again from Blenheim, he three times states his pathetic need to see his parents: 'When are you coming? ... Jack and I want you very much ... please do come soon.'

Winston's emotional sensibility is demonstrated by his affection towards brother Jack, younger by six years. In the early letters from Blenheim Winston makes a point of reporting on Jack when he was with him: 'Baby is quite well', 'Baby sends you his love'. If they were separated, there is frequent reference to him: 'I had a nice letter from Jack', 'Give my love to him'. This fondness remained with Winston all Jack's life.

From the boarding preparatory schools, where Winston was sent at the age of seven, his letters were dominated by the same theme: a pouring out of love and desperate requests to be visited, again virtually unheeded by Randolph and Jennie. After his eighth birthday, when they failed to visit him, the need for his parents is so great that he urges his mother not to forget to collect him for Christmas, before concluding with his usual 'Love and kisses'. He and baby brother Jack, aged only two, were subsequently left with their grandmother while Jennie and Randolph pursued interests elsewhere. It was not the custom for Victorian parents to visit their children at school. Frances may have feared to run the risk of Jennie's disapproval by visiting herself, but there are certainly on record visits by Lady Marjoribanks, Winston's aunt, who had a son there.

Winston's distress was reflected in poor behaviour. At St George's, Ascot, where he was desperately unhappy, a rather sadistic regime does not seem to have controlled his behaviour: beatings were frequent and his reports were critical. In one letter in particular his emotional needs got the better of him: in a state of high tension he scrawled 46 crosses for kisses and added desperately, 'I am coming home in a month.'

During all this time Frances supplied the warmth, affection and security he was crying out for. Together with his much loved nanny, Mrs Everest ('Woomany'), she was his major support. Her kindly nature, sense of responsibility and experience as the mother of her own large family made her a remarkable surrogate mother. His letters from Blenheim are peppered with indications of how he is enjoying himself there: 'I am enjoying myself very much', he writes at Christmas 1881, and the following spring: 'I am enjoying myself here; it is so nice being in the country.'

Winston's poor health, hitherto ignored by his parents, finally necessitated his removal from St George's, but his relief was only temporary: in the autumn of 1884 he was enrolled at a school in Brighton run by two unmarried ladies. This establishment, in contrast to St George's, had little or no pretension and Winston tells us later it had an element of kindness and warmth which had been completely lacking in Ascot. It made no claims to be academic, however, as Winston was to find to his cost.

When he was ten he was involved in an exchange with another boy which could have had serious consequences. The headmistress wrote to Jennie, explaining that Winston and the boy had been arguing about a knife which one of the masters had lent them when Winston received a small wound in the chest. The headmistress was considering the expulsion of the other boy but Jennie would not hear of it. She wrote to Randolph, who was in India at the time, 'I have no doubt Winston teased the boy dreadfully – and it ought to be a lesson to him. Of course, as I thought, he began by pulling the other boy's ear.' Randolph agreed. 'What adventures Winston does have,' he answered. 'It is a great mercy he was no worse injured.' Winston was no angel, and Frances knew this. There is a story about Jack, who was a relatively innocent child, being asked by a visitor if he were a good boy. 'Yes,' he replied apologetically, 'but Winston is teaching me to be naughty!'

The Churchills' family doctor, Robson Roose, had his main practice at Brighton and was able to keep an eye on Winston. The boy's health caused considerable concern: ears, tummy, teeth, all gave him misery, aggravated no doubt by the fact he was unhappy. In 1886 he wrote to Mrs Everest after she and Jack had been on a visit, complaining of weakness and a tendency to cry at everything. He was going down with pneumonia, and his life was in danger. The letter was badly written, as usual when he was upset and miserable, and he became the concern of the whole family. Dr Roose did not leave his side for several days, finally reporting the passing of a critical night when Winston struggled through delirium with a temperature of 101. At last Jennie and Randolph arrived. There was concern from friends, including the Prince of Wales, and Moreton Frewen, Jennie's brother-in-law, wrote in reproach, hoping that now that Winston had been given back to them they would find the time to make more of him. He had certainly had a narrow escape.

That was certainly a critical year for Winston. He spent the summer at Blenheim, as usual, chasing butterflies and basking in happiness, but the following November Randolph, caught up in the heavy schedule of the General Election, was actually in Brighton and failed to visit his son. Grandmother Frances and two cousins visited and he was taken to Blenheim for the New Year while Randolph and Jennie went on a seven-week visit to Russia. Mrs Everest was ill with diphtheria at this point, looked after by Dr Roose. Frances, always anxious when she was in charge of the boys, wrote to Randolph in January 1887:

> It has done them good and I keep Winston in good order as I know you like it. He is a clever boy and really not naughty but he wants a firm hand. Jack requires no keeping in order. They stay at 46 till you return.[1]

Later in January she took them all to her London home at 46 Grosvenor Square, and they had a wonderful time, going to see the new Gilbert and Sullivan, *HMS Pinafore*. This was their latest production, the toast of London at the time. Frances understood perfectly what a boy of Winston's age would enjoy and gave him the colour, excitement, fun and spectacle he would love:

> Winston is going back to school today. *Entre nous* I do not feel very sorry for he is certainly a handful. Not that he does anything seriously naughty except to use bad language which is bad for Jack. I am sure Harrow will do wonders for him for I fancy he was too clever and too much the boss at that Brighton school.[2]

One of the main comforts that Frances provided for him at Blenheim was to remain a pleasure throughout his life. She 'gave' him the Park, which he loved. The magnificent 2,100-acre Park was a restorative in his troubled childhood and was to remain so. As an adult he wrote of Blenheim that Vanbrugh and 'Capability' Brown had created there 'an Italian Palace in an English landscape with perfect harmony'. Blenheim was too dangerous a place during the bombing years of the Second World War, and he had to stay at nearby Ditchley Park. Nevertheless, he took every opportunity to walk or drive in the Park at Blenheim in order to refresh his spirits.

From the age of seven he wrote regularly of childish play in the Park, making encampments using an umbrella as a tent. His time there with Frances instilled in him an appreciation and love of the natural world. He found primroses and put them in a basket, gathered wild hyacinths, caught butterflies and dragonflies. He saw a snake but was not allowed to kill it. He told his parents that the Park was 'so much nicer to walk in than Green Park or Hyde Park'. Frances had him taught the countryside skills. He learnt to ride the pony she gave him: 'I rode Rob Roy today around the Park.' He learnt to fish, writing to his parents in excitement when he 'caught his first'. Appreciation of the natural world sustained him for the rest of his life, either studying butterflies as a subaltern in India or designing and enjoying his gardens at Chartwell.

An important moment in his later life he owed particularly to the influence of the Park. It occurred nearly ten years after Frances' death. The young Clementine Hozier was daunted and hesitant about visiting Blenheim in August 1908, but Winston strongly urged her to come. His letters go into detail about the beauty of the Park and gardens. He describes the great lake surrounded by huge trees, sunlit rose gardens and plenty of places to talk … just the place, a lovely spot, in the Temple of Diana, overlooking the Park and the lake, on the way to the Rose Garden, where a young man might hesitantly propose to a girl!

Frances was no indulgent grandmother, however; she also attended to important, practical matters. When he was seven, Winston wrote to his parents, 'I do lessons every morning with Grandmama.' In later years at Blenheim, a governess was in attendance from ten in the morning until seven in the evening.

By the time he was nine Winston's behaviour was so difficult that Jennie was confessing to Randolph she could not control him without Mrs Everest. At Blenheim, however, Frances did her best to instil sound values and discipline. In contrast to Randolph, whose idea of discipline seems to have been to criticise Winston aggressively, Frances was eminently practical. On one occasion, she wrote to Randolph that Winston needed discipline and made it clear that she kept Winston in order and dealt with him with a firm hand. Even when she was caring for him in London, her firmness continued: 'I fear Winston thinks me very strict.'

Frances clearly understood her grandson, writing to his father more than once that he was a clever boy who just needed handling. By contrast, Randolph regularly disparaged him, seeing no ability at all. Winston himself recounted that the only assessment Randolph ever made of his ability happened when he was 14. He had drawn up his large collection of model soldiers on parade for formal inspection. After studying what he had done, Randolph asked him if he would like to go into the army. Winston agreed, thinking his father had detected military genius in him, and only later did he realise that his father had concluded he was not clever enough to go to the Bar. At the same time Frances was writing that Harrow would bring out the best in him: 'He was too clever for that Brighton school.'

Frances' natural warmth and affection predisposed her to the maternal role and the fact she was strict, probably because her own mother had been, enabled her to manage Winston when his own mother had to admit she could not. Jennie wrote later that Frances was a very remarkable and intelligent woman, with a warm heart, particularly for members of her family, but added that she ruled Blenheim and all those in it with a firm hand: 'at the rustle of her silk dress the household trembled.' Jennie's intention here was not to be critical of her mother-in-law. And in later life, when Randolph's illness was of great concern, the close relationship between the two women to whom Winston owed so much of his personality was not in doubt. His physical health and stamina he owed to Jennie, but his mental energy, determination and fortitude were inherited from his grandmother Frances.

In 1888 Winston arrived at Harrow, ready for a new beginning. According to most he was fortunate to make it, as his Brighton school was not renowned for academic success. His own well-documented account of the experience with his Latin paper describes how, after two hours, his name, the number of the question and a large blot were his sole contribution to the answer paper. Also, getting into Harrow was only the beginning of the problem, because he would not survive there with neither the academic grounding nor the self-discipline he should have acquired by this time. His housemaster's first report outlined the situation clearly:

Winston, I am sorry to say, has if anything got worse as the term passed. Constantly late for school, losing his books ... he is so regular in his irregularity that I really don't know what to do; and sometimes think he cannot help it. But if he is unable to conquer this slovenliness he will never make a success of a public school ... As far as ability goes he ought to be at the top of his form, whereas he is at the bottom.[3]

So much for the rumour that Winston was a dunce at school. His housemaster agrees with his grandmother! Frances wrote to him regularly, urging him to work. His protracted stay with her in London had increased his self-confidence and she wanted to build on the fact that his physical health was improving: 'Take care of yourself and work well and keep out of scrapes and don't flare up so easily!!!' It is a tribute to Winston's resilience and determination that things improved. His letters home were now full of drawings, usually of a military nature, because the first influence was the school Corps; the discipline and physical activity brought out a new attitude in him. The school songs were a great pleasure to him, too, and sung with gusto on special occasions. He found he had an excellent memory and actually won a prize for reciting 1,200 lines of Macaulay's *Lays of Ancient Rome*. At this point he wrote home for his best trousers, jacket and waistcoat, determined to appear at his best when he went up for his presentation. His confidence was evidently growing. It was Frances who had the pleasure of telling him the results of his army preliminary examination, which he passed in all subjects: 'I am very pleased to hear the good news,' she wrote. 'I hope it will encourage you to continue to exert and distinguish yourself and make us all proud of you.'

There were still disappointments, however. In April 1889 the Harrow headmaster, J.E.C. Welldon, found a diplomatic way of reminding Randolph and Jennie they had not yet visited their son:

It has occurred to me that as you are naturally occupied through the week it would perhaps not be disagreeable to Lady Randolph and yourself to come here from Saturday to Monday some time when Winston is in my House and the weather is warm enough to make life enjoyable. Is there any time in May or June that you could come? You would have, if nothing else, at least the opportunity of seeing what Winston's school life is like.[4]

The visiting was covered to some extent by his aunt, Lady Fanny Marjoribanks, who was visiting her own son. In 1889 he begged his mother to visit him after he had fallen off his bicycle and suffered concussion, but had to settle for the devoted Mrs Everest. Speech Day, the most important date in the Harrow calendar, came and went without either parent. Also in 1892, when Winston won the National Public Schools' Fencing Championship at Aldershot, Randolph 'could not make it'.

Winston was fortunate in having a grandmother who understood him. The time she found for him at Blenheim, in his parents' absence, did much to alleviate the hurt he felt at their neglect; she supplied the things that would give him pleasure. She showed the same care for him in his later years. The Eton-Harrow match at Lords was a highlight of the schools' calendar, when boys were given an exeat to visit London to watch the match or celebrate with their parents. To Winston's intense disappointment he was told rather brutally, via Mrs Everest, that he could not stay with his mother as she was occupied with a large house party they were planning for the races at Epsom; he would have to stay with his grandmother. In the face of such heedlessness, Frances rose to the occasion. Winston was taken out for the day by a family friend, Count Kinsky, who was just the kind of dashing young man to capture the imagination of a 16-year-old: an Austrian diplomat, a handsome, glamorous, sophisticated, urbane darling of society, as well as accomplished and daring horseman who had recently won the Grand National on his own horse. Kinsky took Winston to one of the wonders of the time, the Crystal Palace, where there was a special exhibition in honour of the German Emperor. The heads of the Emperor and Empress were outlined in a special fireworks display. There was a wild beast display and a special drill by the Fire Brigade. In short, everything calculated to entrance and excite an impressionable Winston.

One of the delights was to be driven by Kinsky in his phaeton, the fashionable carriage of the young man-about-town and Victorian equivalent of an Aston Martin; Kinsky's fast horses passed everything else on the road. The evening ended with dinner at a splendid restaurant where, after the head waiter had said there were no tables, Kinsky spoke to him in German and a table magically became available. The final highlight was when Kinsky decided that Winston was old enough to share some champagne!

It was because of Frances that the Palace exerted its own influence on Winston. From his early days there, at least part of Winston's youthful enjoyment at Blenheim was in the Palace building itself. Since Frances had so many grandchildren there were always cousins and friends with whom to play, and one of his pleasures was a game he invented for them called 'French and English'. It was a rough and tumble romp played in the corridors with only two rules: he was always General of the English army, and there was no promotion! As he grew older, however, Winston became aware that the Palace's appeal lay in the sum of its parts: Palace, Park and Gardens in harmony. The happy familiarity with Blenheim he had gained as a boy was only a beginning. Frances had set in motion a growing awareness of the historic significance of the Palace, and he developed an admiration, almost a veneration, for the achievement of his great ancestor, the 1st Duke of Marlborough, who destroyed Louis XIV's hopes for world domination at the Battle of Blenheim in 1704. His history exercise books reveal that by the age of 14 Winston was steeped in the Duke's achievement. He wrote a vivid account, with maps, of the Duke's strategy at Blenheim, which demonstrated an accuracy and understanding that modern opinion says matches the best that today's military historians could achieve.

Later in life Winston summed up the importance of the Duke's victory, saying it 'changed the political axis of the world'. By crushing French ambitions to dominate Europe, Marlborough's victory paved the way for Britain to emerge as the confident and outward-looking nation which, over the next 200 years, created the greatest power the modern world has known, the British Empire. The Duke became Winston's inspiration. He wrote of his illustrious ancestor as 'being aware of a thousand years of history at Woodstock'. He was emphasising the fact that the Park at Blenheim spanned the years from Saxon kings, through Henry II, Queen Elizabeth I, Cromwell and the Stuarts to the present.

Winston felt himself part of that continuum of history. This was what lay behind his own sense of purpose in life and his belief he was born to achieve something great. It was the source of the courage and determination which underpinned his Second World War achievements. Of the moment he became Prime Minister, on 10 May 1940, he later wrote: 'I felt as if I were walking with destiny and that all my past life had been but a preparation for this hour and this trial.' If Frances had not enabled Winston to respond to the historic events embodied at Blenheim, to acquire the belief in his destiny that he did, would Winston have become 'the protector of the freedom of Europe' that he did? Would he have merited the words which are carved on the south front of Blenheim Palace to record the achievements of his ancestor and inspiration, the 1st Duke?

Frances gave Winston one other advantage of inestimable value in his later life. He had been so happy at Blenheim in his early years that he remained a frequent visitor throughout his life. Often this was as a family member, but equally often it was as a guest at the formal country-house parties. On these occasions he mixed on personal terms with the most notable and influential people in Britain and beyond. His name appears regularly in the Visitors' Book alongside national and international leaders, among names from the aristocracy, politics, industry, the press, royalty, society and entertainment. One particularly graphic entry is for the weekend of 26-8 August 1936. One page shows a single signature: Edward R.I. On the facing page the signatures include Wallis W. Simpson, Ernest A. Simpson, Diana and Duff Cooper, the Duke and Duchess of Buccleugh, Emerald Cunard, as well as Winston and Clementine Churchill. The contacts he made at Blenheim were of enormous value throughout his political career.

Chapter Twenty-Three

... AND OTHERS

O ther children from the family benefited from the dutiful and responsible yet sensitive and compassionate care of Frances, who eventually had 24 grandchildren. So many of them were happy to stay with her at Blenheim that one of Jennie's family referred to it as 'that great dumping ground for children', reflecting the warmth of the welcome that Frances provided.

Her care for Winston's brother Jack, younger by nearly six years, was probably on a more practical level than had been necessary for Winston. Placid and easy-natured, Jack had a less demanding temperament than his brother. At the same time Frances was writing to Randolph about Winston requiring a firm hand, she remarked that 'Jack requires no keeping in order' and 'he is a good little boy'. Even their letters contrast. At 13 Winston's writing could deteriorate into an urgent scrawl as he beseeched his mother 'Please, as you love me and as I have begged you'. At the same time seven-year-old Jack was writing tidily and in perfect French 'Maman, j'espere que vous allez bien.'

One of the children whom Frances took under her wing as soon as she became Duchess was her orphaned sister-in-law Clementina, who was only nine years old. Their father, the 6th Duke, had married three times and Clementina was the younger of the two children by his second marriage at the age of 53. Her mother had died when Clementina was only two, and six years later her brother Almeric, older by one year, also died. Within 18 months of her mother's death the Duke married for the third time and there was another child, making rather a complex household. This third marriage was not a successful one, especially for the new Duchess. Within a few months of the birth she left, taking legal action to secure the custody of the four-month-old baby.

These years were not happy ones for Clementina. After her mother's death, she lived an unsettled and lonely life in a bleak, unwelcoming Palace with an elderly father and the tensions of the failing third marriage and a new baby around her. The Duke's death, in the year after her brother's, left her orphaned and alone. Instinctively, Frances reached out to this 'lost' child and welcomed her warmly into her care. Clementina was brought into a new world, as John Winston and Frances, now the 7th Duke and Duchess, moved into the Palace; she became part of a lively family of six cousins around her own age, with two babies still to come.

Frances, only 35, was more a mother to her than a sister-in-law. She gave Clementina nine happy years at Blenheim, treating her as one of her own daughters until she married. An important responsibility for an aristocratic Victorian mother was the managing of suitable marriages for her daughters and Frances' sons-in-law included a duke, an earl, a viscount and two barons. She extended this aspect of motherly care to Clementina who, at 18, made what proved to be a happy and highly suitable marriage to the Marquess of Camden. She repaid Frances' love and care with devotion and loyalty. As the Visitors' Book reveals, Clementina and her husband were regular visitors at Blenheim, and she was there when Jennie went into premature labour with Winston, staying by the bedside and comforting her throughout the birth. During Frances' years as Vicereine in Ireland, Clementina was one of the family members who frequently made the crossing to Ireland to lend her support.

The 6th Duke himself caused problems for Frances at her first introduction to the Marlborough family. Despite the fact that John Winston himself was admirable, sensible, industrious and capable, Frances had to overcome considerable parental opposition to her marriage in 1843. Not all the reasons are clear although an episode in the Duke's life which had caused a public scandal a few years before Frances' engagement must have been hard for her parents to overlook.

In 1838 *The Satirist*, a magazine which looked for scandal in high places, published an article which drew attention to a dubious incident in the 6th Duke's life some 20 years earlier, when he was Marquess of Blandford. In March 1817, apparently, the 23-year-old Lord Blandford had gone through a marriage ceremony with 16-year-old Susannah Law at her parents' house. The ceremony was supposedly performed in the Church of England rite by Lord Charles, a brother of Lord Blandford, who, it was (falsely) claimed, was a clergyman. The couple then lived openly in Lord Blandford's house in London as Captain and Mrs Lawson. Blandford settled £400 a year on Susannah, which she later claimed she had always regarded as a marriage settlement. When the deception was revealed, Blandford placated the girl's parents by promising to take her to Scotland where, according to Scottish law, a marriage was legal if publicly recognised as such. After Susannah had given birth to their baby, they all went to Scotland and lived together publicly. Soon after Susannah had returned to London with their baby, Blandford informed her rather brutally, via a friend, that their relationship was at an end. A few weeks later he married his first cousin, Jane Stewart, who subsequently became his Duchess. Four years later, however, he returned to Susannah and begged her to resume the relationship. The 'marriage settlement' of £400 a year was later reduced to £200, but Susannah was forced to surrender many letters from Blandford which he had signed 'Your affectionate husband, Blandford'.

Shortly before Frances met John Winston *The Satirist* had made the whole story public, declaring that since the marriage had been recognised in Scotland it was consequently valid, and so the marriage to Jane Stewart was bigamous. The appalling consequences of this for the Marlborough family would be that the children of Blandford's marriage to his Duchess, John Winston, his brothers and sister, were illegitimate. Therefore John Winston was not a true heir and would not inherit the title.

Furthermore, the Act conferring the Marlborough title on the 1st Duke, because he had no male heir, had legislated that in the event of no male heir the title would pass into the female line. Thus the legal heir to the title now would be Susannah, the girl Blandford had fathered with Susannah Law. The family were forced to act and they took out a case for libel. All the details of Blandford's deceitful behaviour and betrayal were paraded in court, to the embarrassment of the whole family. However, two of Blandford's friends swore that, during the stay in Scotland, on no occasion had Blandford actually paraded openly with Susannah as his wife, and since the letters he had signed as her husband had been surrendered years earlier *The Satirist* lost its case.

The prospect of an unsavoury father-in-law must have been part of the reason Frances' parents resisted her marriage. Yet the financial future of

Frances and her husband depended on him and so there was constant contact with him, the more so when the children arrived and the Park became their playground. The stability and common sense that characterised Frances were a perfect complement to her husband's good judgement. They had what was generally a sound working relationship with the Duke, and at his father's death John Winston was able to step smoothly into the ducal role. It also says much about Frances' strength of character, the depth of her feeling for John Winston and her confidence in him, that she stood firm in her love. Her judgement was well founded; she had a strong and happy marriage of 41 years. Theirs was a mutually supportive relationship, which enabled both to weather the many family anxieties and worries that those years brought.

Frances was a remarkable woman. Her warmth and sensitivity may have made her vulnerable, yet she had the resilience and strength of character to absorb shocks and responsibilities which would have overwhelmed a lesser person. This was just as well: the problems caused by her errant sons pursued her and her husband. No sooner had they returned from Ireland, where Randolph's mistakes had precipitated them, than their eldest son presented his mother with yet another responsibility. She had already had to weather the public humiliation of his adulterous nine-year affair with Lady Aylesford. Now Lady Aylesford bore Blandford a son, Guy, and was then left to bring him up alone when Blandford deserted her. He was quoted as saying, 'Mistress, yes; but future Duchess of Marlborough, never!' Later, after the Marchioness had divorced him in 1883, he married a rich American widow. Frances once again provided a refuge at Blenheim for a child in need and is said to have given the unfortunate Edith Aylesford a pension.

On her husband's death in 1883, Frances' determination and resolution were called upon once more, again on behalf of a child. Earlier that year Bertha, Blandford's wife, had been given custody of their three daughters on their divorce. Blandford was now the 8th Duke and the heir was his only son by marriage, Charles, now the new Lord Blandford. The 7th Duke had sensibly wished that Charles, his grandson, should not leave with his mother but be brought up in contact with Blenheim in order to develop in him a proper awareness of the Palace and of the duties and responsibilities he would have there later as Duke. To this end he had effected part legal guardianship of the boy. When he died Charles was only eleven years old and so, at the age of 61, Frances, who understood and supported her husband's wishes for Charles, steeled herself to go to court to replace her husband as guardian.

She was successful in this, although she had to accept the condition that she should live at Blenheim to supervise the boy and be responsible for a large part of the staff and household expenses. To all this she dutifully agreed.

It could not have been easy for Frances to oppose Bertha on the guardianship issue. Apart from an inclination to play practical jokes, Bertha had been a responsible and conscientious member of the family; Frances had welcomed her as a daughter-in-law, and liked her. But Frances had a strong sense of duty and an understandable desire to carry out her husband's wishes. So oppose Bertha she did, and Charles came partly into her care. Yet Bertha clearly respected Frances' principles and altruistic motives because she maintained a strong and loyal relationship with her. In Frances' years as Vicereine in Ireland, Bertha was the family member above all others who regularly stayed with her to give support. She appeared regularly at Frances' official functions.

Over a period of some 34 years, from the orphaning of Clementina, through Winston's gradual maturity, to the adulthood of her grandson Charles, later the 9th Duke, between the ages of 35 and her late sixties, the love and commitment Frances gave to children who needed her, as well as her own eight surviving children, is clear and admirable. She had what Jennie described as 'a warm heart, particularly for members of her own family'.

In her last decade, alone after her husband's death, Frances accepted more responsibility. Her daughter Annie, Duchess of Roxburghe, was widowed at the age of 53 with quite a young family of three. Inevitably she received some support from her mother, including financial. She was one of only two daughters to whom Frances left money in her will. The other was youngest daughter Sarah, who had made a happy marriage to an army officer, Lt Colonel Wilson. He was not a rich man, however, and they became so short of money he was compelled to ask his wife's trustee to release money from her marriage settlement; he was refused. Frances provided for Sarah in her will, and also left her the valuable London house in Grosvenor Square.

Chapter Twenty-Four

AN ERROR OF JUDGEMENT

In 1886, when Lord Salisbury and his Tory government regained power, Randolph became Chancellor of the Exchequer and Leader of the House of Commons. At long last, it seemed, the anxieties that had besieged his mother for so many years could finally be put to rest. She could take pleasure in her son's achievement. He had reached one of the three great offices of state (Prime Minister and Foreign Secretary being the others), more than his father had done, worthy politician though he was, and promised to go yet further. He was only 37, the youngest politician to achieve such a meteoric rise since the younger Pitt. It was no surprise he was talked of as a future Prime Minister. His appointment to the Cabinet Office, however, was accepted in spite of medical advice: he was taking digitalis as a sedative, he smoked continually and he was living on his nerves. In addition, his youth and inexperience meant he worked longer hours than usual, driving himself extremely hard. Frances' concerns now were over his health and the fact that he and Jennie had still not mastered their financial affairs.

Their extravagance was noticeable: both Randolph and Jennie dressed fashionably and of course entertained lavishly. Despite the fact they were dependent on what had been settled on them by John Winston and Jennie's father, they showed no sign of being frugal or of heeding expense. Randolph's letters were addressed from many quarters as he pursued the fashionable and expensive country house round: as well as Blenheim, they were guests at Wynyard Hall (the Londonderrys' main home), Seaham Hall (Frances Anne's retirement home on the North Sea coast), Branksome Dene (his sister Cornelia's home after her marriage), Floors Castle (his sister Annie's lovely home in the Scottish borders) and several others. Randolph was an accomplished raconteur and a gift to any hostess's dinner table, while Jennie was still an accomplished pianist.

Frances enjoyed his House of Commons performances. He was a worthy opponent to Gladstone, the 'grand old man' renowned for his eloquence and passion. Randolph, with his rapier wit and charismatic personality, was the perfect foil. Winston, who suffered more than most at his father's hands, constantly being rebuffed, was to write in 1930 that, having read over all his father's letters and speeches, he understood and appreciated him much more. Randolph's approach to work was equally illuminating. The staff at the Treasury, who had been dismayed by his appointment, soon discovered that he was very different from what they had expected. Welby, then secretary to the Treasury, spoke warmly of him:

> He ruled as well as reigned. He had a mind and made it up, a policy and enforced it. He was quick in acquiring information, quick in seizing the real point, and quick in understanding what one wished to convey to him; impatient in small matters and details and contemptuous if one troubled him with them. Above all he was accessible, ready and willing to hear what one had to say, whether it accorded with his own views or not.[1]

Randolph's greatest weakness as a member of the Cabinet was that he was no team player. Perhaps this was the greatest loss he suffered when he neglected his education; he lacked self-awareness and the ability to see another's point of view. His behaviour, as well as his health, was a cause for concern with colleagues; his old weaknesses of impetuosity and lack of self-criticism began to emerge once more. He was discreet in public but quarrelled openly with colleagues and gave way to temperamental outbursts at home. He was warned not to pass information to the press, which he ignored, threatening to resign if he could not have his way in Cabinet. His tendency to argue or pontificate on matters which should have been left to others was unlikely to endear him to colleagues; ominously, he risked alienating the leader who had defended him so often. He frequently interfered with Salisbury's role as Prime Minister and often pursued an independent line when he should have been representing either the country or the party. Salisbury complained to a colleague that he had had no choice about appointing Randolph to lead the House, given the danger the government might collapse otherwise, and compared his situation to 'the task of leading an orchestra in which the first fiddle plays one tune and everybody else, including myself, plays another'.²

Unknown to Frances, clouds were gathering. In mid–December 1886 a crisis was finally precipitated by a minor incident. As Chancellor of the Exchequer, Randolph was persistently complaining about the War Office budget proposals, for which W.H. Smith, as War Minister, was responsible. Smith stood his ground on the issue, just as Randolph was preparing his Budget. An irritable, abusive exchange between them led to Smith's permanent personal enmity and Randolph's threat to resign if he did not get his way, a fatal decision. Queen Victoria, kept informed about everything by Salisbury, said that Randolph should not be given in to.

Randolph had confided in friend and Cabinet colleague Hamilton that he intended to resign. Hamilton was shocked: had Randolph consulted anyone? Had he spoken to the Duchess? Absolutely typically, he had consulted no one. Hamilton had been sensitive for some time to the unrest in the Cabinet about Randolph's behaviour and was certain that Salisbury would seize the opportunity to accept his resignation. On 20 December 1886, at Windsor Castle, Randolph wrote to the Prime Minister without, it would seem, too much consideration. In uncompromising style, he gave his views on the Budget proposals on military expenditure he had just received. The total was £31,000,000, which he said could well be exceeded. He urged a considerable reduction, the costs of defence of various military posts, mercantile ports and coaling stations being abandoned or considerably reduced. He maintained that he saw no chance of any agreement to this, so, without leaving room for discussion or compromise, he declared that he could not continue to be responsible for the finances.

There was no doubt in Salisbury's mind about what to do. Randolph had been a thorn in the side of many people over the last few months and suddenly the solution was handed to him on a plate. He was a wise politician, however, who knew he had to make sure there were as few repercussions as possible if he accepted the resignation. It was better that Randolph should go, but the manner of his going and the result of it had to be primary considerations. Salisbury consulted several colleagues before he replied to Randolph on 22 December. He began by summing up Randolph's argument, wisely ensuring there should be no escape for him by claiming any misunderstanding. He restated Randolph's argument about the £31,000,000

Army and Navy budget being too much and then converted what had been a vague statement of intent by Randolph into a clear resignation request: 'You feel ... you must resign your office and withdraw from the Government.'[3]

He then cleverly included in his reasoning the views of Lord Hamilton and the War Minister concerning the absolute need for the money. Salisbury knew the letter would become public and so skilfully argued from a position he knew would receive popular support: national security. He emphasised that the outlook in Europe was extremely black and the chances were in favour of war at an early date; a strong Commission had already recommended the strengthening of the coastal defences and both parties had agreed. He maintained that Smith's request was moderate, implying that Randolph was unreasonable, and referred to Randolph's aggressive manner, which had already alienated so many.

It is the letter of an experienced and skilful politician. Even its conclusion allowed Salisbury room for manoeuvre. He did not accept the resignation explicitly but stated that he could only express his profound regret, throwing all the emphasis and any blame on to his Chancellor. It was far too clever for Randolph, a demonstration of political acumen only serving to emphasise how unperceptive and headstrong Randolph had been.

Randolph had also made a very foolish mistake. He showed a copy of his letter to the editor of *The Times* and it was published next morning, when Jennie first heard of it. 'Quite a surprise for you,' he said to her when she opened the newspaper, with the uncritical self-satisfaction that was so typical of him. This had two serious consequences for Randolph: as the resignation had been made public it gave Salisbury less room for manoeuvre and angered him more; it also infuriated the Queen that Randolph had broken with protocol. As a Minister of the Crown he should have informed the sovereign first of his resignation. He had no support, therefore, even though Queen Victoria was a friend of his mother. In fact, she had already advised Salisbury that Randolph should not be allowed to have his own way.

There was not the public outcry in Randolph's support that he might have expected. The Christmas recess meant that many people were away or relaxing from their labours. Salisbury's decision to play on concerns about national security worked, the opinion that Britain's defences needed strengthening being widely held. The effect on Frances was, of course, appalling. Randolph's success had lifted her so high that the disappointment and dismay were the greater. He had neither consulted her nor given her the courtesy and consideration of a warning to mitigate the shock she now suffered. There was humiliation too. She was actually at Hatfield House, the Salisbury home, attending a Christmas Ball when Salisbury received Randolph's letter. He did not break the news to her but allowed her to leave next morning in ignorance. Frances wrote to Lady Salisbury, whom she thought of as her friend, only to have her letter returned unopened. She kept the true depth of her hurt to herself, however, revealing it at Randolph's death in 1895. In a reply to Salisbury's letter of condolence, she then revealed the shock and sadness that had overwhelmed her. Her letter is uncharacteristically bitter in tone but is all the more telling for being so. She formally thanked Salisbury for his sympathy but could not restrain herself from expressing her true feelings: 'Oh, it is too late, too late ....' The pathos is understandable in a mother who deserved better from her son.

There was much speculation about what had occurred. Randolph had been in office less than a year but the strain on his health must have been considerable. Also, his temperament was the opposite of Salisbury's, the shrewd, pragmatic operator. Lord Rosebery, Randolph's closest friend, described him as always impatient of opposition and irritated into an act of violence when doubted by his colleagues. The manner of his communication with W.H. Smith had won for him an unforgiving enemy. Furthermore, he had refused to listen to his friend Lord George Hamilton, who knew that Salisbury wished him gone. There is an opinion that Randolph had never meant to be taken seriously when he threatened to resign; Salisbury had always suggested a meeting in the past and some agreement had been reached. Perhaps Randolph was expecting this to happen again, but failed to realise that on this occasion he had pushed Salisbury too far.

Ever a wily politician, Salisbury was careful to place his reasoning on record. In a letter to Sir James Stephen, the Lord Chief Justice, he pointed out how Randolph disagreed with colleagues and how combative his manner could be. He cleverly drew attention to the fact that it was widely felt among colleagues that they had done their best to work with him, but that Randolph had insisted Budget considerations should overrule the needs of other departments. Unless he could balance his judgements better, and have more consideration for colleagues, he would not be able to work with any Ministry.

In writing to Frances, who was respected and admired and had the sympathy of all, Salisbury tried to soften the blow. He painted a more favourable portrait, bringing out Randolph's qualities and trying to give her hope:

> Nothing has happened seriously to injure or damage a career of which you are so justly proud or to deprive the country of the value of his services in the future.[4]

This was little consolation to the stricken mother. Randolph's career was over. He left with some dignity, however, making it clear that:

> I shall make no further attempt to defend my action, lest by any such attempt I might, even by one iota, increase the difficulties which surround him; but, recognising to the full my great fallibility of judgement, I shall watch silently and sadly the progress of events.[5]

Chapter Twenty-Five

MIXED EMOTIONS

The sudden death of their father in 1883 had drawn Randolph and George, who now became the 8th Duke, closer together than they had been for some years – to Frances' quiet satisfaction. Her commitment to the upbringing of her young grandson, Charles, now Marquess of Blandford, meant she remained at Blenheim after her husband's death and could again enjoy Randolph's presence. After his father's death he had sought solace there, spending hours reading over his father's letters. Also, at his brother's prompting, he started up the Blenheim Harriers again. To Frances' pleasure this activity was now shared by both her sons, who also enjoyed a holiday together in Switzerland. Her sons worked together as they took forward plans their father had had for bringing the railway to Woodstock, which they accomplished in 1885 on land originally set aside by John Winston.

At this time Randolph's political career was still prospering, but clouds were gathering around Frances after her husband's death, and her eldest son George was at the heart of them. John Winston and Frances had more or less given up all hope in him and tried to protect themselves from the succession of hurts he inflicted on them by raising no expectations. He was a rebel against the proprieties of his parents and their generation, seeing himself as a 'modern man'. His values and attitudes were very different from their own. The things they held dear, such as the traditional morality based on Christian belief, especially in things such as marriage, and the importance of his family heritage, duty and responsibility, meant little to him. A directive in his will makes clear how great was the gap between himself and a saddened, uncomprehending Frances: he wished not to be buried in the vault in the Blenheim chapel because he disliked the sense of exclusiveness it symbolised.

For Frances, the mother of six daughters and a wife in a devoted and happy marriage of 40 years, the purity of womanhood was sacrosanct. In this regard, in particular, her eldest son had caused her much hurt and humiliation. He once expressed the view that the only thing in life worth pursuing was women, and his intentions were far from honourable.

George had pleased his parents at first by making a very suitable marriage into one of the best connected families in the country, the Abercorns. He soon tired of Bertha (Albertha), the Duke's daughter, preferring the charms of his mistress, Lady Aylesford. Tiring of his infidelity, Bertha left him, finally obtaining a deed of separation which ensured she received maintenance; previously he had not given her a regular income, even though there were four children to support. After Edith Aylesford bore him an illegitimate son he deserted her, then Bertha divorced him. Undaunted, he embarked on another extra-marital relationship, this time with Lady Colin Campbell, whose husband cited him as one of four co-respondents in a well-publicised divorce case. He maintained this relationship until his death, despite marrying Lilian Hammersley in the interval, an American widow whose only attraction was her fortune of 5,000,000 dollars and an income of 150,000 dollars a year. Lilian took the view, not uncommon in wronged Victorian wives, including Princess Alexandra, that her husband's infidelity was to be ignored. But the succession of public scandals was not something that Frances could dismiss so easily; such activity offended so much that she held dear. Her characteristic steadfastness and fortitude were needed. However, Duchess Lilian did (immediately after the 8th Duke's death) tear down the life-size portrait of a nude Lady Colin Campbell that her husband had kept in his bedroom throughout their marriage.

There was one step that George took, however, that was too much for his mother. In 1886 he put up for sale a major part of the magnificent Blenheim picture collection. This was something Frances found distressing; an act of such despoliation undermined the glory of Blenheim. She saw the collection, gathered largely by the 1st Duke, as integral to Blenheim, an essential part of the historic symbolism of his great achievement; it was unlike the later gem collection of the 4th Duke or the Sunderland Library sold by John Winston, which were never part of the original Palace inheritance. A further sadness for Frances was the fact her wayward son had indirectly betrayed his father, by manipulating John Winston's breaking of the entail in a way which John Winston had never contemplated and would never have done himself.

In order to finance such things as his scientific experiments, the installation of electricity and a telephone system, and the development of the farms, George ruthlessly disposed of some 227 major paintings, as well as fine porcelain, in major sales in the summer of 1886, despite Randolph's and Frances' protests. He eventually raised some £400,000 in a depressed market. The paintings included works by Rubens (18 paintings), Rembrandt, Raphael, Breughel, Jordains, Van Dyck, Teniers, Wouvermans, Cuyps, Reynolds, Gainsborough, Watteau, Claude, Poussin, Stubbs, Mytens, Caracci, Maratti, Giordano, Carlo Dolci, Titian, Veronese.

Only two were bought for the nation: Raphael's 'Ansidei Madonna' (for £70,000) and Van Dyck's 'Equestrian Portrait of Charles I' (for £17,500), both of which are now in the National Gallery. The Rothschilds bought Rubens' 'Three Graces' (for 25,000 guineas) and self-portraits of the artist and of his wife (55,000 guineas). Randolph violently opposed the sales and fell out with his brother over them. Years later he was enraged to come across three great Blenheim paintings in a Berlin gallery: Raphael's 'Fornarina', and Rubens' 'Andromeda' and 'Bacchanalia'. Some paintings were lost sight of altogether. Only in 2006 did Van Dyck's fine 1635 portrait of Katherine, Lady Stanhope, later Countess of Chesterfield, part of the 1st Duke's collection, come to light, having 'disappeared' after being sold to a New York dealer in the 1886 sale.[1]

Frances registered her disapproval in the most forceful way available to her: she left Blenheim, where her agreement over the guardianship of George's son and heir Charles had kept her, and returned to her London home.

Now another problem arose for Frances. Brought into close contact with her daughter-in-law through their joint activity in the Primrose League, Frances' relationship with Jennie had steadily improved. Because of this, in the summer of 1886 Jennie was able to confide in Frances her worries about her marriage: she was convinced there was another woman. A number of long letters from Frances to Jennie at this time have survived and in them Frances reveals much of herself. The first letter, of 8 September 1886, is typical, characterised by warmth and readiness to help:

Huntercombe [Frances' country house near Henley]
8 September 1886

Dearest Jennie,
I thought so much about you that I was very glad to get your letter; I will
begin with the end of it. Rely on one thing which is – I may not be able
to do any good but I will do no harm and not like poor Cornelia [her
eldest daughter] put the fat in the fire in my desire to help you. Meantime
I pray you do not breathe thoughts of revenge against any one. It will
bring you no blessing. Accept your present worry and anxiety patiently
and strive to dispel it by the exercise of domestic virtues!!! looking after
the children and the new cook etc. – avoiding excitement and the society
of those friends who while ready enough to pander to you would gladly
see you vexed or humbled as they no doubt are jealous of your success in
society. How dull and tiresome you will think me and how little comfort
– I think Lady Mandeville would be true – but oh she is indiscreet and
things do come round so. I wish so much that you had your sisters for
they are to be trusted and I would really trust no one else. Try dear to keep
your troubles to yourself – this is hard for you for you have a tell-tale face
– though you do tell little fibs at times – It is a horrid time of year for
you to be in town. If you do not go to Scotland with him dear Jennie do
come and vegetate quietly here. Bring Jack and we will try to make you as
happy as possible. I am sure it will show Randolph you care for him and
he has a good heart and will give you credit for it. If I were you I would
not if it killed me let the heartless lot you live with generally see there
was 'a shadow of a shade of a shred' wrong, only he should know it and
feel that it makes you miserable. And meantime though it is a humdrum
task try to make yourself so essential to him that he must recognise it …
God bless you, I pray for you and my dear R. every day that God may
give you patience, strength and gentleness and that He may watch over
dear R. and keep him straight.

Believe me, Yours most affectionately
F.M.[2]

Wise in knowledge of human affairs, she advised patient virtue rather
than revenge and acknowledged a long-lasting worry, Jennie's choice of

friends: 'the heartless lot'. She was aware of how different from herself Jennie found her, 'dull and tiresome', and urged one of her own principles and priorities on her: discretion. Frances had suffered too much from publicised family indiscretions. Typically, she extended a warm invitation to Jennie and Jack to stay quietly with her in the country. Her essential Christian belief in God's goodness, which characterised both herself and her husband, was clear.

Frances faced a difficult challenge, trying honestly to make clear to Jennie where the problems and solutions lay, while maintaining a caring relationship. She succeeded remarkably well. For some weeks her letters continued in the same vein, her affection constant if rather dutiful: 'I do not see how I can show you more affection and sympathy than I do.' But, as so often in the past, she was concerned with Randolph's lack of financial prudence ('more money borrowed'). Directly, as was her way, if rather tactlessly in the circumstances, she laid the blame at Jennie's door ('he said he relied on you doing for him'), and made clear just how much she worried about Jennie's undesirable friends: 'You must sacrifice yourself and lead a different life.' She seems to have had a clear idea of Jennie's lifestyle, but did not refer to it directly.

The undiminished love Frances had for Randolph shines through these letters: 'He has a good heart'; 'my dear Randolph'. She went to see him on Jennie's behalf and reassured her daughter-in-law there was no other woman. Randolph seems offhand in his letters to Jennie at the time, but there is no evidence of another woman. The reason for their unhappiness is more likely to have been the tensions of his political life at the time as both Chancellor of the Exchequer and Leader of the House.

On 3 October Frances wrote to Jennie of her delight in Randolph's success: she called it 'statesmanlike, tactful and forcible'. Almost immediately, of course, Randolph's impetuous resignation began his political decline, which it was Frances' ordeal to witness over a number of years. Then suddenly, in November 1892, she was stunned by the news that the 8th Duke had been found dead in his rooms at the age of 48. It was a shock to everyone but there was particular anxiety about the Dowager Duchess. Two letters sent by Randolph to his mother from Blenheim, where he had arrived to take charge of things, survive. He wrote with consideration and affection ('Dearest Mama ... Ever your most affectionate son') and appears to know what his mother's overriding concerns would be. He assured her that he was looking after the widowed Duchess, Lily, and young Charles, now the 9th Duke. He sought to comfort his mother by describing George's death gently and sympathetically ('He looked very peaceful'), and giving the probable cause of death as loss of consciousness following acute indigestion, from which he suffered: his brother had actually died of a heart attack. He quelled any anxiety about practicalities by clarifying all the arrangements: coroner, post-mortem, lawyer, will, funeral. All in all it is a well-judged letter, revealing Randolph's care for his mother and explaining why she lavished her love on him.

His second letter three days later was much more personal, written out of genuine love and concern. It is a letter of consolation, unsentimentally calculated to bring Frances peace of mind by assuring her that all the distress and anxiety his brother George had caused her in life was now at an end. Randolph reminded her how hard she had tried with the recalcitrant George: 'for long and weary years you lavished upon him all that duty required – or affection and love inspired'. No longer would she suffer the shame and disgrace he brought upon the family. 'Much wrong will now be righted,' he says and 'a great name will be well sustained'. She would no longer have the anxiety of worrying what George would do next, and a particularly raw wound could heal: 'there will be quieter and more orderly times at Blenheim'. He ended by deliberately giving Frances an especially strong expression of his love: 'Ever your most affectionate son ...'

Although his impetuosity had by now ruined his political career and his health, the effort Randolph made to support his mother was impressive. There was one further service he did for Frances: despite George's wish to the contrary, Randolph's advice and support determined her to bury her eldest son in the family vault below the chapel at Blenheim. She had at last the satisfaction of restoring him to the family tradition and heritage he had so disregarded, which she and John Winston held so precious.

George's talents were never properly fulfilled. He had the reputation of being gifted, particularly in scientific matters, and had taken his own path in life while Randolph and the six sisters came together in a close family way. Very little is known of his early life except that he was expelled from Eton for using a catapult. While Randolph pursued his university studies, his elder brother was serving as an Army officer in the Household Cavalry and thoroughly enjoying himself. His intellect and ability were never in doubt; Lord Redesdale called him:

a youth of great promise, marred by fate, shining in many branches of human endeavour, clever, capable of great industry and within measurable distance of reaching conspicuous success in science, mathematics and mechanics.[3]

With his own laboratories at Blenheim and a level of scientific knowledge which enabled him to produce his own telephone system, much seemed possible. But his failure to express himself through the achievement he desired created in him 'an inner source of restlessness incapable of satisfaction'. It is difficult to understand why, with all his intellectual and social advantages, he preferred the company of the Marlborough House set and chose to neglect his own particular gifts.

Chapter Twenty-Six
THE LAST DAYS

In the summer of 1892, a few months before his brother's death, Randolph was showing odd signs of irritability. One week he had a particularly pleasant dinner with Joseph Chamberlain, a long-time friend; the very next week, however, at another dinner and apparently without reason, he spoke rudely and aggressively to Chamberlain and ordered that a bowl of flowers be placed to separate them. Shortly after Blandford's death more serious signs appeared of Randolph's declining mental health. For the next two years Frances had the grim ordeal of watching her son's mental deterioration, and not just in private. Rosebery, his lifelong friend, summed it up: 'He died in public, by inches.'

The excessive length and shaky writing of his letters at the time confirms the beginning of the decline, although for a short while his political fortunes rose. He was invited back on to the Front Bench and joined meetings of the Tory party leaders, the Shadow Cabinet as it would be called today. The penetrating wit and dramatic style which had characterised his speeches and made his mother so proud, did not return, however, and his doctor began to be concerned about his mental condition. Dizziness, palpitations, numbness of the hands, difficulty in speaking and deafness seemed to indicate a serious brain condition. There has been over a century of speculation as to its nature. Popular opinion enjoyed the sensational possibility of its being syphilis, the idea even being used by his political enemies to denigrate Winston years later. As one of his granddaughters later recorded, 26 years after Randolph's death one of Winston's enemies within the Conservative party tried to keep him from office by describing him as 'the alcoholic son of a syphilitic father'. The foundation for the theory rests on very unreliable sources, such as Frank Harris, a journalist and writer, and members of Jennie's family who resented Randolph. Informed medical opinion has now made it clear that Randolph died of an undiagnosed and inoperable brain tumour, which has similar symptoms.[1]

The mercurial and confused state of Randolph's mind at the time are demonstrated by two encounters he had with Winston, quite close together, in which he revealed himself in totally different mental states. On a happy occasion in the autumn of 1892, Randolph spoke to Winston rationally and calmly in a situation when he could well have flown off the handle. It was a moment of intimacy Winston had never previously shared with his father, and which he relished:

Only once did he lift his visor in my sight. This was at our house at Newmarket in the autumn of 1892. He had reproved me for startling him by firing off a double-barrelled gun at a rabbit which had appeared on the lawn beneath his windows; he had been very angry and disturbed. Understanding at once that I was distressed, he took occasion to reassure me. I then had one of the three or four intimate conversations with him which are all I can boast. He explained how old people were not always very considerate towards young people, that they were absorbed in their own affairs and might well speak roughly in sudden annoyance. He said he was glad I liked shooting, and that he had arranged for me to shoot on September 1st (this was the end of August) such partridges as our small property contained. Then he proceeded to talk to me in the most wonderful and captivating manner about school and going into the Army and the grown-up life which lay beyond. I listened spellbound to this sudden departure from his usual reserve, amazed at his intimate comprehension of my affairs. Then at the end he said, 'Do remember that things do not always go right with me. My every action is misjudged and every word distorted ... so make some allowances.'[2]

Only a few months later Randolph had deteriorated to the extent that when, in August 1893, Winston wrote to tell him he had passed into Sandhurst at the third attempt, the reply was irrational, caustic, even brutal. In a tirade that goes on relentlessly for 47 lines, Randolph entirely dismissed Winston's success, condemning him in terms no father should ever use to a son. Winston's failure to pass high enough for the infantry was 'slovenly', an achievement fit 'only for the second or third rate'. With vicious sarcasm he ridiculed his son and complained that his getting into the cavalry would cost an extra £2,000 a year. He told Winston not to write about such so-called successes in future, as he would not attach the slightest importance to anything he might say. He describes Winston as leading an 'idle, useless, unprofitable life', becoming a 'social wastrel', who will lead 'a shabby, unhappy and futile existence'. This was clearly the outpouring of a mind at least temporarily unhinged. If there is any doubt of this, Randolph ended his letter with the words 'Your mother sends her love, Your affectionate father ...'

There was also the unhappy episode in 1894 of the watch which Randolph had given Winston and over which he accused his son of carelessness. Winston, wounded, wrote at length to his father:

I placed the watch last Sunday in my breast pocket – not having with uniform a waistcoat to put it in – and while walking along the Wish stream I stooped to pick up a stick and it fell out of my pocket into the only deep place for miles.

The stream was only about five inches deep – but the watch fell into a pool nearly six feet deep. I at once took off all my clothes and I dived for it but the bottom was so uneven and the water so cold I could not stay in longer than ten minutes and had to give it up.

The next day I had the pool dredged – but without result. On Tuesday therefore I obtained permission from the Governor to do anything I could provided I paid for having it all put straight again.

I then borrowed twenty-three men from the Infantry Detachment – dug a new course for the stream – obtained the fire engine and pumped the pool dry and so recovered the watch. I tell you all this to show you that I appreciated fully the value of the watch and that I did not treat the accident in a casual way. The labour of the men cost me over three pounds.

I would rather you had not known about it. I would have paid for its mending and said nothing. But since you know about it – I feel I ought to tell you how it happened in order to show you that I really valued the watch and did my best to make sure of it. I quite realise that I have failed to do so and I am very sorry that it should have happened. But it is not the case with all the things. Everything else you have ever given me is in as good repair as when you gave it first.

Please don't judge me entirely on the strength of the watch. I am very sorry about it.

I am sorry to have written you such a long and stupid letter, but I do hope you will take it in some measure as an explanation.

With best love,
I remain ever your loving son

Winston S. Churchill[3]

At the age of 19 Winston was showing a talent for positive action on a substantial scale, an anxiety to please his father, and an astonishing lack of self-esteem in spite of his considerable resourcefulness and clear command of the English language. The watch was confiscated and given to Jack.

The public face of Randolph's mental unbalance came to a head when he spoke in the Commons on 17 February 1893 on the Irish Home Rule Bill. As he stood up to speak, members were appalled by his pale and prematurely aged face. His trembling hands and inaudibility were so severe that many left the House, some, with cruelty, talking loudly to each other as they went.

The problems with his health, together with more serious financial difficulties than usual, forced Randolph and Jennie to give up their London house in Connaught Place. Frances generously invited them to share her own house in Grosvenor Square, thus providing yet another significant opportunity for Winston. Though still only 18, he was able to meet and mix there with influential political figures of the day whom his well-connected mother invited to dinner, just as years later at Blenheim he heard men of the calibre of Rosebery, Balfour, Asquith, all future Prime Ministers, discuss the issues of the day. Jennie encouraged him also to attend the House of Commons and listen to the debates. Once again Frances was instrumental in developing the future politician.

Randolph was insisting on persevering with political speeches, but by the spring of 1894 had only to rise to speak and the Commons emptied. Frances was at close quarters to see all this. Rosebery actually begged her and Jennie to persuade Randolph to stay away from the House and Winston records hearing them trying to persuade Randolph to take a rest; they did not succeed.

Around this time occurred the only known occasion when Frances' kindness and concern for the vulnerable seem to have deserted her. Just before Christmas 1893 she dismissed Mrs Everest, much loved nanny to Winston and Jack and family servant for 20 years. She first sent her on holiday, without the customary board wages, then dismissed her. By letter! Winston was incensed: 'cruel and mean' he called it. He acknowledged that the Duchess had the right to dismiss a servant no longer needed, and Frances maintained there was no room for her at Grosvenor Square, but it was the manner of dismissal and lack of future support that angered him.

It seems, however, that Frances had long found her a problem; perhaps her long service had made her familiar and dictatorial and hard to bear. Mrs Everest had offended her where she was most sensitive, by coming between her and her grandchildren. She had tried to prevent Winston and Jack coming to Blenheim as children, describing it as cold and damp and unhealthy for them. 'Horrid old Everest', Frances had called her on one occasion. With the emotional shock of her eldest son's early death only weeks earlier, personal and practical problems now bore in on her: Randolph's health and political future; his and Jennie's marriage and their carelessness with money, which had forced them to leave their country and London homes; pressure on space at Grosvenor Square, which was the reason given for the dismissal. Winston insisted that Jennie should find provision for Mrs Everest, which she finally did at the home of an Essex bishop.

Randolph's condition had become so unpredictable, often uncontrolled, that his doctors believed that time abroad might ease his distress. On 27 June 1894 Randolph and Jennie left for a world tour, planned to last for perhaps a year; it was hoped the constantly changing scene could be an antidote to Randolph's symptoms. Removing him from the public demonstration of his illness was desirable, a relief for Frances and his family and friends.

Whatever criticism might be levelled at Jennie elsewhere, her conduct over the months that followed and her commitment to the man she once loved were admirable. Without hesitation, she left the society world and devoted herself to Randolph, sometimes in terrifying circumstances; on one occasion he brandished a revolver in her face, threatening to shoot her. For some parts of the journey he seemed to recover quite significantly, but generally he worsened. It was the indefatigable Frances who maintained contact with Winston, now at Sandhurst, passing on news to him of his parents. By the time they reached Singapore, Randolph's condition had worsened to the extent that a lead-lined coffin was added to their luggage. By the time they reached Madras, Randolph's condition had become impossible. The journey had to be cut short and by Christmas Randolph and Jennie were home.

His mental state was now very serious indeed, moving Jennie to write to her sister, 'Even his mother wishes now that he had died the other day.' Frances had persevered to the end, but now even she had to give up. On 24 January 1895 Randolph died peacefully in his sleep at his mother's house. Winston records later that at the moment of his father's death he ran across the snow in Grosvenor Square in the early hours of the morning. He was always aware of his father, sometimes as a physical presence. Seventy years later he was to die on the same day of the year. Jennie is said to have refused to return the Chancellor's robes, as was customary, saying she was keeping them for Winston. He did wear them with pride when he became Chancellor 34 years later.

It was Randolph's death that finally defeated Frances. Her calm and self-control disappeared and she now wrote from the heart. Once dismissed as a formidable and rather cold Victorian matriarch, she was in fact a woman of intelligence, energy and emotion. Her grief at her son's death was expressed openly. Salisbury had respected and liked Randolph, and now he wrote a sincere and moving letter of condolence to Frances. Overcome by her feelings, she could not refrain from pouring out her heart in a letter of reply. She expressed her love for her dead son most movingly: 'I would have given my life for him,' she insists. Her grief reaches a climax in her last sentence: 'Now it is too late, he seems to be understood and appreciated.' Even more powerful are the six handwritten pages, bordered in mourning black, of the 'Recollections' she wrote, at Gladstone's urging, to assuage her grief. No one reading them could fail to be moved by her deep sadness and nostalgia for the days now gone. In one passage she summed up all she had loved in Randolph and her pride in his achievement, talent and zest for life:

When I look back in sadness to his youth and remember his ready wit, his warm affection and his bright spirits and his energy in carrying out any undertaking, I feel how great was the want of foresight and intellect on my part in his training and management, for one of his most endearing qualities was his extraordinary affection for his father and me and his constant interest and pride in his family and especially his sisters Cornelia, Rosamund and Fanny in his earliest days and later in his younger sisters also. Alas, had I been a clever woman I must have had more ability to curb and control his impulses and I should have taught him patience and moderation. And yet at times he had extraordinary good judgement and it was only on rare and fatal occasions he took what the French call 'Le Mors aux Dents' and then there was no stopping him. He was by nature a leader of men and had a wonderful power of organisation. This was evident in his leadership of the so-called Fourth Party which began to some extent as a joke and yet was among the causes which first shook the power of Mr Gladstone. Later on it was displayed in the machinery of the Primrose League which Sir Algernon Borthwick and Sir Henry Wolfe managed. At an earlier period I had felt the power of his organisation when in Ireland he drew up the system of relief in the famine-stricken districts and made the Fund which I had managed for that relief a great success.[4]

She also reveals what had hitherto not been suspected: that the move to Ireland to extricate the family from the consequences of the Aylesford affair had been the result of her appeal to her mother's old friend, Disraeli. The last word, appropriately enough, belonged to Lord Rosebery, Randolph's closest friend from childhood. In 1906 he published a biography of Randolph, the closing paragraph echoing his own personal grief:

This [book] may, of course, be a wholly mistaken estimate of Randolph's character. Misgivings may well beset the pen that traces it, for it is written by one who feels for him all the affection of a long friendship, but who was always his political opponent. I see, as all the public saw, many faults; but I remember what the public could not know, the generous, lovable nature of the man. I cannot forget the pathos of the story; I mourn, as all must mourn, to whatever party they belong, that he has not had time to retrieve himself, not time to display his highest nature; I grieve, as all must grieve, that that daring and gifted spirit should have been extinguished at an age when its work should only have just begun.[5]

Randolph's funeral was held in Westminster Abbey, Londoners crowding the silent streets in his honour, and he was then brought home on a cold winter's day, the snow lying deep over Oxfordshire, to be buried in Bladon churchyard, close to the small village school named after his mother. In due course he was to be joined in that quiet English churchyard by his son Winston and other members of his family.

Some months later Winston visited his grave and wrote to Jennie:

I went this morning to look at Papa's grave. The service in the church was going on and the voices of the children singing all added to the beauty and restfulness of the spot. The hot sun of the last few days has dried up the grass a little – but the rose bushes are in full bloom and make the churchyard very bright. I was so struck by the sense of quietness and peace as well as by the old world air of the place – that my sadness was not unmixed with solace. It is the spot of all others he would have chosen. I think it would make you happier to see it.[6]

Chapter Twenty-Seven
LOOKING AHEAD

———————————

F rances found herself facing the end of her life without the support of her cherished son Randolph. She had had to face stoically the deaths of all five of her sons, having shed many tears in her ambitions for the family. However, she did have the comfort of her six daughters, all of whom outlived her and became a strong support.

In 1896, the year after Randolph's death, Frances faced a further family challenge with the arrival of a new Duchess, Consuelo Vanderbilt, the 19-year-old wife of her grandson Charles, now the 9th Duke. In her autobiography, *The Glitter and the Gold*, Consuelo describes her first meeting with Frances and presents a surprisingly poor view of her. So unsympathetic is her account of Frances that an assessment of its validity is long overdue. Frances, she wrote, received her in Grosvenor Square and welcomed her with a kiss like 'a deposed sovereign greeting her successor'. Frances had 'cold grey eyes' and hoped to see Blenheim restored 'to its former glories' and 'the prestige of the family upheld'. She told Consuelo her first duty was to produce an heir in order to prevent Winston, 'that little upstart', from becoming Duke. Frances apparently asked her then if she was in the 'family way'. This account has led subsequent writers to draw over-simplistic conclusions about the relatively complex Frances. Consuelo's account of her challenging reception misses the warmth, care and family generosity that was characteristic of Frances. The Dowager Duchess was indeed a strong, forthright character and when necessary could be blunt and direct; as Duchess and Vicereine she had known occasions when formality and something of the 'Grande Dame' would have been appropriate. But the circumstances of her first meeting with Consuelo make her reaction more understandable. Some 22 years earlier another attractive 19-year-old American girl had been presented to her as the proposed wife of her much loved son Randolph. The months of struggle to dissuade Randolph from an unwise marriage were followed by the anxiety and stress brought her by Jennie over the next 20 years: of flirtation, infidelity, extravagance, self-indulgence, inadequate parenting and disharmony with Randolph. As Consuelo noted, Frances was still in mourning for her son, and so the reminder of Jennie must have been painful, even bitter. It is unsurprising that her response to the new American girl was a cool one.

Furthermore Frances came from a generation for whom the arrival of what came to be called the 'Dollar Princesses' was viewed with mistrust. Queen Victoria did not receive them at Court until protocol was relaxed to enable her to do so. Frances' stiff attitude was understandable. She was also making sure the priorities of an heir and the restoration of Blenheim to its former glory were impressed upon the young girl, something the reserved Charles might not have done.

Her comment on her beloved grandson Winston is more difficult to understand: it simply does not fit with other known facts. Frances had loved, protected and championed Winston all his life. Just 18 months earlier she had again taken him into her care at Christmas time while Randolph and Jennie were on their world tour. She wrote to them then, remarking on Winston's being 'affectionate and pleasant … difficult to refuse him anything'. She had enough confidence in him to accept his word he would not gamble, when she gave him permission to go to the races at Sandown because 'it's a great thing to keep him in good society.' Out of all the family, Frances had expressed unflagging confidence in Winston's ability, refusing to accept Randolph's low opinion of his son. Not long before Consuelo's visit her confidence had proved well founded: having scraped into Sandhurst near the bottom of the list, Winston passed out in the first 20 from 150 candidates. And why 'upstart'? He was the grandson of a Duke and the son of dearly loved Randolph!

An explanation may lie in the fact that Consuelo was well into her seventies when she wrote her autobiography; recalling events of over 50 years earlier, her memory would not have been perfect. Although she loved her sons dearly and enjoyed Blenheim later in life, her period there in Frances' time had been unhappy and had possibly coloured her recollection. But her unflattering picture of Frances has since become central to Frances' reputation. Two details in particular correspond with the overall picture of Frances that has been established here. Her wish to 'see Blenheim restored to its former glories' is a vivid reminder of the pain caused her by the 8th Duke's insensitive disposal of Blenheim's magnificent collection, particularly of the pictures, and perhaps of the Aylesford affair, which had forced her husband to break the entail unwillingly, thus allowing the sale of the Churchill inheritance. Her desire to 'see the prestige of the family upheld' recalls the humiliation she suffered when her eldest son repeatedly dragged the family into public disgrace.

In summary, then, Frances' reservations were justified. The marriage between Consuelo and Charles did not work out; it lasted only ten years and a divorce followed which Frances would have found abhorrent. Other aspects of Consuelo would have pleased her greatly: her love for her children and, particularly, her social conscience. Her compassion and help for the vulnerable echoed Frances' own endeavours. At Blenheim she continued the tradition, begun by Frances, of sending leftover food to the villages each day. She won public love and affection, whether it was by reading to an old lady in the 4th Duchess's almshouses or ensuring medical aid to the sick. She was a regular visitor to the school, particularly the one built by Frances at Bladon, and actively encouraged the children by hearing them read and sing. She brought the girls to the Palace to be taught cookery, and Blenheim gardeners were sent to the school to teach their skills to the boys.

During the 15 years Consuelo lived alone in London, social work was the centre of her life. She used her title and position to generate finance to relieve any need she perceived, especially those involving women and children. A list of her involvements includes the Waifs and Strays Society, the Anti Sweated Labour League, the YWCA, Dr Barnardo's, the Church Army, Prisoners' Aid and Royal Holloway College. She discovered that no relief existed for children of women whose husbands were imprisoned; the streets were often their only recourse. Consuelo set up laundries where the women could work, and provided nurseries for their children. To further all these and other activities she became a London county councillor. Living in France during her second marriage, her support for sick and hungry French children before and immediately after the Second World War earned her the award of the Legion d'Honneur. Frances would have greatly respected her.

The two ambitions Frances had expressed to her new granddaughter-in-law were subsequently fulfilled. With Consuelo's fortune, Blenheim 'was restored to its former glories' by Charles, the 9th Duke. Gilded ceilings, exquisite furniture, extensive new Italian and Water Terrace Gardens and restoration of the Great Court all contributed to a rejuvenated environment which once more welcomed the family, their friends and political figures, just as it had in Frances' own time.

'The prestige of the family' was more than upheld, too. Frances' sons had disappointed her, but her daughters did much to compensate. Cornelia's family produced a further Viceroy of Ireland, two Privy Counsellors, a Secretary of State, a Paymaster General, a Lord-in-Waiting to the King and four MPs. Her other daughters produced three further MPs, another Privy Counsellor, a Lord Privy Seal, a Lord President of the Council, a Comptroller of the Royal Household and a First Lord of the Admiralty. Frances would have been particularly pleased with Fanny, in whom she saw something of herself. She married the 2nd Baron Tweedmouth, and the *Dictionary of National Biography* records that his success as a Liberal politician was in no small measure a consequence of her being 'endowed with a natural gift for society [who] shared her husband's labour in bringing together Liberal politicians of all shades of opinion'. Annie, Duchess of Roxburghe, became Mistress of the Robes and Lady of the Bedchamber to Queen Victoria, receiving, as her mother had done, the Royal Order of Victoria and Albert. As Dowager Duchess, in 1906 she launched the *Mauretania* from Swan Hunters, first of the great transatlantic ocean liners and holder of the Blue Riband for the fastest Atlantic crossing for 28 years. Frances' greatest delight would have been in Sarah, her youngest daughter: inheriting her mother's intelligence, strength of character and resilience, she became a woman of the new century. As the first woman war correspondent, she covered the Siege of Mafeking in the field for the *Daily Mail*. Her reports gained a huge following in London, promoting, it was said, 'the bulldog spirit' among a population depressed by the poor news of the war.

Above and beyond all these, of course, was the achievement of Frances' grandson Winston. After he joined his regiment, the 4th Hussars, in February 1895 his arduous training as a regimental officer and his subsequent service abroad meant contact with his grandmother was very limited. Also, distracted by all the exciting activity, he was a little careless about remaining in touch, as he later admitted himself. Fortunately, two important letters exist, hitherto unpublished, which he wrote to Frances when he became more settled. Vividly revealing, with him at the exciting beginning of his career, and her very near the end of her life, the letters confirm many aspects of Frances' character of which her life is a testimony. At the same time, they provide telling insights into Winston's activities and the important decisions he was making at this critical time of his life.

The first letter is from India, where he was with his regiment in October 1897, after well-recorded adventures in Cuba, Sudan and on the North West Frontier. Whatever Consuelo might have noted, the tone of both letters confirms the affection Frances had always shared with her grandson. In the first he leaves her with 'I trust that you will regard affectionately, Your loving grandson'; the second ends 'Goodbye, my dear Grandmama, with best love, I remain, Your affectionate grandson'. Even though he is apologising for having been out of touch, the tone in the first letter is so sincere and purposeful it indicates a confidence the affection he feels will be returned:

> I feel that I was very wrong not to have come to see you. Nor is there perhaps anything that I can say that can wholly explain or excuse my omission. I heard however that you disapproved very much of my having come home at all and this led me to put off coming from one day to another – until it was too late – and all intentions were involved in the hurry of departure. I will not say more, but will only beg you to believe that I regret and have regretted my neglect very much – and hope that in spite of it you still think of me with kindness.

The account he gives Frances of what he has been doing, in particular the military activity, is a vivid foretaste of the drama in his writing to come, more so perhaps because it is so personal:

> ... both in enabling me to get to the one brigade that was the most severely engaged – and bringing me safe back. I was with the unfortunate General Jeffreys on the big action of 16th September – and was myself with the 35th Sikhs, who as you perhaps remember were nearly cut to pieces. Indeed so close and critical did affairs become that I was forced to fire my revolver nine times in self-defence. However, though, a third of those troops at this point were either killed or wounded.

His descriptions of conflicts in which he was engaged confirm what is now well known: Winston's personal courage. He is quite indifferent to danger. Later in the letter, he writes almost casually, 'If I live [sic] I intend to …'. Winston found the excitement of battle exhilarating, but throughout his life was sharply aware of the horrors of war, its human suffering and cost:

I wonder if people in England have any idea of the savagery of the warfare that is being carried on here. It is so different from what one has been led to expect that I do not doubt that there are many people who do not realise, for instance, that no quarter is ever asked or given. The tribesmen torture the wounded and mutilate the dead. The troops never spare a single man who falls into their hands, whether he be wounded or not. The field hospitals and the sick convoys are the especial targets of the enemy and we destroy the tanks by which alone their water for the summer can be obtained – and employ against them a bullet – the new Dum-Dum bullet of which you may have heard – the shattering effects of which are simply appalling.

His judgement on the horror of war as 'appalling' remained with him for life: 'Jaw, Jaw is better than War, War!' was his later dictum. He already anticipates this belief here, aged only 22. He also reveals a maturity when he judges his experience on the frontier to have been valuable in many ways, and well worth having from an educational point of view.

In another of his characteristics revealed in the letter Frances must have recognised Randolph. Like his father Winston was ready, often unwisely, to challenge those he thought were in error, despite the possible consequences. Both he and Randolph damaged their careers seriously because of this, Randolph irretrievably. Only the overwhelming threat of the Second World War rescued Winston from the same descent into political oblivion. He was critical of the generals and politicians behind the war in a way that recalled Randolph's campaign against his leader, Stafford Northcote:

I wish I could come to the conclusion that all this barbarity – all these losses, all this expenditure – had resulted in a permanent settlement being obtained. I do not think, however, that anything has been done that will not have to be done again. It seems that many years of war and disturbance await the Indian Frontier.[1]

When Winston confesses that he intends to leave the Army and stand for Parliament he shows he understood his grandmother: 'I am afraid you will disapprove of all this.' A political career for him would have been attractive to her, but stability, order, a sense of responsibility and perseverance were virtues of immense importance to her. She had seen both her sons fail conspicuously to achieve them, and rightly judged that her preference would be for him to stick with what he had begun. When he mentioned that he had left his regiment in India and come back to England on leave he knew this further example of his not being fully committed would bring her disapproval.

Family meant much to Frances. All her life she looked after and supported its members, and Winston was careful now to give her news of another of her grandsons, Cornelia's son Ivor. Winston had received several letters from him and was soon to spend a week or two with Ivor at Bangalore, where he was stationed with his regiment. Winston was looking forward to the visit as he found Ivor a congenial companion.

Only two or three weeks before she died, Frances received a second, equally illuminating letter from Winston, this time from Suez. Now she learned of another momentous decision in his young life, an intention to embark upon a writing career: '... how much writing my new book has entailed. I have now finished eighteen of the twenty three chapters, 135,000 words.' He reaffirms his decision to leave the Army but now puts forward a reason for it he knows will appeal to Frances. Throughout Randolph and Jennie's marriage, their extravagance, their heedlessness of the need to establish security had caused her anxiety, so Winston's thinking now could only be a pleasure to her. He tells her:

Had the Army been a source of income to me instead of a channel of expenditure, I might have felt compelled to stick to it. But I can live cheaper and earn more as a writer, special correspondent or journalist.

Infinitely more pleasing to her would be Winston's hard-headed assessment of his financial situation and his determination:

You will be glad to hear that the serial rights of *Affairs of State* have been bought by Messrs Macmillan for their magazine – for £100. The story is to begin publication next month and will run for six months, after which it becomes again my property and I shall make Longmans publish it in book form in the autumn. This serial publication is very satisfactory from a financial point of view as it means an extra hundred pounds – for the value of the book is rather enhanced than depreciated by it.[2]

Never, even in her most optimistic moments, could Frances have foreseen the prestige he was to bring to the family name. His breadth of achievement as politician, statesman, writer, orator and painter brought him the nation's, and the world's, highest honours: Order of Merit, Companion of Honour, Knight of the Garter, Nobel Prize, even the offer of a Dukedom (declined!). Her pleasure would have been to recognise in him so much of Randolph at his best: the crackling wit and power of his oratory, his energy, industry and phenomenal memory, his adherence to the principles of Tory Democracy and the Primrose League. She would recognise, too, something of herself in him, especially the humanity, compassion and love of family and home. His great Marlborough ancestor, the 1st Duke, had his rescue of Europe from French domination recorded by the inscription carved into the South Front of Blenheim Palace: 'Protector of the Freedom of Europe'. Winston's rescue of a virtually defeated nation, and of much of the rest of the world, earned him a parallel accolade, 'The Greatest Briton', by popular acclaim. His grandmother would have been both proud and satisfied.

Frances died on 16 April 1899, aged 77, at 45 Portman Square, London, but was brought back to Blenheim for burial next to her husband in the vault beneath the chapel. Above her, in the chapel itself, are the two monuments she had raised at particularly sad times: to her husband John Winston and to her son Randolph. Winston lies close by in Bladon churchyard.

This intelligent, loyal, principled and compassionate woman was a true Victorian, of an age eloquently described by Winston himself:

I was a child of the Victorian era, when the structure of our country seemed firmly set, when its position in trade was unrivalled, and when the realisation of the greatness of our Empire and of our duty to preserve it was ever growing stronger. In those days the dominant forces in Great Britain were very sure of themselves and of their doctrines.[3]

This supreme confidence was to be shattered, but the foundations had been laid for Winston to become a worthy descendant of his great ancestor

John Churchill, 1st Duke of Marlborough; he would be an elder statesman who raised the courage of his countrymen and led them to victory in that same glorious spirit. If she could have looked ahead, Frances would have seen her faith in Randolph justified and fulfilled in his son, and possibly been content with her own contribution. Certainly, she could not have wished for a greater memorial.

Notes and References

Chapter One, pp.1–7

1. Castlereagh to his father, Lord Londonderry, April 1819, cited in *Ladies of Londonderry* by Urquhart, p.16.
2. Martha Bradford to Viscountess Ennismore, and to Lady Bloomfield, December 1819, cited in *Ladies of Londonderry* by Urquhart, p.17.

Chapter Two, pp.8–13

1. Letter from Frances Anne to her mother, Countess of Antrim, 1822, cited in *Frances Anne* by Edith Londonderry, p.68.
2. Private letters of Princess Lieven to Prince Metternich, 1820-6, ed. Peter Quennell 1937, cited in Urquhart, p.18.
3. *Journal of Frances Anne*, cited by Edith Londonderry, p.73.

Chapter Three, pp.14–18

1. Letter from Frances Anne to her mother, Countess of Antrim, 27 October 1822, cited by Edith Londonderry, p.91.
2. *Journal of Frances Anne*, cited by Edith Londonderry, pp.89-90.

Chapter Four, pp.19–25

1. Letter from Frances Anne to her mother, Countess of Antrim, Verona, 26 December 1822, cited in *Frances Anne* by Edith Londonderry, p.114.
2. *Journal of Frances Anne*, p.14, cited in *Ladies of Londonderry* by Urquhart, p.11.
3. Letter from Charles Stewart to Emily Castlereagh, 7 June 1823, cited by Edith Londonderry, p.123.

Chapter Five, pp.26–32

1. *Durham Advertiser*, 1828.
2. Letters of Lord Londonderry, 1831-2, cited by Edith Londonderry, pp.173-4.

CHAPTER SEVEN, PP.41-8

1. *Durham Advertiser*, 1853.

CHAPTER EIGHT, PP.49-56

1. *The Later Churchills*, by A.L. Rowse, pp.215, 223.
2. *Reminiscences* of Lady Randolph Churchill, pp.61-2.
3. *Jackson's Oxford Journal*, 1.5.1858, cited in *History of Bladon School* by Wendy Heppell and Carol Browning, 2008, p.8.
4. Log book of Woodstock School, cited in *History of the Woodstock Schools* by Norman Roast, pp.24, 25, 31.

CHAPTER NINE, PP.57-66

1. *Victoria County History* vol.12, pp.257ff.
2. *Life and Times of F.M. Muller*, ed. by his wife, 1859, cited in *The Later Churchills* by A.L. Rowse, p.217.
3. Diary of Mrs Jeune, 1859, cited by A.L. Rowse, p.224.
4. Undated newspaper cutting, Bodleian, G.A. Oxon. 73 (5,6).
5. FA to people of Seaham 1854, cited by Edith Londonderry, pp.260-1.
6. Disraeli's letters to Frances Anne, cited by Edith Londonderry, p.268.
7. Last Will and Testament of Frances Anne, 3rd Marchioness of Londonderry.

CHAPTER TEN, PP.67-72

1. I Corinthians Ch. 9, v. 22.
2. *Recollections of My Dear Son*, by Frances, 7th Duchess of Marlborough, Blenheim Archives.
3. *Recollections of My Dear Son*, by Frances, 7th Duchess of Marlborough, Blenheim Archives.

CHAPTER ELEVEN, PP.73-7

1. Letter from H.G. Liddell, Dean of Christchurch, cited by Robert Rhodes James in *Lord Randolph Churchill*, pp.27-8.

CHAPTER TWELVE, PP.78-82

1. Randolph to Marlborough from Blenheim, 20.8.73, cited by Churchill and Mitchell, pp.23-5.

CHAPTER THIRTEEN, PP.83-90

1. Marlborough to Randolph 31.8.73, Blenheim Archives A IV/21.
2. Randolph to Jennie 7.9.73, Churchill Archives.
3. Jennie to Randolph 16.9.73, Churchill Archives.
4. Randolph to Jennie 18.9.73, Churchill Archives.

5. Jennie to Randolph 18.9.73, Churchill Archives.
6. Randolph to Jennie 19.9.73, Churchill Archives.

CHAPTER FOURTEEN, PP.91-6

1. Marlboroughs to Randolph (from Cowes), Blenheim Archives A IV/23.
2. Frances to Jennie (from Portarlington) 7.1.74, Blenheim Archives A IV/23.

CHAPTER FIFTEEN, PP.97-106

1. Marlborough to Randolph (wedding day) 14.4.74, Blenheim Archives A IV/21.
2. Frances to Clara Jerome 30.11.74, Blenheim Archives A IV/23.

CHAPTER SIXTEEN, PP.107-11

1. *Reminiscences* of Lady Randolph Churchill, pp.58-9.

CHAPTER EIGHTEEN, PP.119-30

1. All quotations in this chapter from Blenheim Archives: Book of Press Cuttings.

CHAPTER NINETEEN, PP.131-40

1. Frances' letter to *The Times*, 18 December 1879.
2. Frances' final letter to *The Times*, 21 April 1880.
3. Queen Victoria to Frances, 7th Duchess of Marlborough, with grateful thanks to the Library of Congress in Washington and by kind permission of the Royal Archives, Windsor Castle.

CHAPTER TWENTY, PP.141-9

1. *Vanity Fair*, 1883.

CHAPTER TWENTY-ONE, PP.150-8

1. In Birmingham, cited by Robert Rhodes James, p.133.
2. In Blackpool, cited by Robert Rhodes James, p.136.
3. Cited by Robert Rhodes James, pp.136-7.
4. Cited by Robert Rhodes James, p.137.
5. Cited by Robert Rhodes James pp.137-8.
6. To the Primrose League, cited by Robert Rhodes James, p.162.
7. To the electors of Paddington, cited by Robert Rhodes James, p.246.

CHAPTER TWENTY-TWO, PP.159-69

1. Cited by Celia Sandys in *From Winston with Love and Kisses*, p.104.
2. Cited in *From Winston with Love and Kisses*, p.104.
3. Cited in *From Winston with Love and Kisses*, p.118.
4. Cited in *From Winston with Love and Kisses*, p.124.

Chapter Twenty-Four, pp.175–80

1. Cited by Robert Rhodes James in *Lord Randolph Churchill*, p.267.
2. Cited in *Lord Randolph Churchill*, p.277.
3. Cited in *Lord Randolph Churchill*, p.293.
4. Cited in *Lord Randolph Churchill*, p.304.
5. Cited in *Lord Randolph Churchill*, p.312.

Chapter Twenty-Five, pp.181–7

1. Tate Britain Exhibition 'Van Dyck and Britain', Spring 2009.
2. Frances to Jennie, 1886, cited by Churchill and Mitchell in *Jennie*, pp.142–3.
3. Lord Redesdale, *Memoirs II*, p.685.

Chapter Twenty-Six, pp.188–95

1. *From Winston with Love and Kisses* by Celia Sandys, p.207.
2. *Winston and Jack* by Celia and John Lee, pp.150–3.
3. Cited in *From Winston with Love and Kisses*, p.173.
4. *Recollections of My Dear Son*, by Frances, Duchess of Marlborough.
5. Lord Rosebery, *Lord Randolph Churchill*, Humphreys 1906.
6. WSC letters 23.6.08, Churchill Archives, cited in *Winston S. Churchill* by Randolph S. Churchill, companion volume 1, part 1, 1874–1896, p.578.

Chapter Twenty-Seven, pp.196–204

1. WSC from Bangalore (1897), Churchill Archives.
2. WSC from Suez (1899), Churchill Archives.
3. *My Early Life* by Winston S. Churchill, Preface (1930).

BIBLIOGRAPHY

PRIMARY SOURCES

Blenheim Archives, Blenheim Palace
Blenheim Papers, British Library, London
Churchill Archives Centre, Churchill College, Cambridge
Log Books, Bladon C.E. Primary School, Oxfordshire
Londonderry Papers, Durham County Records Office
National Library of Ireland Archives, Dublin
Spencer-Churchill, Frances Anne Emily: *Recollections of My Dear Son*

SECONDARY SOURCES

Aldous, Richard, *The Lion and the Unicorn: Gladstone and Disraeli* (Hutchinson, 2006)

Balsan, Consuelo Vanderbilt, *The Glitter and the Gold* (Heinemann, 1953)

Bond, James and Tiller, Kate (eds), *Blenheim: Landscape for a Palace* (Budding Books, 2000)

Bonham-Carter, Violet, *Winston Churchill As I Knew Him* (Reprint Society, 1966)

Buczacki, Stefan, *Churchill and Chartwell* (Frances Lincoln Ltd, 2007)

Churchill, Peregrine and Mitchell, Julian, *Jennie, Lady Randolph Churchill* (Thames Television and Collins, 1974)

Churchill, Randolph, *Winston S. Churchill Vol. 1 Youth (1874-1900)* (Heinemann, 1966)

Churchill, Lady Randolph, *Reminiscences* (Edward Arnold, 1905)

Churchill, Winston S., *Lord Randolph Churchill* (Macmillan, 1906)
My Early Life (Odhams, London 1930)

Cornwallis-West, Mrs (Lady Randolph Churchill), *Reminiscences* (Edward Arnold, 1908)

de Courcy, Anne, *Life of Edith, Marchioness of Londonderry* (Sinclair-Stevenson, 1992)

Disraeli, Benjamin, *Letters from Benjamin Disraeli to Frances Anne Londonderry 1837-1861* (Macmillan, 1938)

Fletcher, Anthony, *Growing up in England: The Experience of Childhood 1600-1914*

Forster, John and Bapasola, Jeri, *Winston and Blenheim* (Blenheim Palace, 2005)

Fowler, Marian, *Blenheim: Biography of a Palace* (Viking Penguin, 1989)
    In a Gilded Cage: from Heiress to Duchess (St Martin's Press, New York, 1994)

Garnett, Oliver, *Chartwell* (National Trust, 1992)

Gilbert, Martin, *Churchill, A Life* (Heinemann, 1991)

Girouard, Mark, *Life in the English Country House* (Yale University Press, 1978)
    The Victorian Country House (Yale University Press, 1985)
    A Country House Companion (Yale University Press, 1987)

Goldsmith, Annabel, *Annabel: An Unconventional Life* (Weidenfeld and Nicholson, 2004)

Green, David, *Blenheim Palace* (Country Life, 1951)
    The Churchills of Blenheim (Constable, 1984)

Heppell, Wendy and Browning, Carol, *A History of Bladon School 1858-2008* (Bladon School)

Hibbert, Christopher, *Disraeli* (Harper Collins, 2004)
    The Marlboroughs (Viking, 2001)
    Queen Victoria (Harper Collins, 2000)

Higham, Charles, *The Dark Lady: Winston Churchill's Mother and her World* (Virgin Books, 2006)

Hyde, H. Montgomery, *The Londonderrys* (Hamish Hamilton, 1979)
    Londonderry House and its Pictures (Cresset Press, 1937)

James, Robert Rhodes, *Lord Randolph Churchill* (Weidenfeld and Nicholson, 1959)

Jenkins, Roy, *Churchill* (Macmillan, 2002)

Kehoe, Elisabeth, *Fortune's Daughters* (Atlantic Books, 2004)

Kingaly, Christine, *A New History of Ireland* (Sutton Publishing, 2004)

van der Kiste, John, *The Romanovs 1818-1959* (Sutton Publishing, 1998)

Lee, Celia and John, *Winston and Jack: the Churchill Brothers* (Lee, 2007)

Leslie, Anita, *Jennie: Mother of Winston Churchill* (Hutchinson, 1969)
  Edwardians in Love (Hutchinson, 1972)
Londonderry, Edith, Marchioness of, *Frances Anne: Her Life and Times* (Macmillan, 1958)
Longford, Elizabeth, *Wellington* (Weidenfeld and Nicholson, 1992)
McColl, Gail and Wallace, Carol McD., *To Marry an English Lord* (Workman Publishing, New York, 1989)
McInstry, Leo, *Rosebery* (John Murray, 2005)
Magill, Paul, *Garron Tower* (Magill, 1990)
Martin, Ralph G., *Lady Randolph Churchill 1854-1895* (Cassell, 1969)
Massingberd, H. Montgomery, *Blenheim Revisited* (Bodley Head, 1985)
  Blenheim and the Churchills (Jarrold, 2004)
Masters, Brian, *Wynyard Hall and the Londonderry Family* (Hartlepool, 1976)
Montgomery, Maureen E., *Gilded Prostitution* (Routledge, 1989)
Roast, Norman, *A History of the Woodstock National Schools* (privately published, 1983)
Rosebery, Lord, *Lord Randolph Churchill* (Humphreys, 1906)
Rowse, A.L., *The Later Churchills* (Macmillan, 1958)
Sandys, Celia, *From Winston With Love and Kisses* (Sinclair Stevenson, 1994)
Scarisbrick, Diana, *Ancestral Jewels* (Andre Deutsch, 1989)
Scharf, George, *A Catalogue Raisonné of the Pictures at Blenheim Palace* (National Portrait Gallery, 1862)
Sebba, Anne, *Jennie Churchill: Winston's American Mother* (John Murray, 2001)
Shaw, Matthew, *The Duke of Wellington* (British Library, 2005)
Soames, Mary, *Clementine Churchill* (Cassell, 1979)
  The Profligate Duke (Collins, 1987)
  (ed.) *Speaking for Themselves: the personal letters of Winston and Clementine Churchill* (Doubleday, 1998)
Spencer-Churchill, Henrietta, *Blenheim and the Churchill Family* (Cico Books, 2005)
Stuart, Amanda Mackenzie, *Consuelo and Alva* (Harper Collins, 2005)
Urquhart, Diane, *The Ladies of Londonderry* (I.B. Tauris, 2007)
Waller, Maureen, *Sovereign Ladies: The Six Reigning Queens of England* (John Murray, 2006)
Watney, John, *The Churchills: Portrait of a Great Family* (Gordon and Cremones, 1977)
Wilson, A.N., *The Victorians* (Hutchinson, 2002)

REFERENCE

Burke's Peerage and Baronetage (Fitzroy Dearson, 1999)

Hansard: British Parliamentary Debates 1874ff. (Government Publishing Office)

Oxford Dictionary of National Biography (Oxford University Press, 2004)

Victoria County History Who's Who (Oxford University Press, 2009)

NEWSPAPERS AND PERIODICALS

The Chronicle
The Daily News
The Freeman's Journal
The Irish Times
Jackson's Oxford Journal
The Oxford Times
The Standard
The Telegraph
The Times
The Graphic
Illustrated London News
Vanity Fair
The World

INDEX

Numbers in **bold** refer to illustrations in the plate section.